THE PINK BOOK:
Legislation

for tourist accommodation and attractions

11TH EDITION

Published by VisitEngland,
3 Grosvenor Gardens
London
SW1W 0BD
Publishing Manager: Hannah Lowe

Written and edited by Kurt Janson Ltd
Cover design and typsetting by Consider This UK Ltd

Disclaimer

No advice

This Pink Book contains general information about laws applicable to your business. The information is not advice, and should not be treated as such.

Limitation of warranties

The legal information on the Pink Book is provided "as is" without any representations or warranties, express or implied. VisitBritain/VisitEngland makes no representations or warranties in relation to the information in the Pink Book. Without prejudice to the generality of the foregoing paragraph, VisitBritain/VisitEngland does not warrant that:

- the information in this Pink Book will be constantly available, or available at all; or
- the information in this Pink Book is complete, true, accurate, up-to-date, or non-misleading

Professional assistance

You must not rely on the information in this Pink Book as an alternative to legal advice from your attorney or other professional services provider.

If you have any specific questions about any legal matter you should consult your attorney or other professional services provider.

You should never delay seeking legal advice, disregard legal advice, or commence or discontinue any legal action because of information in this Pink Book.

Liability

Nothing in this disclaimer will limit any of our liabilities in any way that is not permitted under applicable law, or exclude any of our liabilities that may not be excluded under applicable law.

Legislation for tourist accommodation and attractions

Welcome to the eleventh edition of VisitEngland's *Pink Book: Legislation for tourist accommodation and attractions,* which now includes information for visitor attraction operators.

Published ten times previously, the Pink Book has always been recognised as providing significant support to the tourism sector. It provides a common sense approach to helping tourism businesses understand their legal obligations.

The guidance contained here is also available online at **www.visitengland.org/pinkbookonline** – this is updated as legislation changes.

Keeping up to date with legislation

If you run a tourist accommodation business or visitor attraction, or are involved with running or advising tourism businesses, you need to be aware of the legislation that applies. There is a wide range of applicable legislation. Customers are increasingly demanding higher quality and are becoming more aware of their rights. Complying with legislative requirements helps you to meet these expectations and avoid claims, prosecution and fines.

This book provides practical guidance on the legislation relevant to accommodation and visitor attraction providers in England. For legislation relevant to those outside England, please contact the relevant National Tourist Board.

Using the book

This book is arranged into eight main sections, as follows, each of which contains a number of topics. Page tabs have been provided to help you quickly reach the section you need:

- Licences & Consents
- Marketing
- Customers

INTRODUCTION

- Food & Drink
- Health & Safety
- Staff
- Business Management & Tax
- Further Information

The final section, Further Information, provides details of where to go for further help and a list of useful websites and definitions.

See the Contents page or **www.visitengland.org/pinkbookonline** for an immediate pointer to these main sections and topics or go to the Index at the back of the book for an alphabetical listing of the subjects and legislation covered.

Legislation which has been updated since the 10th edition of the Pink Book (published 2019) is identified by an 'Updated' tab in the margin. New information is identified by a 'New' tab in the margin. All content is correct as of January 2021.

Disclaimer

No advice

This Pink Book contains general information about laws applicable to your business. The information is not advice, and should not be treated as such.

Limitation of warranties

The legal information on the Pink Book is provided "as is" without any representations or warranties, express or implied. VisitBritain/VisitEngland makes no representations or warranties in relation to the information in the Pink Book.

Without prejudice to the generality of the foregoing paragraph, VisitBritain/VisitEngland does not warrant that:

- the information in this Pink Book will be constantly available, or available at all; or
- the information in this Pink Book is complete, true, accurate, up-to-date, or non-misleading

Professional assistance

You must not rely on the information in this Pink Book as an alternative to legal advice from your attorney or other professional services provider.

If you have any specific questions about any legal matter you should consult your attorney or other professional services provider.

You should never delay seeking legal advice, disregard legal advice, or commence or discontinue any legal action because of information in this Pink Book.

Liability

Nothing in this disclaimer will limit any of our liabilities in any way that is not permitted under applicable law, or exclude any of our liabilities that may not be excluded under applicable law.

Welcome to the 11th Edition
of the *Pink Book*

First of all, I would like to thank all the owners and operators of attractions, accommodation, travel and hospitality businesses for your hard work over the last year. You've implemented COVID-safe measures to protect customers and staff, complied with the rules and restrictions that have been necessary to implement and you've provided feedback on the issues that you have faced during these unprecedented times. I recognise that the past year has been exceptionally difficult, but with the vaccine rollout I believe that there is now light at the end of the tunnel and we can look forward to tourism returning to a more normal footing in the near future.

At the Department for Digital, Culture, Media and Sport (DCMS) we are focused on restarting the tourism industry as fast as possible in order to rebuild local communities and economies. To do this I have been working with the industry through the Tourism Industry Council to develop a Tourism Recovery Plan which we hope to publish shortly. The Plan will cover how we reopen business safely, how we stimulate demand, how we support businesses back to profit and, in the longer term, how we build back better. As part of this Recovery Plan I have commissioned a review of Destination Management Organisation structures so that small local businesses in the sector can more easily access the development and marketing support that they need to maximise future opportunities.

I very much believe that tourism will bounce back strongly to lead the UK's economic recovery and I look forward to working with you to achieve this.

Nigel Huddleston MP *Minister for Arts, Heritage and Tourism*

Contents

LICENCES & CONSENTS

Alcohol and Entertainment Licensing — **1**
TV and Copyright Licences — **13**
Planning and Building — **21**
Signs for Your Premises — **29**

MARKETING

Unfair Trading Practices — **33**
Direct Marketing — **39**
Holiday Packages — **45**

CUSTOMERS

Pricing and Charging — **51**
Bookings and Tickets — **57**
Registration and Data Protection — **61**
Cancellations and No-shows — **75**
Accepting Customers — **81**
Disabled Customers — **85**
Luggage and Belongings — **93**
Childcare — **99**
Alternative Dispute Resolution — **103**

FOOD & DRINK

Food Safety and Hygiene — **107**
Food Labelling — **117**
Single Use Plastics — **121**

HEALTH & SAFETY

Health and Safety at Work Act 123
Health and Safety Liabilities 129
Safety Management 135
Hazards from Work Activities 141
Legionnaires' Disease 147
Hazards in the Workplace 149
Product Safety 157
Swimming, Gym and Outdoor Safety 165
Fire Safety (General) 169
Fire Safety of Furniture and Furnishings 179
Smoking in Public Places 185

STAFF

Working Hours 189
National Minimum Wage 193
Discrimination 199
Time Off for Parents 203
Migrant Workers 209
Employing Under 18s 217
Workplace Pensions 221

BUSINESS MANAGEMENT & TAX

Income Tax, VAT and Legal Form of Business 225
Tax Status of Accommodation Businesses 231
Business Rates 235
Self-Catering Letting Options 241
Houses in Multiple Occupation 245
Utilities and Waste Collection 249

FURTHER INFORMATION

253

LICENCES & CONSENTS

Alcohol, Entertainment and Gaming Licensing

KEY FACTS

- If you wish to sell alcoholic drinks you will need a licence.
- There are two types of licence: premises licences and personal licences.
- It is illegal to buy alcohol from a wholesaler who is not registered.
- For gaming machines, other than skills with prizes (SWP) machines, you will need a licence or permit from your local licensing authority and possibly from the Gambling Commission.

Note: due to COVID-19, there have been significant short-term changes to licensing rules, including hours of operation and the ability to sell alcohol for off-premises consumption. This section does not include these temporary changes and businesses are advised to check the latest Government COVID-19 updates for any temporary restrictions or permissions.

Does the legislation apply to me?

If you wish to sell alcoholic drinks you will need an alcohol licence. It is an offence to sell intoxicating liquor without one.

Providing 'free' alcohol to customers

You need a licence to sell alcohol – this includes providing 'free' alcohol because it is an incentive to purchase and/or is included in your pricing structure. If you charge the customer to enter or stay at your premises or for some other product that must be purchased in order to receive the free alcohol, this means that they are essentially paying for the alcohol that is provided. In other words, the customer has effectively paid a 'consideration' for that service. It is not free.

> **Note:** in 2014, through the Deregulation Act, the Government announced that it would introduce Community and Ancillary Sales Notices (CANs), which would allow accommodation businesses to sell small amounts of alcohol for a nominal fee. However, there is no indication as to when they will be introduced.

The Licensing Act 2003

The **Licensing Act 2003** rationalised the previous licensing systems (in England and Wales) to produce a simpler system that is easier for all involved to understand.

Local authorities are required to consult on their statement of licensing policy every three years. Before applying for a licence, it is therefore important for you to read this policy. This will enable you to tailor your application to the local authority's policy and thereby reduce the risk of your application being rejected.

Administration and enforcement

Administration and enforcement of the Licensing Act lies with local authorities (and other agencies where appropriate), e.g. fire safety, police, licensing officers, and environmental health. Each local authority has a licensing committee of between 10-15 locally-elected councillors who decide on licensing applications.

In practice, their responsibilities are devolved to a licensing manager and staff who deal with the administrative functions. All contested applications will be heard before a sub-committee of at least three members of that committee.

Licensing objectives

There are four principles which underpin the Licensing Act and impact on everyone. These are:
- the prevention of crime and disorder
- public safety
- the prevention of public nuisance
- the protection of children from harm (including sexual exploitation).

These principles are the key elements to be addressed by applicants, local authorities, police and other statutory authorities, and objectors to your licence.

Licensable activities

Activities regulated by the **Licensing Act 2003** fall into one of the following four categories:

- the sale of alcohol
- the supply of alcohol by or on behalf of a club
- provision of regulated entertainment
- provision of late-night refreshments.

The activities that tourism businesses should be familiar with are as follows:

Provision of regulated entertainment

Regulated entertainment includes many of the activities offered for the benefit of your customers in, for example, attractions, public houses, hotels, guesthouses or club rooms at caravan parks, including:

- dancing either as a show for customers or as an activity for them to take part in
- films (defined as any showing of moving pictures) not being shown in a community premises
- plays
- all indoor sporting events (physical skills must be a factor)
- music – the public playing of recorded music (e.g. DJs) as an accompaniment to dancing. (See *Live Music Act 2012* below).

Provision of late night refreshment

Provision of late night refreshment covers the supply of hot food or drinks from premises for consumption on or off premises between 11pm and 5am. This aspect is mainly focused on late-night takeaway premises, so an exception is made for the provision of refreshments by hotels, guesthouses, hostels and caravan sites.

However, if you have a restaurant which serves hot food and drinks to members of the public after 11pm or are staging an event at an attraction where hot food and drink will be provided to customers such as a midnight movie, you will need to nominate this as one of your licensable activities. Should you have any doubts about what should be included as licensable activities, your local licensing authority will be able to give advice.

Temporary Event Notices (TENs)

A Temporary Event Notice (TEN) is a licence to hold one-off licensable activities in an unlicensed premises and are particularly useful for attractions that want to stage a limited number of licensable events during the year. A single event can last up to 7 days and you are limited to a maximum of five per year if you do not hold a personal licence and 50 if you do. No more than 15 TENs can be

UPDATED

given to a single premises in any calendar year and the total length of the events cannot exceed 21 days. Events covered by a TEN can only be attended by a maximum of 499 people and there must be a minimum of 24 hours between consecutive events.

The Temporary Event Notice section of the Gov.uk website gives more information related to TENs and how to apply for one: www.gov.uk/temporary-events-notice.

Types of licences

There are two licences.

- **Premises licence:** required for any premises that offer any of the licensable activities previously described.
- **Personal licence:** a separate, portable system of personal licences that provides authority to sell alcohol. Personal licences are valid indefinitely and do not need to be renewed. A designated premises supervisor, who must be a personal licence holder, must be nominated for any premises where the licence includes permission to sell alcohol. In order to obtain a personal licence the applicant must be:
  - 18 or over
  - possess an accredited licensing qualification
  - not have forfeited a personal licence within five years of the application and
  - not have been convicted of any relevant offence.

To sell alcohol on your premises, you are required to have a premises licence and for at least one person to have a personal licence. That person does not have to be present on the premises to oversee the sale of alcohol, but is responsible for any sales made by other members of your staff.

Applying for a premises licence

Your application must embrace the four licensing objectives and you will need to assess any risks associated with each activity you propose to offer.

Advice can be obtained from the relevant statutory authority to achieve this, e.g. a fire safety officer in respect of means of escape under the public safety objective. The police may require CCTV or door supervisors (usually for premises which stay open until the early hours) under the prevention of crime and disorder objective.

Environmental health officers may offer advice on noise arising from any associated music under the prevention of public nuisance objective.

All statutory authorities and your neighbours/local businesses must also confine themselves to the four licensing objectives if they make any representation or objections.

Application process

Applications are made to the local licensing authority where the premises are located. The forms will be available from the local authority's website and can be downloaded for completion together with guidance notes.

While the forms are relatively straightforward, you may wish to engage the services of a specialist licensing solicitor or consultant to assist you. The application can be made by anyone who undertakes, or proposes to undertake, any business involving licensable activities. It includes limited companies or partnerships. If the application is made by an individual, that person must be at least 18 years of age.

You can apply for any of the licensable activities which are applicable to your business. Be mindful, however, that you also have to serve a copy to the following statutory authorities:
- the Chief Officer of Police
- the body recognised as responsible for the protection of children
- Trading Standards officers
- local planning authority
- environmental health authority
- health and safety authority
- fire and rescue authority.

They will all wish to see that your premises and the activities you ask for are compatible.

For details of the responsible authorities in our area, contact your local licensing team. Details may also be available on your local authority's website.

Consultation

You are required to consult with your neighbours and local businesses in the area when seeking to gain a licence or to vary an existing licence. This can be done by placing an advert in a local newspaper, setting out the brief details of your application and displaying a notice on your premises advertising details to passers-by. The guidance notes will give advice on these procedures.

The consultation process lasts for 28 days commencing on the day you submit the application to the local authority. Copies to the other statutory authorities (mentioned above) must be served at the same time.

Providing there are no objections or representations that have not been resolved, the licensing authority will automatically issue your premises licence without you having to attend any meeting. Should there be any representations or objections which cannot be resolved by negotiation, the licensing authority will hold a hearing within 20 working days (from the end of the consultation period) to determine the application.

Fees

There are two sets of fees when applying for a premises licence. Both are based on rating bands and whether the primary or main purpose of the premises is to sell alcohol.

- the first fee is the cost to apply or to vary a licence
- the second fee is the annual charge once the licence has been granted.

Once issued, the licence effectively lasts for as long as your business operates. The licence can be transferred from one licence holder to another. Again, the forms and guidance notes can be accessed on the local authority's website.

The Alcohol Licensing section of the Gov.uk website offers information related to the Licensing Act and the application process: www.gov.uk/guidance/alcohol-licensing.

Variations to licences

Once a licence has been granted, licensees are required to operate within the conditions of the licence. If you would like a minor variation to these conditions, a simplified application process exists for this purpose. This process can only be used for variations that **could have no adverse impact on any of the four** licensing objectives.

For example, a Minor Variation Application could not be used in the following situations:

- to extend the period for which the licence or certificate has effect
- to transfer the licence to other premises
- to specify, in a premises licence, an individual as the premises' supervisor
- to add the sale by retail or supply of alcohol as an activity
- to authorise the sale of alcohol at any time between 11pm and 7am
- to authorise an increase in the amount of time on any day during which alcohol may be sold.

The cost of applying for a Minor Variation Application has been set at £89 and the maximum time that licensing authorities are able to take to process the application has been set at 15 days. Unlike a major variation to a licence, there is no requirement to advertise or make other "responsible authorities", such as the police, aware of your intention to seek a minor variation.

Mandatory Code for the sale of alcohol

In addition to the Provisions of the Licensing Act, if you sell alcohol you are also required to comply with a Mandatory Code. This code:

- bans businesses from undertaking irresponsible promotions that encourage people to drink quickly or to drink more than they otherwise would. Examples include 'all you can drink for £10' or 'free drinks when a football team scores'
- ban drinks being poured directly into customers' mouths, i.e. 'dentist's chairs'
- requires operators to supply free tap water to customers
- requires businesses that sell alcohol to have an age-verification policy in place, and to check the ID of anyone who looks under 18
- requires businesses to sell alcohol in small measures (a half pint for beer and cider, 25ml or 35ml for spirits and 125ml for wine) as well as larger measures
- bans the sale of alcohol below the "permitted price", which is defined as alcohol duty plus VAT. The Home Office has produced the guide *Guidance on banning the sale of alcohol below the cost of duty plus VAT* to help businesses calculate the cost of duty and VAT for a range of products.

How long can I stay open?

While the Licensing Act created the opportunity to stay open 24 hours, very few premises (with the exception of supermarkets) actually operate these hours. You can apply to have any of the licensable activities on your premises starting and finishing at any time to suit you and/or your customers.

Bear in mind that the statutory authorities and neighbours have to be notified and may not agree with your proposals. Common sense usually applies and many establishments have extended their operating hours by perhaps one or two hours.

Who can I sell alcohol to?

Children aged 16 and 17 can consume alcohol providing it is only beer, cider or wine, it has been purchased for them by an adult and it is consumed with a table meal. The adult must be with the child at all times.

You can also decide at what age children are allowed into the licensed areas of your premises. Therefore babies and very young children can now be in your bar/restaurant, providing that they are accompanied by an adult.

Alcohol Wholesaler Registration Scheme

In response to the growing problem of counterfeit alcohol, the Government has introduced the Alcohol Wholesaler Registration Scheme. All wholesale sellers of alcohol are required to register with HMRC. On registration, wholesalers receive a Unique Reference Number (URN) as proof that they are legally able to sell alcohol to businesses.

It is illegal to buy alcohol from a wholesaler who is not registered and able to provide you with their URN (which you are able to check online: www.gov.uk/check-alcohol-wholesaler-registration). If you buy your alcohol from an unregistered business, then you may be liable to a criminal or civil penalty and your alcohol may be seized. You must keep records to prove you have checked that your supplier is registered with HMRC.

Note: there is one important exemption to this scheme. Retailers who make occasional trade sales of alcohol are excluded, meaning that if you buy your alcohol from a supermarket or off-licence, then they will not be registered and you don't have to check their URN registration.

Live Music Act 2012

The Live Music Act exempts small licenced venues with audiences of up to 200 (including attractions, accommodation establishments, pubs, restaurants and community halls) from requiring a separate special licence to hold live shows with amplified music between 8am and 11pm. It also removes the need for a licence for unamplified live performances between 8am and 11pm in all venues.

However, operators will still have to gain a licence for any alcohol sales at such an event and comply with any restrictions on the performances that are imposed by the Licensing Authority.

Gaming Machines

The installation and use of Gaming machines is covered by the **Gambling Act 2005**. Under this Act, 'gaming' means 'playing a game of chance for a prize'.

Skill with prizes machines (SWPs)

There are some machines that fall outside the Gambling Act. Skills with prizes machines (SWPs) are not classified as gaming machines because they are deemed to be a game of skill rather than a game controlled by chance.

These are machines where the customer displays a skill in order to win, rather than there being a large element of chance. An example of an SWP machine is a quiz machine found in pubs that tests the customer's knowledge. Some crane grab machines can also operate on a skill only basis but must utilise a 'compensator' to regulate the number of prizes and are therefore games of chance and rules apply to their location, maximum permitted stake and prize (see below).

The vast majority of skill-based games, such as basketball-type games, are found in Family Entertainment Centres (more commonly known as seaside amusement arcades) but can be sited anywhere.

Gaming machine classification

The legislation regarding gaming machines is complex and there are a wide range of categories for gaming machines.

Category A, B1, B2, B3, B3A and B4 machines

Machines in categories A – B4 can only be used in a limited range of premises such as casinos, betting shops, some membership clubs and Adult Gaming Centres (B4 machines).

Category C and D machines

This section relates to Category C and D gaming machines, which are mainly found in Family Entertainment Centres and pubs. The following table shows the range of Category C and D machines and the maximum stake and prizes for each type of machine.

Category	Max Stake	Max Prize
C	£1	£100
D money prize	10p	£5
D non-money prize (other than crane grab machine)	30p	£8

MARKETING CUSTOMERS FOOD & DRINK HEALTH & SAFETY STAFF BUSINESS MANAGEMENT & TAX FURTHER INFORMATION

LICENCES & CONSENTS

NEW

Category	Max Stake	Max Prize
D non-money prize (e.g. crane grab machine)	£1	£50
D combined money and non-money prize (other than coin pusher or penny falls machines)	10p	£8 (of which no more than £5 may be a money prize)
D combined money and non-money prize (coin pusher or penny falls machines)	20p	£20 (of which no more than £10 may be a money prize)

Category C machines must be restricted to people aged 18 and over. There is no age restriction related to the use of category D machines.

Return to player (RTP)

Category C and D machines must display the 'theoretical target percentage return to player' as well as a declaration of their category.

RTP is an average measured over a large number of games and will vary over a typical session due to normal game volatility. It is up to the manufacturer to decide upon the game RTP and there is no minimum requirement, but the minimum average return must be displayed to the player for the game.

Gaming Licensing

Family Entertainment Centre Operating Licence

Premises which are entirely or mainly used for making gaming machines available for use, such as small arcades (whether that be stand-alone arcades or arcades incorporated into larger premises such as a holiday park or attraction) are known as Family Entertainment Centres (FEC).

If you want to install any category C machines, you will need a Family Entertainment Centre operating licence (FEC Licence), which is issued by the Gambling Commission. This licence allows you to operate an unlimited number of Category C and D gaming machines on a location that is open to all ages. However, Category C machines must be in a segregated part of the premises that is supervised to prevent children and young people accessing those machines.

The cost of this licence ranges from £1,464 to £4,394.

Unlicensed Family Entertainment Centres

If you want to run a Family Entertainment Centre that just operates Category D gaming machines, you do not need an FEC licence from the Gaming Commission. However, you will need an Unlicensed Family Entertainment Centre permit from your licensing authority.

Premises licence

If you have an alcohol licence for the premises, you are automatically entitled to install two Category C or D gaming machines upon notification to the local licensing authority of your intention to make gaming machines available for use. If you would like further machines you need to apply to the licensing authority. Once you have installed machines you will also have to inform the licensing authority if you change the number or category of machines sited.

If the provision of gambling facilities is not the primary function of your business, and you would like to install just category D machines, then you will only need a gambling permit rather than a premises licence.

You should check the licensing requirements on your licencing authority's website as to the range of licences and permits available and review their gambling statement or policy before you apply.

Further guidance

Alcohol licensing

Further information on all aspects of the Licensing Act 2003 is available on the Gov.uk website: **www.gov.uk/guidance/alcohol-licensing**

Gambling Commission Guidance

The Gambling Commission website has guidance on all aspects of the Gambling Act and the requirements associated with installing gaming machines: **www.gamblingcommission.gov.uk/for-gambling-businesses/for-gambling-businesses.aspx**

Your local authority

Information on licensing authority requirements are available from your local council: **www.gov.uk/find-local-council.**

LICENCES & CONSENTS

MARKETING

CUSTOMERS

FOOD & DRINK

HEALTH & SAFETY

STAFF

BUSINESS MANAGEMENT & TAX

FURTHER INFORMATION

TV and Copyright Licences

KEY FACTS

- If you play recordings of any copyrighted music on your premises (this includes playing background music or made available on devices such as TVs and radios on which music can be broadcast) or if the music is performed live, you may need TheMusicLicence from PPL PRS Ltd.
- If you play a TV in public areas with the sound on, you will need TheMusicLicence from PPL PRS Ltd.
- If you offer short-stay accommodation (of any kind) to overnight visitors and have installed television sets in the accommodation, you need a 'Hotel and Mobile Units Television Licence' (hotel licence).
- If you offer a DVD film library, you need a DVD Concierge licence.
- If you operate an in-room entertainment system you will need a Hotel Vision licence.
- If you show films or TV programmes, including channels such as ITV or BBC1, you need an MPLC licence.
- If you use images in your marketing, you must have permission to use them from the copyright owner.

Television licences

Do I need a special licence?

- **Maybe:** for non-accommodation businesses, you will need a licence if you provide a TV or a programme streaming service such as Now TV, ITV Hub or BBC iPlayer for either staff or customers on any part of your premises. If your premises are a single unit then you will only need a single TV licence at the standard rate of £157.50. However, if your business has multiple units (e.g. corporate boxes at a football stadium) then you will need a special Hospitality Licence which costs £157.50 for the first 15 units and £157.50 for each further 15 units.

- **Yes:** If you offer short-stay accommodation to overnight visitors, whether in serviced or self-catering accommodation, and you provide a device on which your guests can view TV programmes, you need to apply for a 'Hotel and Mobile Units Television Licence' (hotel licence). It should be noted that a licence is required regardless of whether the TV programmes are viewed through a TV, computer, mobile phone, games console, digital box, DVD/VHS recorder or any other device.

Note: despite its name, the hotel licence encompasses accommodation ranging from hotels, guesthouses, bed and breakfasts and inns to holiday cottages, flats and chalets through to camping and caravan sites and narrowboats.

The TV Licensing Authority says that you should always take out a hotel licence if you are providing televisions for the use of paying guests. While staying on your property, guests are not covered by their home licence. There is one exception: long-term hotel residents (i.e. those staying over 28 days) are not covered by a hotel licence, but they must have an ordinary television licence.

Note: while accommodation provided in sited caravans falls under the hotel licence scheme, there are different rules for touring caravans or mobile homes. The hirer of a touring caravan or mobile home may be covered by the licence for their home address as long as the television receivers are not being used at their home and caravan or mobile home at the same time.

Hotel licence fees
Your licence fee will be based on the number of units of overnight accommodation you have to let.
- if you have up to 15 units with televisions installed, you will pay one full fee of £157.50
- if you have more than 15 units, you will pay one full fee for the first 15 and an additional £157.50 for every extra five units (or fewer)
- the hotel licence is available only from TV Licensing (See *Further guidance* below for details).

What does it cover?
It will cover any equipment that can be used to watch or record TV programmes in:
- hotels, inns, guest houses, holiday villages, caravans and campsites
- the owner's private rooms on the site
- on-site staff accommodation (if provided by the hotel/ accommodation owner)
- lounges or other common rooms that are open to people staying on the site.

UPDATED

It does not cover:
- TV equipment which is not provided by the proprietor of the accommodation
- TV equipment in long-term letting accommodation and for permanent residents.

> **Note:** an important feature of the regulations is that a TV licence only covers one or more units if they are 'on the same site' or 'within the same premises'. That means a site or premises that is not divided or separated by any public thoroughfare such as a road or footpath or by another private property. For example, if you have a chain of businesses or your attraction spans two sides of a road, or your hotel has an annexe in a separate property next door or if you let holiday cottages in different locations, you will need a Company Group TV Licence.

If you have a TV in public areas, such as a bar or breakfast room, which has the sound turned on, you will also need TheMusicLicence from PPL PRS Ltd.

Copyright licences for music

The **Copyright, Designs and Patents Act 1988** states that any use of copyrighted music in public is possible only with the permission of the person who holds the copyright to the music being played.

"In public" means anything outside a family/domestic situation and includes all areas of a tourism accommodation property, including guests' rooms. So, even if you just have a radio in the breakfast room or TVs in guests' rooms, you may require a licence.

There are two separate copyright licences that relate to the playing of copyrighted music on your premises. They apply regardless of the device provided by which the music is played and even apply if the music is performed live.

The first music copyright licence fee is to pay the performers and record companies for the use of their recorded music. The fee for this licence is collected by PPL and is known as a PPL Licence.

The second music copyright licence fee is to pay the songwriters, composers and music publishers for the use of their musical compositions and lyrics. The fee for this licence is collected by PRS and the licence is known as a PRS Licence.

LICENCES & CONSENTS

While PPL and PRS licences can be paid separately, the two collection companies also work together to provide a single licence that covers both copyright fees where this is required. This combined licence is called TheMusicLicence.

Do I need a music copyright licence?

No: you are exempt from requiring either a PPL or PRS music licence if:

1. you have a B&B or guesthouse that has three guest bedrooms or less and,
- the premises is the only holiday accommodation business that you own or operate
- the premises is also your domestic residence
- facilities are only available to resident guests.

2. you operate only one self-catering unit and that unit has three guest bedrooms or less.

PRS only: you only require a PRS licence if you operate a self-catering property that comprises more than one unit or one unit with more than three bedrooms.

Yes: you need a combined TheMusicLicence that covers both PPL and PRS copyright fees if you operate a business that is outside the exemptions detailed above.

Is a licence required for copyrighted music in customers' rooms?

Yes: a licence is required where music can be played in guests' rooms via TVs, radios and other devices.

The PPL PRS Code of Conduct clarifies the rights and responsibilities of PPL PRS and businesses that provide music. An ombudsman has also been established to oversee PPL PRS's performance and to adjudicate on complaints.

Tariffs

The tariffs relating to TheMusicLicence continue to be set by both PPL (representing the copyright for recordings) and PRS for Music (representing the copyright for songs being played) separately. Licence tariffs vary in accordance with the type of performance (live or recorded), the type of premises, the occasion and the frequency of performances.

There is a wide range of tariff rates depending on the type and scale of business you operate. They include separate tariffs for:
- amusement parks, saloons, arcades, travelling showmen, funfairs
- parks, open-air places, pools
- cinemas

- theatres
- holiday centres
- holiday caravan parks
- hotels, restaurants and cafés
- pubs
- passenger ships and boats.

You can obtain more information by contacting the PPL PRS Customer Service Centre on 0800 0720 808.

Obtaining a licence

If a licence is required, you can find more information on the costs by viewing the separate tariff cards for each of the categories on the PPL PRS website: pplprs.co.uk/business/other.

PPL PRS has a dedicated section of its website for hotels, B&Bs and guesthouses. You can view all the tariffs which relate to your establishment and a checklist of information needed to obtain a quote, which includes:

- music in bedrooms
- number of bedrooms supplied or provided with recorded music
- background music – all premises
- areas where music is audible, such as receptions, bars etc.
- premises with 16 bedrooms or more
- background music
- the square meterage of each area where music is audible
- number of seats in bar and restaurant areas where music is playing
- types of devices used to play music, such as radio, CDs, TV etc.
- live events
- number and capacity of live events held per year.

Note: there are discounts available for businesses that are only open for part of the year, or only stage events or performances for part of the year.

Note: you are required by law to obtain a licence if you need one. If you apply for a licence before you start playing copyright music in a public place, you will be charged a standard rate. If you apply later, or are caught playing music without a licence, you will be charged a higher rate for the first year of the licence.

Discretionary charging policies

PPL and PRS for Music each separately operate a number of discretionary charging policies setting out circumstances in which, whilst legally entitled to do so, they choose not to apply a charge. Due to the specific nature of these policies, it is advisable to contact them for more information and to check if any of them apply to you.

Copyright for showing films and TV programmes

A copyright licence is needed if you show films on your premises or provide a service whereby you provide films to guests through a DVD or streaming service.

There are two main film licencing companies, Motion Picture Licensing Company (MPLC) and Filmbank Media, who each collect copyright royalties on behalf of different film studios in different circumstances. For example, while both MPLC and Filmbank Media both license the showing of films to audiences, MPLC collects the copyright for films shown on TV in commercial settings while FilmBank Media provides films for businesses like hotels to show on in-house entertainment systems.

Previously there has been an exemption for showing films and TV programmes via free-to-air services, e.g. if you have TVs that play films on channels such as BBC or ITV.

However, you now need to gain a licence through the Motion Picture Licensing Company (MPLC) to provide this service to your customers. As with PPL PRS Ltd for audio copyright licencing, MPLC is a collection society which licenses rights on behalf of various film companies and TV producers.

There are three main licence types:

Showing films

If you have a business where you have a limited number of public screenings of films each year or want to stage a one-off event, both MPLC and Filmbank Media offer a Single Title Movie Licence with different rates depending on the number of times the movie is shown, the size of the audience and whether the audience pays an admission charge. For paying audiences, the MPLC cost is the greater of either £75 or 35% of the total ticket sales.

Communal areas

The MPLC operate an Umbrella Licence for businesses that show films on TV in public communal areas (e.g. bar, guest lounge, gym or reception) on an ongoing basis. The fee is set by the type of business and size of the area. For example, the fee for restaurants and cafés up to 500 sq m is £102.62 +VAT. A full table of the charges is available on the MPLC website: www.mplcuk.com.

Alternatively, Filmbank Media offer an annual Public Video Screening Licence (PVSL), which allows organisations to legally screen films to create background ambience within their premises.

Guest bedrooms

If you have TVs in guest bedrooms you will be required to pay the Hotel/Guest Bedroom tariff rate of £5 + VAT per bedroom, per year. There is a 25% concession available where accommodation is available for less than 9 months of the year and there is no minimum fee. This new tariff does not currently apply to bedrooms in self-catering properties. You can find more information on the MPLC website: hotel.themplc.co.uk.

> **Note:** an MPLC licence is not required if you only have a TV in a public area of your establishment that is locked onto a channel that does not play films or TV programmes (e.g. the BBC News channel or Sky Sports). However, you cannot just say that "we only show the news channel" – the test is that the TV is not able to be switched to film-playing channels.

DVD libraries and in-house services

If you offer films to guests, either through an in-room entertainment system or simply by providing a DVD film library, you need a licence to do so.

Licences are taken out on a different basis depending on the type of guest accommodation:
- bed and breakfast accommodation, guesthouses, small hotels and boutique hotels are required to take a licence out on a per room basis
- serviced apartments require one licence per apartment
- chalets and holiday homes require one licence per chalet/home.

The main form of licence applicable to small accommodation businesses is the DVD Concierge Licence which allows businesses to provide DVDs for their customers' use. There are two forms of this licence:
- annual properties (those open year round) – £30 plus VAT per room/unit
- seasonal properties (open for eight months or less) – £20 plus VAT per room/unit
- the fees payable are for the licence only and accommodation providers would continue to purchase DVDs as usual. The licence fees quoted for guest accommodation apply when no extra charge for the DVD is made to the guest. If a charge is levied, as in most hotels, then a higher licence fee applies.

Avoiding DVD licences

Smaller businesses may choose to avoid the purchase of a licence by removing DVDs. A licence is not required if guests bring their own DVDs to watch.

Imagery and copyright

The **Copyright, Designs and Patents Act 1988** treats all imagery – including photographs on websites – as 'artistic works' subject to copyright. This copyright applies to any image, whether it has been produced by a professional photographer or a member of the general public, regardless of the image source i.e. the Act also applies to images found in an online image search.

Under the Act, you need the permission of the copyright owner to use the image, for whatever purpose. If you use an image without permission you could be taken to court and be required to compensate the copyright holder for the illegal use of the image.

To ensure you are using images legally you can:
- take images yourself (meaning you are the copyright owner)
- hire a professional photographer, ensuring image usage is included in your contract with them
- download licence-free images from online image libraries. However, check the conditions attached to any images you wish to use, as some may not have permission to be used for commercial use (i.e. selling something, which includes hotel rooms).

Further guidance

TV Licensing

Check what type of licence you need and pay online on the TV licensing website: **www.tvlicensing.co.uk**

PPL PRS

Find more about TheMusicLicence and how much it will cost on the PPL PRS website: **pplprs.co.uk**

Filmbank Media

Find out which licences you need to show films on the Filmbank Media website: **www.filmbankmedia.com/licences**. You can also call Filmbank Media on **020 7984 5965** or email **dvdconcierge@filmbank.co.uk**

Motion Picture Licensing Company

Find out if you need an MPLC licence on the MPLC website: **www.mplcuk.com**. You can also call the Motion Picture Licensing Company on **01323 649 647** or email: **ukinfo@mplc.com.**

Planning and Building

KEY FACTS

- Planning permission and building regulations apply if you are considering starting a business, if you plan to convert, extend or make structural alterations to an existing property or construct a new building.
- Contact the planning department of your local authority for advice on planning permission.
- Asbestos can be found in buildings and can pose a serious health risk. You must identify whether the building contains asbestos, keep an up-to-date record of the location and condition of asbestos-containing materials, assess any risk, and prepare a plan to manage that risk.

Note: the Government is currently undertaking a fundamental review of planning legislation in England, aimed at streamlining and modernising the planning process. This review covers plan-making, development management, development contributions and other related policy proposals.

Essential first steps

Planning permission and building regulations are the essential first steps if you are considering starting an attraction or serviced accommodation business. Serviced accommodation includes:

- hotels
- guesthouses
- bed and breakfasts
- farmhouses
- inns.

Planning permission

You should contact the planning department of your local authority for advice on planning permission at a very early stage if you are considering:

- starting a new business
- converting or extending your premises.

LICENCES & CONSENTS

Planning policies on providing tourism businesses, especially visitor attractions and accommodation, will be set out in the authority's Local Development Framework.

'Change of use'
The Town and Country Planning (Use Classes) Order 1987 (as amended) puts uses of land and buildings into various categories known as 'Use Classes'. Accommodation is Use Class C, with the provision of serviced tourism accommodation such as hotels and guesthouses being Use Class C1.

Attractions such as museums and galleries are Use Class F1, while attractions such as theatres, amusement arcades/centres or funfairs are outside this classification system and have their own specific Use Class. Always check with your council whether the property that you are planning to use for your business is the appropriate Use Class for your purpose.

If the existing Use Class is not appropriate for your intended use, you will have to apply to the Council for 'Change of Use' consent. Change of Use is required both within a Use Class (e.g. changing a property from residential use (C3) to a guesthouse (C1)), or from one use class to another (e.g. changing a property from a retail store (E(a)) to a museum (F1)).

Depending on the specifics of any proposed change of use, including any building work associated with the proposal, it may require an application for planning permission or prior approval.

Even if you only wish to start offering a simple bed and breakfast in your home or open a small museum or visitor centre in an outbuilding on your property where no structural alterations to the building will be carried out, you may need 'change of use' planning permission to do so.

Change of use consent and B&Bs
There is sometimes confusion about whether converting a property from a residential dwelling to a bed and breakfast establishment requires the owner to gain 'change of use' approval. This confusion stems from two sources - the first being that there are no hard and fast rules as to what constitutes 'change of use' and the second from the fact that there are two change of use requirements:
- the first is related to planning permission
- the second is related to building regulations.

Planning permission change of use consent

In planning terms, consent from the council must be gained if there is any 'material' change of use to a property or building. In most cases, it is relatively straightforward as to what constitutes a material change of use (e.g. converting a house into a commercial building or a block of flats).

However, there is a grey area as to how much change is allowed before that change materially affects the purpose for which the building is used. That is, at what point does a residential house become a premises whose main purpose is to offer accommodation for visitors? This issue is particularly relevant for bed and breakfast properties where the property is simultaneously a residential property and a commercial property.

To clarify this area, local authorities have developed a range of measures to determine whether a material change of use has occurred and planning consent is required. These rules generally relate to the proportion of the property that has been given over to the business. This can be determined in a number of ways, the most usual relating to:

- the number of bedrooms as a proportion of the total number of bedrooms in the property, or
- the area of the building used for the B&B as a proportion of the total building.

However, some local authorities use the 'six-bed rule', i.e. consent for change of use must be sought where the business provides six or more bedspaces (not to be confused with bedrooms) for customers.

If you are considering operating a B&B, you should consult with the local authority planning officers to determine whether change of use consent is required. Even if you have previously operated a similar B&B in another destination where no consent was required, you should contact the council as their interpretation of a material change to the use of a property could be different.

Building regulations change of use consent

The second change of use requirement is under the **Building Regulations 2000.**

Under the Building Regulations, there is a material change of use where there is a change in the purposes for which, or the circumstances in which, a building is used, so that after the change 'the building is used as an hotel or a boarding house, where previously it was not'. As with determining whether planning consent is required, different local authorities have different guidelines as to whether a property is deemed to be a hotel or boarding house under these regulations. Potential B&B operators should check with their local authority to determine whether change of use consent is required.

You should also note that the Building Regulations' definition of 'material change of use' differs substantially from the meaning of 'material change of use' in the **Town and Country Planning Act 1990**, which has given rise to a great deal of litigation. Planning permission may be required for a change of use where Building Regulation approval is not needed and vice versa.

If consent is required, you must make an application using the 'Full Plans' application process, as domestic buildings that are not exclusively used as private dwellings (e.g. holiday accommodation and dwellings providing bed and breakfast) are subject to the **Regulatory Reform (Fire Safety) Order 2005**.

> **Note:** even if planning consent is not required, you may still require building regulations consent. You may also require building regulations consent even if you are not contemplating any structural changes in turning your house into a Bed and Breakfast establishment.

Granting planning permission

Local authorities' policies on granting planning permission vary and any proposal will be checked against these policies. When deciding whether or not to grant planning permission, where it is needed, the council will take into account the effects on neighbours and the environment, the loss of residential accommodation, traffic generation, access from the highway, car parking facilities and the number of bedrooms offered for letting.

Restrictions on what you can do are usually stricter in specially designated areas such as:
● National Parks
● Green belts
● Conservation areas
● Areas of Outstanding Natural Beauty (AONB).

> **Note:** you may also need consent for any signage for your property (see the '*Signs for Your Premises*' section).

Building regulations

Building regulations apply whenever a building is erected, extended, materially altered or made subject to a material change of use. They also cover other works and fittings such as:
● new drainage and sanitary installations
● new heating installations
● structural alterations to a building

- alterations which have an effect on the existing means of escape in fire
- replacement windows and external doors
- electrical installations
- change to a building's energy status and renovation or replacement of thermal elements of a building (such as re-roofing, replacement cladding, re-plastering, dry lining, external render, and renovation or replacement of existing floors).

Permitted Development Rights

Permitted Development Rights are the ability to undertake certain types of building work without needing to apply for planning permission. In August 2020, the Government extended permitted development rights to include the ability for homeowners to increase the size of their homes by adding:

- up to two additional storeys, where the existing house consists of two or more storeys; or
- one additional storey, where the existing house consists of only one storey.

However, there are a large number of restrictions on the operation of this right including the following:

- the house was constructed before 1 July 1948 or after 28 October 2018
- additional storeys have already been added to the original house, whether by operation of this right or otherwise
- following the development, the height of the highest part of the roof does not exceed 18 metres.

Bear in mind that the Permitted Development Rights which apply to many common projects for houses do not apply to flats, maisonettes or other buildings. Similarly, commercial properties have different permitted development rights to dwellings.

It is important to note that Permitted Development Rights are more restricted in specially designated areas like National Parks and AONBs.

Contact the planning department of your local council to check the Permitted Development Rights that apply to your area and your particular building.

> **Note:** even if you are not thinking of altering your house to accommodate bed and breakfast guests, and planning permission is not required, you may still be required to do work to your property in order to meet building regulations requirements. Again, you need to contact the building control department of your local authority as early as possible.

LICENCES & CONSENTS

MARKETING

CUSTOMERS

FOOD & DRINK

HEALTH & SAFETY

STAFF

BUSINESS MANAGEMENT & TAX

FURTHER INFORMATION

UPDATED

Energy Performance Certificates

All properties that are newly built, sold or rented are required to have an Energy Performance Certificate (EPC). These certificates provide information on a building's energy use and carbon dioxide emissions and are accompanied by a report with suggestions on how to reduce them. A certificate is valid for 10 years, after which it must be renewed.

A building's EPC must be provided to any person who wishes to purchase or rent the building. However, an EPC is not required where a property is:

- rented out for less than a cumulative period of four months within a 12 month period, or
- rented out through a licensing arrangement whereby the holiday-maker does not have exclusive use of the property during the period of their booking
- a listed building
- a stand-alone building with total useful floor space of less than 50 square metres.

This means that accommodation operators are not required to gain and provide EPCs for customers, provided that the agreement under which the property is let is a 'licence to occupy'. A licence to occupy is the type of agreement that hotels have with customers, whereby staff can enter the property to undertake essential work, rather than a tenancy agreement whereby the landlord must gain the permission of the tenant to enter the property.

Managing asbestos

Many buildings throughout the country contain asbestos, which can pose a serious health risk if not managed properly.

Regulations governing the management of asbestos in non-domestic properties are the **Control of Asbestos Regulations 2012**, which provide a framework for the management of asbestos/asbestos-containing materials (ACMs) in existing non-domestic premises and during any work activity involving asbestos. Dutyholders must make sure anyone who carries out any work in non-domestic premises and any occupants of the premises are not exposed to asbestos from ACMs that may be present.

The legal duty relates to its management, not necessarily its removal. The regulations require you to:

- identify whether the building contains asbestos
- keep an up-to-date record of the location and condition of asbestos-containing materials
- assess the risk and prepare a plan to manage that risk.

All parts of your property that are non-domestic will be subject to the regulations. Any private areas used only by the owner will be considered to be domestic and therefore not subject to the regulations.

If you think that your property contains asbestos, seek advice from an expert. Asbestos is only dangerous when disturbed - if it is safely managed and contained it does not present a health risk.

Further guidance

Your local authority
Information and advice on whether you need planning permission is available from the Planning Department of your local authority: **www.gov.uk/find-local-council**

Planning Portal
The Government's online service offers free guidance on all aspects of planning: **www.planningportal.co.uk**

Guidance on asbestos
The Health and Safety Executive has guidance on asbestos, including identifying whether it is present and how to manage it, which can be found in any building built before 2000: **www.hse.gov.uk**.

LICENCES & CONSENTS

MARKETING

CUSTOMERS

FOOD & DRINK

HEALTH & SAFETY

STAFF

BUSINESS MANAGEMENT & TAX

FURTHER INFORMATION

Signs for Your Premises

KEY FACTS

- If you display any outdoor signs and/or advertisements you may need to apply to the planning authority for consent to display the proposed sign.
- The need for consent from the planning authority depends on whether signs are fully, partially or non-illuminated and where they are situated.
- You will also need to ensure that any signs displayed are not misleading, as this could constitute a breach of unfair trading and misleading marketing legislation.
- The highways department of your local authority can advise on brown tourism signs.

Background

Do the regulations apply to me?

Yes, if you display any outdoor signs and/or advertisements, you need to comply with:

- the **Town and Country Planning (Control of Advertisements) Regulations 2007**
- the **Consumer Protection Regulations 2008** (CPRs) relating to unfair trading and misleading marketing (see *Unfair Trading Practices* section).

Planning regulations and permission

The display of all outdoor signs and advertisements is controlled by local planning authorities under the provisions of **Town and Country Planning (Control of Advertisements) Regulations 2007**.

Local planning authorities are required to exercise their powers under the regulations with regard to amenity and public safety, taking into account relevant development plan policies in so far as they relate to amenity (including both visual and aural amenity) and public safety, as well as any other relevant factors.

These regulations can be complex and you are strongly advised to seek the advice of the planning department of your local authority (see *Further guidance* below) before commissioning and setting up any signs for your premises.

A very brief summary of the regulations is given here:
- 'express consent' means that you have to apply to the planning authority for consent to display the proposed sign
- 'deemed consent' means that consent is deemed to have been given by the planning authority and you do not have to apply for it.

Signs on your premises

Illuminated and non-illuminated signs
- **Fully illuminated signs** always require express consent from the planning authority (although this is not normally the case if the sign is displayed inside a window, rather than on the wall or doorway outside).
- **Partially illuminated signs** (e.g. where only letters, and not the background, are illuminated) may not require express consent.
- **Non-illuminated signs** can normally be displayed with deemed consent if they are fixed to the building, although there are limitations placed on the height of the sign and on the size of any characters or symbols on it.

Listed buildings
If your property is a Listed Building, you will always have to obtain Listed Building consent before you put up a sign.

Signs at the entrance to your premises
You may normally put a non-illuminated sign by your gate, driveway or within the grounds of your establishment with deemed consent (subject to limitations on overall size, height and size of characters or symbols).

Signs in advance of your premises
If you wish to put up directional signs by the side of the roads approaching your establishment, e.g. in a field overlooking the road (with the landowner's permission, of course), you must always seek the express consent of the planning authority.

Flags

Provided that your premises are not within areas of special control or other areas with protective designations, flag advertisements that do not require express consent are restricted to:

- a single flag from a single flagpole projecting from the premises with either the company name or logo of the company or the advertising of a specific event of limited duration, such as a sale,
- two flags on flagstaffs not attached to a building.

Special controls

In sensitive places, e.g. Conservation Areas, the deemed consent may be removed by an Article 4 Declaration. You will have to apply for consent for signs on or at the entrance to your premises. In some rural localities, an Area of Special Control Advertisements may restrict all outdoor advertising.

Ensuring signs are not misleading

You should also ensure that any signs displayed are not misleading. For example, it is illegal for a non-assessed property to display a Quality Grading Scheme sign or to display a sign showing an incorrect rating.

For more information on misleading signs, see the *'Unfair Trading Practices'* section.

Brown tourism signs

Both attractions and accommodation businesses can apply for brown tourism signs. However, in practice, accommodation establishments have been less successful with their applications than visitor attractions.

The first step is to contact the highways department of your local authority who will advise you about procedures, local policy and the cost of such signs. Each local highways authority will have its own guidelines that balance local environmental and road safety interests with those of the tourism industry.

Your local highway authority controls signs on the local roads in its area and sets local policy on brown signs. Highways England controls signs on trunk roads and motorways.

The standard for tourism signing on the trunk road network and guidance on signage on local roads in England is available on the Highways England website, along with an application form for signs on roads managed by Highways England: **www.gov.uk/ guidance/apply-for-brown-tourist-signs-on-roads-the-highways-agency-manage**. However, it should be noted that the application process can take up to nine months and a sign can be expensive - from £8,000 to £20,000 if it is on a single carriageway and from £17,000 to £40,000 if it is on a motorway.

> **Note:** guidance on tourist signs has been modified to ensure that priority is given to genuine tourist attractions rather than wider retail, sport or leisure facilities. There has also been a move towards greater transparency in the application process and improving processing times. Whilst this guidance only applies to motorways and trunk roads, local highway authorities will be encouraged to apply similar standards.

Further guidance

Your local authority
For informal advice or to apply for consent for signage on your property, contact the planning department of your local authority: **www.gov.uk/find-local-council**

Outdoor Advertisements and Signs
Outdoor Advertisements and Signs - A Guide for Advertisers can be downloaded from the Gov.uk website: **www.gov.uk/government/ publications/outdoor-advertisements-and-signs-a-guide-for-advertisers**

Applying for a brown tourism sign
The Highways England website contains a range of guidance publications related to tourism signage on both trunk and non-trunk roads: **www.gov.uk/guidance/apply-for-brown-tourist-signs-on-roads-the-highways-agency-manage**

Local support
Your local Destination Organisation or your local authority may also be able to advise you on the local situation with white-on-brown signs: **https://www.visitbritain.org/business-advice/find-local-support.**

LICENCES & CONSENTS · MARKETING · CUSTOMERS · FOOD & DRINK · HEALTH & SAFETY · STAFF · BUSINESS MANAGEMENT & TAX · FURTHER INFORMATION

www.visitengland.org/pinkbookonline

MARKETING

Unfair Trading Practices

KEY FACTS

- Businesses have a general duty not to undertake unfair trading practices under the Consumer Protection from Unfair Trading Regulations (CPRs).
- The CPRs aid in determining whether certain advertising and marketing practices are misleading, aggressive or lack due diligence.
- In addition to this general duty, there are 31 business practices that are banned outright, such as displaying a quality mark without authorisation.
- The Business Protection Regulations impose further restrictions on how companies compare their products to rival products from other companies.

Background

The **Consumer Protection from Unfair Trading Regulations 2008** (Consumer Protection Regulations) harmonise legislation preventing business practices that are unfair to consumers.

The aim of the legislation is to make it easier for customers to compare the products and services provided by businesses and make informed purchasing decisions. This is particularly relevant to the tourism sector, where the customer is unable to see the product before making a booking or deciding to visit.

The **Business Protection from Misleading Marketing Regulations 2008** (Business Protection Regulations) tighten restrictions relating to how companies compare their products to rival products from other companies.

Do the regulations apply to me?

Yes, if you are either:

- advertising your business using any form of media (including online and via social media)
- making statements about your facilities to the public.

Unfair trading

What constitutes an unfair trading practice?

The aim of the CPRs is to provide a framework for determining whether certain practices are misleading, aggressive or lack due diligence on the basis that they would alter the behaviour of the average customer. In other words, if it can be determined that the customer made a purchase that they otherwise would not have done had they known the full facts of the matter, then the business has engaged in unfair practices.

This covers engaging in misleading practices such as making false or deceptive statements in marketing material or omitting important information that would have a bearing on the customer's purchasing decision.

Examples

False and deceptive statements could include statements made about:
- the quality of accommodation (see also *Practices banned outright* below)
- the amenities or services available
- the location of the premises.

For example, it would be a false statement if you advertised that your accommodation was "five minutes from the beach", when it is actually a half-hour drive, while a misleading claim would be that "the art museum has the best collection of Turner paintings in the UK" when only one is on public display.

Similarly, if you omitted to notify customers that you were undertaking refurbishment work that either closed facilities or generated considerable noise or dust, or that you had to pay for rides within a theme park in addition to the admission charge, this could be deemed to be misleading.

Another aspect to be aware of in this area is when it comes to the provision of food and descriptions of dishes on menus. For example, it would be a false statement if you say you provide a "champagne breakfast" if you actually served prosecco, or that all meals were organic if the produce used was not certified to be organic. Similarly, it would be misleading to state that seafood is sourced locally if that means that it came from a local supermarket.

UPDATED

Practices banned outright

While much of what constitutes an unfair practice will have to be determined through case law, the legislation lists 31 practices that are banned outright. These practices include:

- *displaying a quality mark (such as a grading scheme mark) or an accessibility rating mark without having the necessary authorisation. This includes displaying a mark that is out-of-date*
- *falsely claiming that a premises or product has been approved or endorsed by a public body such as VisitEngland*
- *falsely stating that an offer will only be available for a limited time.*

So, if you were to display on your premises an incorrect VisitEngland star rating, or an outdated tourist board rating such as a Crown or Diamond classification and grading, this would be regarded as a breach of the regulations.

Unfair comparison

In addition to the Consumer Protection Regulations, the **Business Protection from Misleading Marketing Regulations 2008** tighten the legislation relating to comparison marketing. These regulations specify that companies must not use advertising to:

- compare products or materials that are not designed for the same period
- confuse people as to the advertiser and the competitor
- present imitations or replicas of products bearing a protected trademark or trade name
- take unfair advantage of the reputation of competitors' trademarks, trade names, other distinguishing marks, or country of origin information.

Examples

Unfair comparisons could include:

- taking out an advertisement that unfavourably compares the cost of staying at a neighbouring hotel with staying at your hotel would be deemed to be unfair if you failed to mention that the neighbouring hotel was a five star property while yours was a three star property
- comparing your admission charge with that of another attraction, when their admission includes the use of all facilities and visitors to your attraction have to pay the use of facilities
- describing your guesthouse as "the Torquay Hilton", even if you consider this to be a tongue-in-cheek description.

LICENCES & CONSENTS

MARKETING

CUSTOMERS

FOOD & DRINK

HEALTH & SAFETY

STAFF

BUSINESS MANAGEMENT & TAX

FURTHER INFORMATION

UPDATED

Online reviews and endorsements

If your website allows customers to post reviews, the **Consumer Protection from Unfair Trading Regulations 2008** prevent you from managing or presenting the reviews you receive in a way that misleads your customers. This means that you cannot write or commission fake reviews. 'Commission' includes asking friends to write reviews and offering inducements to customers in return for writing positive reviews.

It also means that, in order not to mislead your customers, the review section of your website must accurately reflect your customers' views, regardless of whether they are positive or negative. Your process for collecting, moderating and publishing reviews must not hinder their impartiality and you must publish all genuine and lawful reviews. For example, you cannot pick and choose which customers you ask to provide a review when they depart – you must either invite all of them or none – and you cannot choose which reviews to publish on your site.

The Competition and Markets Authority (CMA) have issued a guide *Giving a balanced picture: dos and don'ts for online review sites* on the Gov.uk website.

Paid promotions

It is not illegal to pay a person or publication to promote your business online; however, potential customers need to know the endorsement has been paid for. For example, while it is legal to pay a blogger to write a piece about your business, it must be clear that you have paid for this endorsement. This can be done by adding a statement such as 'Advertisement Feature' or 'Advertisement Promotion'.

The CMA have also issued a guide *Online endorsements: being open and honest with your audience* on the Gov.uk website.

Enforcement and penalties

Your local Trading Standards office is responsible for enforcing the regulations.

Anyone who breaches the regulations can be prosecuted for a criminal offence by a local Trading Standards office and subject to a fine and/or, in extreme cases, a sentence of up to two years. In addition, it could lead to a civil claim – see *Misrepresentation* below.

Defence against a charge of unfair trading

Possible defences against a charge of unfair trading include:

- you made an honest mistake and were not given the opportunity to remedy the situation (i.e. you thought that you had the oldest pub in the region)
- your statement was based on information supplied by a third party
- the statement was made by some 'other person' such as a guidebook or newspaper article ('other person' does not mean any of your employees).

However, in any defence, you would still have to show that you took all reasonable care and exercised all due diligence to check that the facts were true in any publication or statement. You should keep written records of those efforts so you can prove what you did (e.g. a copy of your brochure or information sheet marked to show the checks you made).

Misrepresentation

Engaging in unfair trading practices can not only result in a criminal prosecution (see *Enforcement and penalties* above) but it may also result in a civil claim being brought against you by any person who has suffered loss as a result of a false statement. This stems from what is referred to in law as misrepresentation.

When misrepresentation occurs

Misrepresentation occurs where a party is induced to enter into a contract by certain statements that later turn out to be untrue. With respect to tourism businesses, these could again include statements regarding:

- quality
- amenities
- location.

For example, if Mr Anderson and his family had booked into a bed and breakfast with an assurance that it was only 'five minutes from the beach' and it turned out to be a half-hour drive he would be able to either:

- refuse to continue with the booking and claim damages from you for any losses incurred as a result
- continue staying with you but claim damages for his, and his family's, distress and disappointment.

MARKETING

Other considerations

For any promotional material, you should also bear in mind
the following:

- **advertising codes** (for broadcast and non-broadcast media)
  are issued by the Committee of Advertising Practice (CAP)
  and require advertisements and sales promotions to be legal,
  decent, honest and truthful. Advertising codes also deal with
  specific issues, including the availability of products at the
  advertised price and VAT inclusion in prices
- the requirements of the **Package Travel and Linked Travel
  Arrangements Regulation 2018** – see the *'Holiday Packages'*
  section for more information.

Social media

Many operators advertise and market their business through social
media – for example, having a Facebook account for the business
and/or a Twitter feed attached to their website.

It is important to realise that while you may use a far more relaxed
or 'chatty' style of communication when using social media than you
would in print or on your main website, everything that you post
via social media must still comply with all aspects of the CPRs. It is
therefore essential to re-read anything that you are about to post
using social media to make sure that it is accurate, is not open to
misinterpretation and does not make unfair comparisons.

Further guidance

Your local Trading Standards office

Your local Trading Standards office is responsible for enforcing the
regulations and should be able to give you further guidance:
www.gov.uk/find-local-trading-standards-office

Consumer Protection: a basic guide

The guidance publication The Consumer Protection from Unfair
Trading Regulations: a basic guide for business can be downloaded
from the Gov.uk website

Advertising codes

Further information on the advertising codes can be obtained from the
Committee of Advertising Practice (CAP) website: **www.asa.org.uk.**

Direct Marketing

KEY FACTS

- If you make direct marketing calls to individuals, or send direct marketing faxes to individuals or businesses, you are required to comply with direct marketing legislation.

- As a business, you are not allowed to make direct marketing calls to individuals who have declined to receive such calls or who have registered with the Telephone Preference Service (TPS).

- If you send email and text/picture/video marketing messages to advertise your business, the **Privacy and Electronic Communications (EC Directive) Regulations 2003** apply.

- The **Consumer Contracts (Information, Cancellation and Additional Charges) Regulations 2013** came into force in June 2014, replacing the **Consumer Protection (Distance Selling) Regulations**. These regulation apply to goods and services sold over the internet, by phone or by mail order. However, they **do not apply to contracts to provide accommodation, transport, catering or leisure services.**

Direct marketing by telephone or electronic media

The **Privacy and Electronic Communications (EC Directive) Regulations 2003** were introduced to protect individuals, and in some cases businesses, against receiving direct marketing material by phone or electronic media (e.g. internet or text messaging) without their prior approval.

Under the 2003 regulations you are not allowed, by law, to send unsolicited marketing material by email to an individual subscriber without previous consent or send any marketing material by email (whether solicited or unsolicited) to any subscriber without revealing your full identity or a valid address to which the recipient can send an opt-out request.

MARKETING

The regulations are overseen and enforced by the Information Commissioner's Office. This is an independent authority established by the Government.

Do the regulations apply to me?
Yes: if you make direct marketing calls, emails, texts or other electronic communications to individuals or businesses.

What do the regulations cover?
Direct marketing phone calls
As a business, you are not allowed to make a direct marketing call to any individual (including sole traders and, except in Scotland, partnerships), if they have told you that they do not want to receive such calls or they have registered with the Telephone Preference Service (TPS). If you do undertake marketing calls, you are required to ensure that your phone number is displayed on the customers' phone (i.e. you are not allowed to make calls using a private line).

TPS is a service set up by the Direct Marketing Association (DMA). They maintain registers of all those who have stated that they do not want to receive direct marketing calls or faxes.

Emails and text messaging
The regulations define electronic mail as "any text, voice, sound, or image message sent over a public electronic communications network" and includes messages sent via social media.

The regulations require you to obtain individuals' prior consent before sending unsolicited direct marketing via e-mail or text messages. When undertaking any marketing you must also identify your business and provide a valid address to which the recipient can send an opt-out request.

Customers must opt-in
There used to be an exemption called the 'soft opt-in' whereby you were allowed to send electronic communications such as emails or texts for marketing purposes to previous customers who had not opted-out of receiving these communications (i.e. the customer had not actively indicated that they did not want to receive them).

This is no longer the case. Customers now have to actively indicate that they want to receive marketing communications. This means that you must provide an empty tick-box on a paper or online booking form for them to fill in rather than a 'pre-ticked' box where they have to remove the tick.

If customers agree to you sending them marketing communications, the material you send them must relate to the similar products and services only (i.e. you cannot send them advertising material for someone else's business). In addition, the material you send must also provide the opportunity for the person to opt-out of any subsequent communications.

How do I comply, and what are the costs?

If you intend to make any 'cold' direct marketing calls (calls where permission has not been given to do so beforehand) to individuals you need to check the numbers first against the TPS register. If you make regular cold calls, you need to check the numbers every 28 days.

The cost of access to the TPS register varies, depending on the type and level of access you require. In order to ensure that you have the most appropriate package, call the TPS information pack line (see *Further guidance* below). There is also useful information on the TPS website: **www.tpsonline.org.uk/tps/index.html**. If you use a telemarketing company to run a telephone campaign for you, you do not need to subscribe.

Penalties for non-compliance

The **Privacy and Electronic Communications (Amendment) Regulations** were introduced in 2018 following reports from the Information Commissioner's Office (ICO) that its penalty imposing powers were not having the intended effect on unsolicited direct marketing. As a result, if a company cannot show that an individual did not 'opt-in' to receive direct marketing, and no other type of consent is obtained, it can be fined up to £500,000 by the ICO.

Using premium rate numbers

Premium rate numbers generally begin with 09, 118, 0871, 0872 and 0873. Mobile text shortcode numbers - the five and six-digit numbers that you can use to enter text competitions, give to charity via your mobile, download mobile games, etc. - are also considered premium rate. The 0870 and 0845 numbers are not affected.

Premium rate numbers are currently regulated by the Phone-paid Services Authority under an Ofcom approved code of practice.

- **Pricing:** pricing information is to be clearly written wherever you display the number. It applies to electronic, website and print information.
- **Undue delay:** there should not be an unfair delay before a caller can access the service required. Callers must be informed of the expected time it will take to have their call answered and, if applicable, of their position in any queuing system.

LICENCES & CONSENTS

MARKETING

CUSTOMERS

FOOD & DRINK

HEALTH & SAFETY

STAFF

BUSINESS MANAGEMENT & TAX

FURTHER INFORMATION

NEW

- **Prior permission licences:** some services require prior permission from the Phone-paid Services Authority before they can operate on a premium-rate line, such as international dial-through services. A list of those services exempt from prior permission can be found on the Phone-paid Services Authority website.
- **Customer care contact number:** a number must be provided for customers with complaints or concerns to call. This number can be the same or an alternative 087 number.

For more information or to register a premium rate service, visit the Phone-paid Services Authority website: **www.psauthority.org.uk.**

The use of 'cookies' on websites

A 'cookie' is a piece of data stored by a website within a browser, and then subsequently sent back to the same website by the browser. Typically, a cookie remembers a user's preferences or settings when they revisit the website. More recently, businesses have introduced 'tracking cookies' as a way to compile long-term records of an individual's browsing history so that products and offers can be targeted to specific customers or so a picture can be developed of a customer's buying patterns.

You are not allowed to use cookies or similar devices unless:
- customers are provided with clear and comprehensive information about the purposes of the storage of, or access to, that information, and;
- have given their consent.

The Regulations are not prescriptive about the sort of information that you should provide but the text should be sufficiently comprehensive and intelligible to allow customers to clearly understand the potential consequences of allowing storage and access to the information collected by the cookie should they wish to do so.

Guidance on the use of cookies and other similar devices is provided on the Information Commissioner's Office website: **ico.org.uk**. The ICO also produces a guidance publication, *Guidance on the rules on use of cookies and similar technologies*, which can be downloaded from the website.

Distance selling

In June 2014 the Consumer **Contracts (Information, Cancellation and Additional Charges) Regulations 2013** came into force, replacing the **Consumer Protection (Distance Selling) Regulations 2000** and the **Consumer Protection (Distance Selling) (Amendment) Regulations 2005**. For small businesses, the new legislation does not provide any significant changes to the existing legislation.

These regulations apply to goods and services that are not sold in 'face-to-face' transactions. That is, items sold over the internet, by phone or by mail order where the customer is not able to inspect the goods and services that they are purchasing.

The purpose of these regulations is to provide additional rights to consumers buying at a distance to encourage confidence in this method of transaction. The information that must be provided in these transactions includes details about:

- the business
- the goods or services you are selling
- payment arrangements
- delivery arrangements
- consumers' right to cancel their orders.

The regulations also require the business to provide those goods or services within 30 days.

However, it is important to note that the regulations do not apply to contracts to provide accommodation, transport, catering and leisure services where the contract provides for a specific date or period of performance (e.g. a concert or sports event that is only being staged on specific dates).

It should also be noted that the regulations do not apply to goods and services sold to other businesses (these are business-to-business contracts) and only apply to transactions that are normally undertaken at distance and where there are systems in place for trading in this way.

So even if you occasionally sell products and services other than the services listed as exempt above, the regulations only apply if this is your normal way of selling these products and services.

Further guidance

The Direct Marketing Association

The Direct Marketing Association runs the TPS and other preference services and provides further information on its website: **dma.org.uk**

Guidance on privacy and e-communications

Guidance on the Privacy and Electronic Communications (EC Directive) Regulations 2003 can be downloaded from the Information Commissioner's Office website: **ico.org.uk/for-organisations/ guide-to-pecr/what-are-pecr**

Guidance on consumer contracts

Guidance on the Consumer Contracts (Information, Cancellation and Additional Charges) Regulations 2013 can be downloaded from the Gov.uk website

Phone-paid Services Authority

The UK regulator for content, goods and services charged to a phone bill: **psauthority.org.uk**

Telephone Preference Service

The official central opt-out register where consumers record their preference not to receive unsolicited sales or marketing calls: **www.tpsonline.org.uk//tps/index.html.**

LICENCES & CONSENTS

MARKETING

CUSTOMERS

FOOD & DRINK

HEALTH & SAFETY

STAFF

BUSINESS MANAGEMENT & TAX

FURTHER INFORMATION

Holiday Packages

Note: the Department for Business, Energy and Industrial Strategy (BEIS) will be reviewing the Package Travel and Linked Travel Arrangements Regulations 2018 during 2021 and the following information could change as a result.

KEY FACTS

- If you offer, or allow customers to buy, at least two of the following elements: transport, accommodation, vehicle hire and other significant visitor service, then you are probably subject to the **Package Travel and Linked Travel Arrangements Regulations 2018**.
- These regulations cover circumstances where you sell different elements yourself, work with another business to sell different elements or provide the customer with a targeted offer to purchase an element from another business.
- These regulations include specific requirements relating to how you market, book and deliver these products.

Package Travel Regulations

The **Package Travel and Linked Travel Arrangements Regulations 2018** (commonly known as the Package Travel Regulations) were introduced on 1 July 2018 and greatly expand the scope of the former Regulations. The main changes are that the Regulations now cover situations where the customer creates their own packages (dynamic packaging) and introduces the concept of a 'Linked Travel Arrangement', whereby a customer is provided with a targeted offer for a service provided by a separate business once they have completed a booking. These changes affect the activities of many accommodation providers.

These regulations concern the marketing, sale and performance of products that are sold together or through a linkage. They apply not only to the big companies offering overseas package holidays, but also to accommodation businesses selling offers that combine or link products (for example, accommodation with tickets to an attraction, a spa treatment, a murder mystery weekend or a round of golf).

Enforcement and penalties

There are criminal penalties for non-compliance. Trading Standards are responsible for enforcing the legislation.

Do the regulations apply to me?

Yes: if you are offering a package of services for sale at an inclusive price which includes at least two of the services listed below and the package lasts for at least 24 hours or includes overnight accommodation, you will probably be offering a 'package' that is subject to the regulations:

- transport
- accommodation
- vehicle hire
- other visitor services that are a significant part of the package and not ancillary to transport or accommodation (e.g. excursions, access to a golf course and theatre tickets, but not educational, business or conference services).

Selling Packages

There are two main circumstances in which an accommodation business may be deemed to be selling a package.

1. **You work with another business in order to provide a package that combines two or more elements.** (This is the traditional package, where two businesses work together to develop a package that is then sold to the customer for an inclusive price. For example, if you sell accommodation and a ticket to a nearby attraction for an inclusive price).

2. **Your business sells two or more different elements to customers.** This applies in situations where you sell different products to customers on your premises – for example, if you operate a hotel which provides accommodation and other services such as restaurant meals, spa treatments, gym use or a round of golf. This covers two different situations:
   - Specific offers your business puts together such as a "romantic weekend package" at a hotel which includes accommodation and a meal, or a "New Year's Eve special" which includes entrance to a party with the accommodation.
   - Self-packaging by the guest where, either by phone or through your website, they book a room and another service such as a spa treatment or meal in the restaurant at the same time.

> **Note:** a package is only formed if the different elements can be purchased separately. Therefore B&Bs are exempt because the price of the breakfast is always included in the room rate.

Selling Linked Travel Arrangements

A Linked Travel Arrangement is deemed to have been formed if, on the basis of booking accommodation with you, the customer is provided with a targeted offer such as a discounted rate for purchasing something from another business or access to facilities not generally available. This applies regardless of whether you gain financially from the arrangement.

Exemptions

There are two main exemptions to the Package Travel Regulations for accommodation businesses:

1. If the 'Other Tourism Service' element does not form a 'significant part' of the package

When the element 'Other Tourism Service' is combined with accommodation, a Package is only deemed to have been formed if the 'Other Tourism Service' makes up 'a significant part' of the package.

What constitutes a 'significant part' of the package is a bit of a grey area but there are two main tests:

- **If the 'Other Tourism Service' constitutes over 25% of the cost of the package.** This requirement provides accommodation businesses with the opportunity to review their pricing structure so that, where they provide a service alongside accommodation, the service is priced in such a way that it comprises less than 25% of the overall cost to the customer, thus excluding the package from the regulations.

- **If the 'Other Tourism Service' is deemed to be an 'essential element' of the package.** It's important to note that even if the service is less than 25% of the total cost, it could still be a 'significant part' of the package if it is deemed to be an essential element. This means that there is good reason to believe that the customer bought the package on the basis of this element. While this can be subjective, it is generally accepted that if the promotion of the package is based on the service, then it is an essential element, compared to where it is promoted as a 'bonus'.

For example, if you sold a combination of accommodation and a round of golf as a 'weekend golf break', then the round of golf would be an essential element regardless of whether it was

MARKETING

more than 25% of the total cost. However, if you simply said that use of a golf course was a benefit of staying at the hotel, this would probably not be deemed as an essential element.

2. The 24 hour period

The other main exemption is that a Package or Linked Travel Arrangement is not formed if the two different elements are purchased at least 24 hours apart.

For example, if a customer books both their accommodation and a table at your restaurant at the same time, this would constitute a Package. However, if they booked the accommodation and then called back a couple of days later to book a spa treatment, this would not be a Package. Similarly, if your guests purchase a meal at your restaurant after they arrive, or you sell them tickets to a local attraction or a round of golf at the local golf club, provided that they booked the accommodation more than 24 hours before arrival, then this would also be outside the scope of the legislation.

What do the regulations require?

The regulations contain significant provisions relating to the marketing, booking and delivery of Packages and Linked Travel Arrangements, including the terms and conditions of contracts for providing these products.

If you are deemed to be selling a Package or Linked Travel Arrangement, there are also significant requirements on the information you must provide to the customer, the terms and conditions that must apply to the sale and the financial proportion that you must have in place. The specific requirements vary between Packages and Linked Travel Arrangements, but the main features are:

1. Pre-contractual information

Before customers book the Package, they must be provided with information on the main characteristics of the Package (i.e. what is included in the package and any exceptions, such as whether service charges are included or whether the offer of a meal includes drinks), the total price of the Package, the name and details of the organiser and information on the cancellation policy.

2. Standard information about the Package Travel Regulations

The pre-contractual information has to be accompanied by standard information forms that make customers aware of the key protections associated with buying a package holiday, including telling them if they are not covered by the regulations.

3. Contractual information

When the customer makes the booking, they need to be provided with further information. This includes contact details if a problem is experienced during the course of the contract, the complaints resolution process and the ability of the customer to transfer the booking.

4. Insolvency protection

You must have insolvency protection that covers all reasonable costs, including the return of all payments for services not performed and repatriation. This can be achieved through buying insurance, keeping customer payments in a trust account or becoming bonded.

Government guidance

The Department for Business, Energy and Industrial Strategy (BEIS) provides guidance for tourism businesses on the application of the Package Travel Regulations: **www.gov.uk/government/publications/package-holidays-complying-with-regulations-guidance-for-businesses**. Although the guidance offers a good assessment of what constitutes a Package, you are advised to seek specific advice if you believe that you are selling Packages or Linked Travel Arrangements as this remains a complex area.

Further guidance

Your local Trading Standards office

Your local Trading Standards office can provide more information on the requirements of the Package Travel Regulations: **www.gov.uk/find-local-trading-standards-office**.

LICENCES & CONSENTS

MARKETING

CUSTOMERS

FOOD & DRINK

HEALTH & SAFETY

STAFF

BUSINESS MANAGEMENT & TAX

FURTHER INFORMATION

CUSTOMERS

CUSTOMERS

Pricing and charging

KEY FACTS

- It is a criminal offence for businesses to provide customers with misleading information on the prices charged for services or goods.
- It is an offence not to do everything reasonably possible to correct a price indication that has subsequently become misleading if it is reasonable to assume that customers will still be relying on the original price information.
- Prices must include VAT if you are VAT registered.
- You cannot charge customers extra for paying by credit/ debit card.

Price statements

Does this apply to me?
Almost certainly yes: the **Consumer Protection from Unfair Trading Regulations 2008** (CPRs) cover all statements you make regarding the provision of products or services.

It will normally apply to all businesses regardless of whether the price is:
- stated in an advertisement, a brochure, a leaflet or on a website
- given in an email or text message
- given by letter or over the telephone.

What does the legislation require?
It is a criminal offence for you to give customers misleading information on the prices charged for services or goods.

It is also an offence not to do everything reasonably possible to correct pricing information that has subsequently become misleading if it is reasonable to assume that customers will still be relying on the original price information.

Good practice

The Chartered Trading Standards Institute's Business Companion website (**www.businesscompanion.info**) contains a series of both quick guides and in-depth publications on all aspects of trading standards. Included on the site is a good practice guide on how to comply with the Consumer Protection from Unfair Trading Regulations. They also produce a guide specifically related to the pricing of goods and services called *Guidance for Traders on Pricing Practices*. This gives practical guidance on how to avoid giving misleading prices. Compliance with the guide, while not an absolute defence, will assist you in showing that you have not committed an offence under the Act.

One important point to note is that you are not allowed to separate out non-optional extras (such as a cover charge) from your headline price. If there is a non-variable charge that a customer cannot avoid paying, then this must be included in the headline price.

Where non-optional charges vary, you should give clear information about the charging structure at the outset to enable customers to easily calculate the cost before agreeing to a purchase.

All prices given to customers should include VAT. The message is that customers should not get any surprises when it comes to paying the bill.

Displaying prices on your premises

The **Consumer Protection from Unfair Trading Regulations 2008** (CPRs) require you to be open and honest in your pricing and to not mislead or leave out information that could affect the purchasing decision of your customers (see the *Unfair trading practices* section for further information).

While there is no specific regulatory requirement regarding the display of prices in a reception area, it is recommended that you do so in order to fulfil your obligations under the CPRs. This price list should be in a prominent position and be easy to read. It is suggested that the price list you display should include:

For accommodation businesses

- the price of a bedroom for one person (for example, £55 per night) if all the rooms are the same price, or the lowest and highest price (for example, £50-60 per night) if there is a range of prices
- the price of a bedroom for two people
- the price of a bed in any other type of room
- whether or not accommodation prices are inclusive of breakfast or other meals.

For attractions
- the price of admission (adults and children)
- the price of admission for groups
- whether the price includes admission to all exhibitions/rides/activities
- the price of components that are sold separately.

All prices must include VAT and any compulsory service charge. You must make it clear if meals are included in the price.

Further information on displaying prices in hotels is available from the Chartered Trading Standards Institute website: **www.businesscompanion.info**

The **Consumer Protection (Amendment) Regulations 2014** give consumers new private remedies where a trader has committed a misleading or aggressive practice under the 2008 regulations. Under these regulations, consumers have simple, standardised remedies against traders who have misled or intimidated them into entering a contract or making a payment.

Importantly, they do not need to demonstrate any loss or show that you have acted dishonestly, recklessly or even negligently. If the trader's actions were misleading or aggressive, then the remedies apply.

Under the regulations there are three remedies:

1. Unwind a contract and get their money back
The right to unwind allows the consumer to undo the transaction they entered in to, restoring the consumer to the position he or she was in before entering the contract or making the payment. This must be done within 90 days of the start of the service being provided (i.e. when they arrive at the property rather than when the booking was made) and it must be possible to reject the service (i.e. this must be done before the booking ends).

2. Receive a discount on the price paid
The right to a discount applies where the right to unwind has been lost, whether due to delay (with a claim made more than 90 days after the relevant day), or because the goods or services have been fully consumed.
For goods or services that cost £5,000 or less, consumers have a right to a fixed percentage discount on the price. There are four pre-set bands of discount which can apply, depending on the severity of the misleading or aggressive practice:
- 25% if it is more than minor;
- 50% if it is significant;
- 75% if it is serious; and
- 100% (full price) if it is very serious.

LICENCES & CONSENTS MARKETING CUSTOMERS FOOD & DRINK HEALTH & SAFETY STAFF BUSINESS MANAGEMENT & TAX FURTHER INFORMATION

3. Claim damages for detriment caused

Consumers can claim damages if they have suffered losses that exceed the price paid for the relevant goods or service. Damages can cover distress and inconvenience, as well as losses suffered by the consumer because of the contractor payment they made as a result of the misleading or aggressive practice.

These damages can only be claimed upon proof of actual loss, or distress and inconvenience. In accordance with general principles, only reasonably foreseeable losses are covered. Under the regulations, a defence can show that the misleading or aggressive practice happened as a result of a mistake or other cause beyond your control, and that you took all reasonable precautions to avoid the misleading or aggressive practise from occurring.

The guidance publication *Misleading and Aggressive Commercial Practices: New Private Rights for Consumers* is available on the Gov.uk website.

Bonds/card payments in case of damage

The practice of accommodation businesses taking bonds (or damage deposits) is separate to taking a deposit on the payment for the booking.

This bond is protection against damages incurred while the guest is staying in the property but is becoming increasingly uncommon, as businesses tend to retain customers' credit or debit card details in case of damage. If you wish to either charge a bond or to retain customers' card details so that you can charge for any damages, you must notify customers of this prior to the booking being agreed (while this can be done verbally, it is far better to do it in writing in case there is any dispute).

It is important to note that you are only able to retain money from the bond or charge a customers' card if the damage has resulted from a deliberate act (e.g. kicking in walls) or negligence (actions whereby it was reasonably foreseeable that damage would occur). You are not able to charge for damage that results from general 'wear and tear', e.g. marks on floors, an electrical item failing or a cup breaking during washing-up.

To protect against disputes, it is good practice to show a customer around a property so that any pre-existing damage can be recognised and agreed (as car hire companies do) and to get photographic evidence of any damage, so this can be used to support your actions if the customer or their credit card company queries the charge.

Also, three quotes should be gained on any repairs to show that the amount being charged is justified.

The requirement for customers to provide a bond or pay for damages must be applied in a fair and consistent manner that does not breach anti-discrimination law. That is, the requirement should be imposed on all customers and cannot just be imposed on the basis of race, disability, sexual orientation, age or gender. For example, you cannot require a bond from a group of young male customers if you do not require it from other groups of customers.

Credit and debit card charges

It is illegal to make any additional charge where payments are made using debit, credit or charge cards, such as American Express and electronic forms of payment such as PayPal.

In essence, this means that the price you advertise a product for has to be the price that the customer pays at the end of the booking process. However, you are allowed to increase the headline cost of your product to compensate for not being able to charge the card fees if you wish.

The law also only applies to purchases made by personal consumers and not to purchases made by businesses. So, if your customer is a business (e.g. a company booking rooms for an away day or to use an attraction for an event) then you are allowed to charge a card processing fee, provided that it is no more than the cost to you of processing the transaction.

However, in this situation it is important to note that a customer must be using a business card for you to charge a fee. You cannot charge a card processing fee if the customer is using their personal card, regardless of whether they will reclaim the cost as a business expense later.

Further guidance

Guidance on pricing practices
Business Companion provides free, impartial legal guidance for businesses on Trading Standards law: **www.businesscompanion.info**

Your local Trading Standards office
Check you are trading legally by contacting your local Trading Standards office: **www.gov.uk/find-local-trading-standards-office.**

LICENCES & CONSENTS

MARKETING

CUSTOMERS

FOOD & DRINK

HEALTH & SAFETY

STAFF

BUSINESS MANAGEMENT & TAX

FURTHER INFORMATION

LICENCES & CONSENTS

MARKETING

CUSTOMERS

FOOD & DRINK

HEALTH & SAFETY

STAFF

BUSINESS MANAGEMENT & TAX

FURTHER INFORMATION

Bookings and Tickets

KEY FACTS

- Once you have accepted a booking from a customer, you normally have to honour the booking.
- All businesses should abide by good practice with regard to booking procedures.

Booking contract

Once you have accepted a booking from a customer, you normally have to honour the booking (see the *Accepting customers* section for circumstances where a booking does not have to be honoured). This is because once you have agreed the terms of the booking with a customer (e.g. the dates, accommodation type or services to be provided and price) and then accepted the booking, a legally enforceable contract exists between you and the customer.

This applies equally whether the arrangement has been made verbally over the telephone, by email or in writing. You may change the terms of the booking at a later date, provided that both you and the customer agree to the change of terms.

To avoid any problems with cancellations, no-shows or curtailment (when a customer cuts their stay short), you are strongly recommended to have a cancellation procedure. For the cancellation procedure to be enforceable, you must make it clear to customers before accepting a booking. See the *Cancellations and no-shows* section for further details.

Booking terms and conditions

Larger businesses may have arranged for their lawyers to prepare full booking conditions, and any operator that needs to comply with the Package Travel Regulations will require them. However, it is recommended that all operators have a policy relating to deposits and cancellations.

If you have any special arrangements like these, you must give customers the full details before they book to ensure the arrangements are part of the booking contract and binding on the customer.

In developing any terms and conditions for the provision of goods and services to customers, there are three important points to keep in mind:

- regardless of your terms and conditions, the law requires you to use reasonable skill and care in providing the underlying services
- you can't contract yourself out of your legal responsibilities. For example, you cannot have a condition which states you are not responsible for any injury a customer may sustain when the Health and Safety Act says you have a responsibility towards your customers. Similarly, you cannot say that that you will only deal with complaints that are brought to your attention while the customer is on the premises
- the law does not allow you to limit your liability to a customer for death or personal injury arising out of your negligence, or that of an employee or agent. In respect of any other loss or damage, you can only restrict your liability towards a guest as far as is reasonable.

The Competition and Markets Authority (CMA) provides guidance as to what constitutes unfair terms in contracts. In general terms, their guidance is:

- a deposit is just to reserve the goods/services and should be no more than a small percentage of the total price
- advance payments should reflect the business' expenses and leave customers with a reasonable amount still to pay on completion
- customers should not lose large advance payments if they cancel
- businesses should set sliding scales of cancellation charges so they cover their likely losses directly from the cancellation.

However, this guidance should be viewed 'in the round'. A special deal which requires a large deposit or payment in full could be justified if there were no cancellation charges or if cancellation charges only applied within a few days of the customer arriving.

A more detailed *Guide on Unfair Contract Terms* is available on the Gov.uk website.

You can also see the *Cancellations and no-shows* section for more information.

Good practice

As a matter of good practice, you should keep a clear, accurate record of the arrangements for each of your bookings. You might also want to have a simple checklist by the telephone or computer, to remind you of the details you need to run through with each guest, e.g.:

- pricing
- deposit
- cancellations
- data protection.

Ideally, you should confirm all bookings in writing to the guest, although this may not always be practical. However, you are advised to confirm in writing/email the booking details for any longer stays, larger groups or bookings that are more complex than usual.

Selling tickets

Selling tickets for entry or for events is covered by the **Consumer Protection from Unfair Trading Regulations 2008**. This means that you must provide full and clear information, including:

- any terms and conditions associated with the ticket
- what the ticket entitles the customer to
- opening hours
- the validity of the ticket (e.g. whether it is for a particular day or can be used on any day)
- if the ticket is for an event, the timing of the event, the location and, if it is seated, where the seats are.

Under these Regulations, it is illegal to give consumers misleading information or claims and to mislead the customer by omitting information that the customer requires to make an informed choice. This could include:

- additional charges not included in the ticket price (e.g. where the price for entry for an amusement park does not include the cost of rides on attractions)
- advertising an event as "A night with Michael Bublé" when the singer is only a guest that performs one song
- the cancellation policy if an event cannot be held
- information on any part of an attraction that is closed for maintenance
- whether seating is allocated, and if so, where it is in relation to the stage and whether the view is restricted.

Pricing

For events where there is a range of pricing for tickets, you can advertise that "prices start from £x". However, when doing this, you must ensure that there are a reasonable number of tickets available at that price. Having a very limited number of tickets at the advertised price is referred to as "bait marketing" and is illegal.

NEW

LICENCES & CONSENTS   MARKETING   CUSTOMERS   FOOD & DRINK   HEALTH & SAFETY   STAFF   BUSINESS MANAGEMENT & TAX   FURTHER INFORMATION

CUSTOMERS

It is also important to note that when you advertise and sell a ticket, the price must include all non-optional extra charges, such as booking fees.

Cancellations

It is important to have a cancellation policy where you are selling tickets ahead of an event and that the terms and conditions are fair to the customer. **The Consumer Contracts (Information, Cancellation and Additional Charges) Regulations 2013** apply to sales over the internet or by phone and generally require businesses to provide a 14 day period in which the customer can cancel a service or return goods.

However, there is an exemption for tickets for events held on a specific date or within a specific time period.

Further guidance

Guidance on ticketing for events

The Society of Ticket Agents and Retailers (STAR) has developed a code of practice for businesses selling tickets for events to the public which is available on their website: **www.star.org.uk**

Professional legal advice

Booking contracts and conditions are a complex area of law. For any detailed information or assistance, you should seek professional legal advice.

Registration and data protection

KEY FACTS

- If you hold any personal information on customers or any other individuals, including employees, the Data Protection Act applies.

- Unless you have an exemption, you are required to pay an Annual Data Protection Fee to the Information Commissioner's Office (ICO).

- The General Data Protection Regulation (GDPR) came into force on 25th May 2018 and enhanced consumer rights, including the ability to access the information you hold.

- All serviced and self-catering accommodation premises must keep a record of all customers over the age of 16. The record should include their full name and nationality. You must keep each customer's details for at least 12 months.

- Surveillance equipment can only be used if there is a legitimate reason to do so. Customers should be made aware that they are being monitored, who is undertaking the activity and the purpose for which that information is to be used.

Data protection

The holding and use of personal information of individuals is regulated by the **Data Protection Act 2018 (DPA)**, which sits alongside the **General Data Protection Regulation 2018 (GDPR)**. As the provisions in the Act are extensive, you should read the paragraphs below to see if they apply to you.

Note: the paragraphs in this section focus on personal data held on customers, as this is perhaps the most relevant situation for smaller tourism businesses. However, the Acts apply equally to personal data held on other individuals, including employees, although the specific provisions vary. For further information, contact the Information Commissioner's Office.

CUSTOMERS

What is the purpose of the DPA?

The Act is to protect the privacy of individuals (data subjects) by preventing the misuse or unauthorised use of personal information (personal data) that is held by others (data controllers). The Act achieves this by:

- regulating the use of personal data held by data controllers, and
- giving rights to data subjects.

Does this Act apply to me?

The Act applies to the 'processing of personal data', for any business purpose, regardless of the size of the business. This includes personal data on either employees or customers.

What is 'personal data'?

Personal data is any information that relates to an identifiable individual. It can range from their name, phone number or email address through to more personal information such as their sexual orientation or whether they are disabled. It is important to note that personal information also includes images, including CCTV recordings. As a general rule, if it is possible to identify an individual directly from the information you process, then that information is personal data.

What is 'processing'?

Processing of personal data is pretty much anything you do from collecting, storing, organising and using that data through to deleting it.

What is a 'controller'?

A controller is the person that decides how and why to collect and use the data. Employees are deemed acting on behalf of the employer, meaning that, as the business operator, you are the controller even if you do not actually process the data yourself.

Data Protection Principles

Controllers are required to follow strict rules called 'data protection principles'. You must make sure that all data is:

- used fairly, lawfully and transparently
- used only for specified, explicit purposes
- used in a way that is adequate, relevant and limited to only what is necessary
- accurate and, where necessary, kept up to date
- kept for no longer than is necessary
- handled in a way that ensures appropriate security, including protection against unlawful or unauthorised processing, access, loss, destruction or damage.

I think the Act applies to me. What must I do?

The three basic requirements are set out below. Please note that even if you are exempt from (a), you still need to comply with (b) and (c).

(a) Pay an Annual Data Protection Fee

No: if you only hold personal data on a manual filing system, you do not need to pay this fee.

Yes: if you hold personal data on a computer (or any other automated system), you must pay this fee. However, you are exempt if you only hold personal data for the following purposes:

- staff administration (including payroll)
- accounts and records (i.e. details of past or present customers or suppliers)
- your own advertising, marketing and public relations (the information must be restricted to just what is necessary for your advertising, marketing and public relations) and your advertising, marketing and public relations are not undertaken by a third party
- you are using the personal data for not-for-profit purposes
- you are maintaining a public register.

It is important to note that if you use CCTV on your premises for crime prevention purposes (i.e. security reasons), then you are required to notify the ICO and pay the Annual Data Protection Fee.

Under the Data Protection (Charges and Information) Regulations 2018, individuals and organisations that process personal data need to pay a data protection fee to the ICO. There is an annual fee of £40 if you have a turnover of less than £632,000 or fewer than 10 staff and £60 for businesses with a turnover of up to £36m or up to 250 staff.

Charities, regardless of their size, are only required to pay an annual fee of £40.

The Information Commissioner's Office has an online assessment tool for determining whether you have to pay the Annual Data Protection Fee: **ico.org.uk/for-organisations/data-protection-fee/self-assessment.**

(b) Follow the data protection principles

All data controllers, whether their records are computerised, automated or manual and whether they have to notify or not, must comply with the eight data protection principles set out in the DPA.

LICENCES & CONSENTS   MARKETING   CUSTOMERS   FOOD & DRINK   HEALTH & SAFETY   STAFF   BUSINESS MANAGEMENT & TAX   FURTHER INFORMATION

NEW

CUSTOMERS

In brief, personal data should be:

- obtained and processed fairly and lawfully, and should not be held or used unless the data subject has given their consent, or it is necessary in performance of a contract to which the data subject is a party, or it is necessary for any other reason specified in the Act (see the *Direct marketing* section)
- obtained only for specified and lawful purposes
- adequate, relevant and not excessive in relation to the purposes for which they are being held or used
- accurate and, where necessary, kept up to date
- kept no longer than necessary for the purposes concerned
- processed in accordance with the rights of data subjects (see *(c)* below)
- subject to appropriate technical and organisational measures against unauthorised or unlawful processing, and against accidental loss or destruction
- not transferred to a country or territory outside the European Economic Area, unless that country or territory ensures adequate level of protection for the rights and freedoms of data subjects in relation to processing personal data.

Consent

If you are going to hold information on a customer for any purpose other than handling their current booking or purchase (e.g. you would like to send them marketing material in future), you need to obtain their consent.

The Act does not specify what form this consent has to be in. It may be an informal, spoken 'yes', but you should give customers enough information for them to make an informed decision (e.g. what personal information you intend to hold and why).

Customers can give their consent at any time - on booking, on entry or check-in or when they leave. You should keep all consents on record in case a customer disputes that they granted permission.

You may want to produce a simple form that can be used either over the telephone, on emails or in writing, which:

- explains to customers the personal information on them that you want to hold and why
- asks customers for their consent
- has a space, such as a tick box, to record whether or not consent was given.

If you intend to keep 'sensitive personal information', you must have the customer's explicit consent to hold and use their personal data for the purposes specified. Sensitive personal information includes the following:

- race, ethnic origins
- religion
- political opinions
- physical or mental health (e.g. disability)
- sexual orientation
- criminal convictions or allegations.

(c) Complying with the rights of data subjects

All data controllers must comply with the rights given to individuals by the Act in relation to the personal information held on them. The Act gives eight distinct rights, of which the most applicable are as follows:
Right of access: individuals have a right to know what information on them you are holding and why you are holding it (called a Subject Access Request). If you receive a written request from an individual for this information, you must respond within 30 days stating:

- whether you hold any personal data on them
- what the data is, the reason you are holding it and those to whom it has/may be disclosed, along with an intelligible copy of the information and details of the manner in which it was collected.

Right to prevent processing for the purposes of direct marketing: if you receive a request from an individual to cease using the personal data you hold on them for direct marketing, you must do so.
Right to prevent processing likely to cause damage or distress: if you receive a request from an individual to cease using the personal data you hold on them because it is causing, or likely to cause, substantial damage or distress to them or another, you must do so.
Right to compensation: any individual who suffers damage or distress as a result of a contravention of the Act by you is entitled to seek compensation from you if you did not take reasonable care to comply.

Note: you have the right to require reasonable proof of identity from a person asking to exercise these rights. You should be satisfied that the person asking is the person concerned, but you must not use excessive identity checking as a way to deliberately make access to the data difficult.

Caution! If you are buying-in any mailing lists, you should ensure that the provider has the consent of the individuals listed to pass on the individual's details to third parties.

The Information Commissioner's Office has produced a helpful online assessment tool that you can use to determine whether you are complying with the Data Protection Act: **ico.org.uk/for-organisations/business/assessment-for-small-business-owners-and-sole-traders.**

The General Data Protection Regulation (GDPR)

The General Data Protection Regulation (GDPR) came into force on 25th May 2018. The main additional requirements from the GDPR are:

1. The Right to be Forgotten

A customer can, at any time, request that you remove all their personal data from your system. If the customer has previously agreed that you could provide their data to a third party, you must also stop doing this if you receive a Right to be Forgotten request. However, it is important to note that any Right to be Forgotten request does not override requirements to hold information under other legislation. For example, you are required by law to keep financial records for seven years, therefore a customer cannot request that you delete records of any financial transactions they undertook within the last seven years.

2. Improving Consent and Withdrawal of Consent

The conditions for consent have been strengthened so that you must be clear and upfront with customers about what exactly they are consenting to when they sign-up. This is to stop companies hiding the details in their terms and conditions. So, if you are planning to pass their information on to a third party and to email them a newsletter, you must tell them in simple and clear language next to the box they are ticking.

Importantly, it must be as easy for customers to withdraw consent as it is to give consent. So, if you have a simple tick-box online where customers give consent, then there should also be a simple tick-box online to withdraw consent.

3. Right to Access

The GDPR also expands the rights of customers to access the information that you hold on them. This has two parts – first, on request from the customer, you are required to inform them if personal data concerning them is being processed, where and for what purpose. Second, if requested, you must provide a copy of all the personal data you hold on the person electronically and free of charge. This includes any information you have made on the person's file, so if you have added notes such as, 'likes the Sunday Times', 'owns a Spaniel called Arthur' or 'gave a donation', you also need to provide this information. You need to provide this information within 30 days.

4. Notification of Data Breaches

The GDPR will require you to notify the Information Commissioners' Office within 72 hours of first having become aware of the breach where that breach is likely to 'result in a risk for the rights and freedoms of individuals'. For any breach, you are required to notify the customers 'without undue delay' after first becoming aware of a data breach.

The Information Commissioner's Office (ICO) has produced several resources to help businesses comply with GDPR on their website:

- a *Guide to the General Data Protection Regulation (GDPR)*
- a small business toolkit to help you check your compliance
- a support helpline aimed at people running small businesses or charities, designed to provide additional, personal advice. As well as advice on GDPR, callers can also ask questions about other legislation regulated by the ICO, including electronic marketing and Freedom of Information. People from small organisations should dial the ICO helpline on **0303 123 1113** and select option 4 to be diverted to staff who can offer support.

Transferring personal data to and from the EU/EEA

If you transfer personal data with other European countries, (for example, you take bookings from an EU based tour operator) the EU-UK Trade and Cooperation Agreement contains a bridging mechanism that allows the continued free flow of personal data between the UK and EU/EEA countries for up to 6 months from 1 January 2021 while new arrangements are negotiated.

As a sensible precaution during the bridging mechanism, it is recommended that you work with EU/EEA organisations who transfer personal data to you to put in place alternative transfer mechanisms to safeguard against any interruption to the free flow of personal data.

More information on this is available as part of the UK Government's Brexit guidance for businesses: **www.gov.uk/guidance/using-personal-data-in-your-business-or-other-organisation.**

Data security and credit cards

The Data Protection Act 2018 says that 'appropriate technical and organisational measures shall be taken against unauthorised or unlawful processing of personal data and against accidental loss or destruction of, or damage to, personal data.'.

If you never receive a customer's card number (i.e. you use a third party to deal with transactions) you probably have little to worry about other than to ensure that the third party is a reputable organisation with a good knowledge of data security issues (e.g. Paypal or Worldpay).

If you do receive customers' data, you should follow the standards of the Payment Card Industry Security Standards Council. This Council is a global consortium of all the main card payment companies, including Mastercard and Visa. Its function is to promote standards of data security so as to make it harder for criminals to steal data. These standards are quite demanding, but compliance is mandatory for retailers who accept card payments. The requirements of the Payment Card Industry Data Security Standard are contractual rather than the law of the land but, if you follow them, you will also be meeting the legal requirement.

If you do handle card data you need to be sure that you know and follow those rules that are applicable to your circumstances. There are twelve requirements, some of which are of limited relevance to small businesses:

1. **Install and maintain a firewall**. Your computer operating system probably has this built in, e.g. Windows Firewall.
2. **Do not use default passwords**. If your password is "password", change it. Passwords should not be obvious.
3. **Protect stored cardholder data**. Do not leave personal data on your laptop and then travel with it, due to the risk of losing it. Keep it secure at all times.
4. **Encrypt internet transmission of cardholder data**. Never use ordinary email to send credit card information.
5. **Use and regularly update anti-virus software**. This really is essential for everyone – set it to update automatically if you can.
6. **Develop and maintain secure systems and applications**. Likely to apply only to larger businesses developing their own systems.
7. **Restrict access to cardholder data on a need-to-know basis** Ensure card data is not available to all your visitors, staff, etc.
8. **Assign a unique ID to each person with computer access**. Do not share identities or passwords or run a database of past clients shared between several people with the same login.
9. **Restrict physical access to cardholder data**. Don't leave a print-out of data in an unlocked location (or a file of manual card data records).
10. **Track and monitor all access to network resources and cardholder data**. This is relevant to businesses with

larger systems, but all businesses should record who has access to card data.

11. Test security systems and processes regularly. At the least, check that your security measures are being adhered to.

12. Maintain a policy that addresses information security. For small businesses the key point is that you give this topic some serious thought, rather than writing a formal policy.

For small business operators, the above list can be summarised as making sure that access to card data, both on paper and electronically, is very well controlled, restricted to people who really need it, and that any computer on which you store it has proper defences such as a firewall and anti-virus software.

Although not a legal requirement, your acquirer may also require you to complete a PCI DSS Self-Assessment Questionnaire (SAQ) in order to validate your compliance to the standards.

Accommodation: keeping a register of your guests

Does this apply to me?
Yes: under the **Immigration (Hotel Records) Order 1972**, all serviced and self-catering accommodation premises must keep a record of all guests over the age of 16.

What do I need to record?
To comply with the **Immigration (Hotel Records) Order 1972** you need to collect the following information from guests on their arrival:

- full name
- nationality.

Note: you are not legally required to take a guest's home address or contact number.

For all who are not British, Irish or Commonwealth guests:

- passport number and place of issue (or other document which shows their identity and nationality)
- details of their next destination (including the address, if known) on or before departure.

Note: diplomats, their family and staff do not have to register.

What about the format of the register?
There is no set format for the register. It could be a visitors' book or an exercise book, but you must keep each guest's details for at least

12 months and have the register available for inspection by a police officer or duly authorised person at all times.

It may be, of course, that you are given the necessary details at the time of booking, but you should check them when the guests arrive and make sure that you have all the information you are required to collect. Even if your local police have traditionally shown no interest in these records, circumstances could change.

Using surveillance equipment on your premises

Over recent years the cost of buying and installing surveillance systems has dropped considerably. Their use is now becoming more prevalent in small businesses who want to safeguard their property and their customers.

However, it is very important to get the right balance between justifiable reasons for surveillance and a customer's right to privacy.

There are two main Acts that cover the use of CCTVs and other surveillance equipment – the **Protection of Freedoms Act and the Data Protection Act**. The first covers when and where it is justifiable to use CCTV equipment and the second covers the treatment of the data that is gained from its use.

Protection of Freedoms Act

The starting point of the Protection of Freedoms Act is that people have a fundamental right to privacy and this can only be encroached upon if there is a legitimate reason to do so. It is not acceptable to install surveillance equipment simply because you 'want to keep an eye on what was going on'.

You **must also only use surveillance equipment if there is no other practical way to solve a problem that doesn't impact on customers' right to privacy.** For example, if there had been thefts from a particular area, ways of restricting access to that area should be considered before you install surveillance equipment.

Surveillance equipment can only be used if the encroachment on people's right to privacy is proportionate to the purpose for which the equipment is being used. However, there are no hard and fast rules as to what is proportionate because each circumstance will involve differing levels of both justification and privacy.

For example, installing CCTV cameras to protect possessions in a museum or to monitor customers' safety in an animal park would be justifiable but it would not be justifiable to put CCTV in customer bedrooms or in changing rooms where customers would expect a very high level of privacy.

Conversely, installing a CCTV in a communal lounge would not normally be justifiable, but could become justifiable if there had been a spate of thefts in this area. However, it is important to note that in this situation the justification would end once the person committing the thefts was identified or the thefts ended.

Importantly, **when you do use surveillance equipment, customers should be made aware that they are being monitored, who is undertaking the activity and the purpose for which that information is to be used.** Again, the greater the extent that a customer's privacy is being encroached, the more important it is that they are fully aware of the surveillance that is being undertaken.

Data Protection Act

Provided that the use of surveillance equipment is justified, there is then the issue of how to use, handle and store the data you collect. This comes under both the Privacy Act and the Data Protection Act.

Again, the handling and storage of this data need to be proportionate to the justification for collecting it in the first place. **You must have very clear guidelines as to who has access to the monitoring equipment and the stored data.** The greater the extent that you are encroaching on customers' privacy, the greater the restrictions should be on access to the monitoring equipment and the data.

The **length of time that you keep the data should also be proportionate to the justification for using the surveillance equipment.** For example, if the equipment is being used to monitor a pool to ensure that there are no accidents, then there would be little justification for storing the data beyond the period that the pool was being used (i.e., it should be deleted at the end of each day as its storage is no longer warranted). However, if the equipment was being used to monitor the carpark, then it could be justifiable to keep the data for longer in case a customer returned home and later found a dent that they thought happened while at your premises.

To help businesses in their use of surveillance equipment, the Home Office has produced the following 12 point code of practice:

1. Use of a surveillance camera system must always be for a specified purpose which is in pursuit of a legitimate aim and necessary to meet an identified pressing need.

LICENCES & CONSENTS

MARKETING

CUSTOMERS

FOOD & DRINK

HEALTH & SAFETY

STAFF

BUSINESS MANAGEMENT & TAX

FURTHER INFORMATION

CUSTOMERS

2. The use of a surveillance camera system must take into account its effect on individuals and their privacy, with regular reviews to ensure its use remains justified.

3. There must be as much transparency in the use of a surveillance camera system as possible, including a published contact point for access to information and complaints.

4. There must be clear responsibility and accountability for all surveillance camera system activities including images and information collected, held and used.

5. Clear rules, policies and procedures must be in place before a surveillance camera system is used, and these must be communicated to all who need to comply with them.

6. No more images and information should be stored other than that which is strictly required for the stated purpose of a surveillance camera system, and such images and information should be deleted once their purposes have been discharged.

7. Access to retained images and information should be restricted and there must be clearly defined rules on who can gain access and for what purpose such access is granted; the disclosure of images and information should only take place when it is necessary for such a purpose or for law enforcement purposes.

8. Surveillance camera system operators should consider any approved operational, technical and competency standards relevant to a system and its purpose and work to meet and maintain those standards.

9. Surveillance camera system images and information should be subject to appropriate security measures to safeguard against unauthorised access and use.

10. There should be effective review and audit mechanisms to ensure legal requirements, policies and standards are complied with in practice, and regular reports should be published.

11. When the use of a surveillance camera system is in pursuit of a legitimate aim, and there is a pressing need for its use, it should then be used in the most effective way to support public safety and law enforcement with the aim of processing images and information of evidential value.

12. Any information used to support a surveillance camera system which compares against a reference database for matching purposes should be accurate and kept up to date.

For more information, see the Surveillance Camera Code of Practice on Gov.uk: **www.gov.uk/government/publications/surveillance-camera-code-of-practice.**

Further guidance

Information Commissioner's Office (ICO)
The ICO provides extensive information on data protection, including a free toolkit for businesses to check their GDPR compliance: **ico.org.uk**. The ICO helpline is **0303 123 1113**

Credit card data
Information on complying with data protection for credit card data can be found on the Payment Card Security Standards Council website: **www.pcisecuritystandards.org**

CCTV data
Information on surveillance cameras can be found in the full surveillance Camera Code of Practice: **www.gov.uk/government/publications/surveillance-camera-code-of-practice.**

LICENCES & CONSENTS

MARKETING

CUSTOMERS

FOOD & DRINK

HEALTH & SAFETY

STAFF

BUSINESS MANAGEMENT & TAX

FURTHER INFORMATION

Cancellations and no-shows

KEY FACTS

- All businesses are strongly recommended to have a cancellation procedure in order to avoid any problems with cancellation, curtailment and no-shows.
- If a customer cancels a booking or checks out early from accommodation, they are in breach of the booking contract they have with you.
- If you cancel a booking that you have already accepted, you are in breach of the booking contract.

Cancellation by customers

Cancellation provisions in the booking conditions

To avoid any problems with cancellation or curtailment (when a guest cuts their stay short), you are strongly recommended to have a cancellation policy. To rely on the procedure you must make this policy clear to customers before you agree on the booking, whether on the telephone, email or in writing. It is also prudent to get confirmation from the customer that they understand and accept the policy. Finally, your booking conditions and cancellation policy should also be clearly stated on your website.

It is recommended to include a cancellation clause in your standard booking terms and conditions (see the Bookings section). Common cancellation procedures are to either charge customers a cancellation fee that varies according to the amount of notice given of cancellation or to forfeit any deposit provided at the time of booking. It is important to note that any cancellation terms and conditions need to be fair to the customer. For example, demanding full payment in advance and having a cancellation policy that would see the customer forfeit the entire payment, regardless of when the cancellation was made, would be deemed to be unfair.

CUSTOMERS

On cancellation or curtailment, you will need to send an invoice to the guest for the amount due. In spring 2019 HMRC changed its guidance on the VAT treatment of deposits when customers cancel a booking or do not arrive (no-shows). The new guidance states that VAT is still chargeable because the deposit was a payment for the opportunity to use your goods or services. Therefore, you will need to send an invoice to the guest for the amount due inclusive of VAT and include the revenue in your VAT filing.

Please note that VAT only applies to deposits made by the customer. If the customer cancels and you have a separately payable cancellation charge as part of your terms and conditions, this is exclusive of VAT as this is a penalty payment rather than a payment for the opportunity to use your goods and services.

Cancellation insurance
One option that is often given to customers on booking is to take out cancellation insurance. A premium covers any payments they are obliged to make for their accommodation in the event of them having to cancel. A typical policy will cover claims as a consequence of illness or injury to the guest or a member of their family, redundancy, a burglary, fire or jury service.

If you need to comply with the Package Travel Regulations (see the *Holiday Packages* section), you are required to tell the customer about the possibility of taking out cancellation insurance in good time before the start of their holiday.

You can contact a local insurance company or broker for details of how to offer this facility.

Deposits
Increasingly, businesses are taking deposits or asking for credit card details to reduce their exposure to cancellations.

Typically, this charge is a 25% deposit at the time of booking with the balance paid between six to eight weeks in advance of arrival, but this will vary depending on the type of business and the ease of replacing lost custom. For example, accommodation providers will charge a higher deposit and require a greater lead time for full payment than attractions, due to it being more difficult to replace cancelled bookings.

If you are VAT registered, you need to remember that any deposit is inclusive of VAT. This means that if you withhold a deposit as compensation for a guest cancelling, you must return the VAT component of the deposit as no service has been provided.

If a customer cancels and refuses to pay

If the customer refuses to pay:

- you may be able to charge the amount to their credit or debit card (as explained below), but if not:
- you will need to consider taking the matter to the small claims court.

Charging a credit card following cancellation or no-show

If you accept a telephone booking made by a credit or debit card and the customer later cancels the booking or fails to turn up, you can charge the customer's card **provided that** you can show that you have clearly communicated to the customer at the time the booking is made that their account will be charged in the case of a cancellation and the customer has accepted this condition.

One way to do this is to include this condition in your cancellation policy within the booking terms and conditions. Ideally, you should confirm this arrangement in writing or, at least, keep a record of the conversation as proof for the credit card company should the customer later challenge the charge. If the customer refuses to acknowledge having made a booking or claims they were not made aware of your cancellation conditions, and there is no proof to the contrary, banks will tend to refund their money, debiting your account. If you take bookings via the internet, it is a good idea to have a 'tick-box' where the customer has to confirm that they have read and accepted the cancellation conditions.

Claiming damages if a customer cancels

If a customer cancels a booking or leaves early when staying in accommodation, they are in breach of the booking contract they have with you. You may be entitled to claim damages for any losses you have suffered from the cancellation/curtailment. This applies regardless of whether you have cancellation/curtailment procedures as a booking condition.

Procedure

If you do not have a cancellation policy and want to make a claim for damages, the procedure is as follows:

- **Minimising your loss:** You must first make every reasonable effort to minimise your loss. This may be by trying to re-let the accommodation or reselling a ticket on which only a deposit was paid. If you re-let the room or resell the ticket at the same price, you should have not suffered a loss and so cannot make a claim.
- **What amount can I claim?** If, despite your efforts, you cannot re-let the accommodation or resell the ticket, you will be entitled to claim damages that reflect the losses you have incurred as a result of the cancellation. This is the value of the booking less the cost of any items that you did not supply.

For example, you cannot charge for food, heating, electricity or cleaning as you did not supply these products or services. You are also not able to include any service charge.

> **Note:** there is a general rule of thumb for accommodation businesses that your loss will be about two-thirds of the value of the booking, but individual cases differ.

- **What about the deposit?** You may keep the deposit, offsetting it against the amount claimed.
- **How soon can I make a claim?** You must wait until the period of the booking has elapsed before you can send the customer an invoice for the amount claimed (this should be exclusive of VAT, as no services have been provided).
- **What happens if the customer does not pay the claim?** If you have any difficulties with a guest refusing to meet your claim, you could consider pursuing the claim through the small claims procedure in the County Court. A small claim can be for any amount up to £10,000. You will have to pay a fee to start your claim which is related to the size of your claim, but this will be added to the money that you are already owed. The appropriate forms and a booklet advising you on how to pursue your claim can be obtained from any County Court.
- **What happens if I lose?** Be aware that if you lose the case, the customer can seek to recover expenses from you (although not the cost of any legal fees they have paid). These expenses include £95/day for loss of earnings or leave to attend a hearing, plus reasonable travelling expenses for each of the other side and any necessary witnesses they take along to court. You can also be required to pay £750 if the judge gave them permission to get evidence from an expert.

What if a customer does not accept your product or service?

Should a customer refuse to accept a product or service that they have booked or any other suitable alternative that you may offer, then, depending on the reasons given by the customer, you may be able to treat this as a cancellation.

Generally, you will not be able to do this if the customer rejects the product or service because they booked it on the basis of untrue statements made about it by you or your staff or if the alternative does not meet the criteria of the customer's booking (e.g. the customer specifically asked for a room with a sea view when booking and the only room available when they arrive overlooks the carpark or the customer booked a dinner/dance on the basis that there was a vegetarian option and that was not available).

UPDATED

What if I cancel a customer's booking?

If you have to cancel a booking that you have already accepted, you are in breach of contract and must refund the customer.

For accommodation businesses, if you cannot accommodate a guest who has made a booking, you must find them alternative accommodation of the same or higher standard. The guest is entitled to claim damages as compensation for any losses incurred in finding alternative comparable accommodation (e.g. extra taxi fares or any extra accommodation costs). However, the guest has a legal duty to keep losses to a minimum, so if your establishment is a bed and breakfast they cannot book into a five-star hotel and expect you to pay the difference. The guest is entitled to claim damages as compensation for any losses incurred in finding alternative comparable accommodation (e.g. extra taxi fares or any extra accommodation costs). However, the guest has a legal duty to keep losses to a minimum, so if your establishment is a bed and breakfast they cannot book into a five-star hotel and expect you to pay the difference.

Further guidance

Professional legal advice

If you have any detailed questions on cancellations or any problems with a customer, you are advised to seek professional legal advice.

Your local Trading Standards office

Your local Trading Standards office may be able to offer some guidance, particularly on cancellation terms: **www.gov.uk/find-local-trading-standards-office**.

CUSTOMERS

Accepting Customers

KEY FACTS

- You cannot discriminate against any customer on the basis of a range of characteristics including race, religion, sexuality and disability.
- A hotel can refuse guests who appear unable or unwilling to pay or who are not in a fit state to be received.
- You are bound to honour a booking unless the booking was made on the basis of false statements that impact on the provision of services or facilities.

Can I turn customers away?

As a service provider, the Equality Act 2010 applies to your business. This means that it is unlawful to discriminate against customers on the following 'protected characteristics':

- disability
- gender reassignment
- pregnancy and maternity
- race – this includes ethnic or national origins, colour and nationality
- religion or belief
- sex
- sexual orientation
- marriage and civil partnership
- age – this applies to guests aged 18 and above i.e. you cannot have a policy excluding under 25s.

Discrimination does not just mean refusing to provide services to people on the basis of their 'protected characteristics'. It also means providing them with different standards of service, different products, charging different prices or having different terms and conditions. For example, it would be discriminatory to only allow gay couples to have a twin bedroom rather than a double bedroom, or to prevent groups of more than 10 men from entering an attraction.

However, you are allowed to provide different products and services for disabled customers provided that there is an objective justification for doing so. Objective justification is said to occur when the difference in the goods or service provided is 'a proportionate means of achieving a legitimate aim'. For example, it could probably be considered justified to only sell ground floor rooms in a listed building to a wheelchair user if the upper floors were only accessible by a staircase. Similarly, it would probably be considered justified to advise pregnant women not to undertake a particularly violent ride at an adventure park on the basis of medical risk.

It should be noted that it is the inability to make alterations rather than the cost of making alternations that provides objective justification – i.e. you cannot provide a discriminatory service on the basis of cost alone.

In addition to not being able to discriminate against customers on the above grounds, you cannot discriminate against anyone on the grounds of association. This means not discriminating against the parent, partner, friend or carer accompanying someone with one of the protected characteristics listed above.

Indirect discrimination

You must be careful not to have booking conditions or rules that would constitute indirect discrimination. Indirect discrimination occurs when any requirement, which in itself is not discriminatory, would have a disproportionate impact on people with a protected characteristic. For example, if you have a requirement that all-male groups had to pay a higher booking fee because you had problems with stag parties in the past, this could be deemed to be indirect discrimination as it would always apply to gay couples but would not apply to heterosexual couples.

To help ensure that you do not discriminate, you are required to undertake reasonable adjustments to your premises or to the way you deliver your services. This, for example, could mean providing improved access, undertaking training staff on equality issues or providing meals that comply with the religious requirements of guests.

For more information on accepting disabled customers, see the *Disabled Customers* section.

Requirements for accommodation providers

For accommodation businesses, there are further requirements related to accepting guests.

LICENCES & CONSENTS

MARKETING

CUSTOMERS

FOOD & DRINK

HEALTH & SAFETY

STAFF

BUSINESS MANAGEMENT & TAX

FURTHER INFORMATION

Guests with prior bookings

When a guest has made a prior booking, you must honour the booking unless there are legal grounds for not doing so. Such legal grounds may include accepting the booking on the basis of false statements made by the guest. For example, if you state that pets are not allowed at your establishment and the guest arrives with a pet, or if they book a room for two adults and they arrive with children who they want to sleep on the sofa. In these situations, you can turn the guests away and you may also be able to claim damages from them if you are unable to re-let the room.

'Walk-in' guests

Under the **Hotel Proprietors Act 1956**, a hotel can only refuse to let a room to a walk-in guest with no booking if that guest appears unable or unwilling to pay or is not in a fit state to be received. This would be the case, for example, if the guest was drunk or if you had reasonable grounds for believing that the guest would be a nuisance to other guests.

However, you have complete discretion to decide which room to allocate to a guest, provided that the guest has not booked a specific room.

Note: the Hotel Proprietors Act 1956 defines a hotel as 'an establishment held out by the proprietor as offering food, drink and, if so required, sleeping accommodation, without special contract, to any traveller presenting himself who appears able and willing to pay a reasonable sum for the services and facilities provided and who is in a fit state to be received'. As such, it is possible for an operator whose premises do not fit this definition to refuse walk-in guests.

Accepting bookings from under 18s

Anyone under the age of 18 does not have the same legal capacity as an adult to enter into a contract, such as making a room booking. You can accept bookings for someone under 18 to stay, but you are advised to be careful. For example, the booking itself should be made by someone 18 or over such as a parent, guardian or another adult who can take responsibility for payment or damages.

Further guidance

How to comply with equality legislation

The EHRC provides comprehensive advice for tourism businesses on how to comply with equality legislation: **www.equalityhumanrights.com**

Under 18s and the law

The Children's Legal Centre website has a good service that answers questions in relation to under 18s and the law on their website: **www.childrenslegalcentre.com**

Guidance publications

A range of guidance publications on the Equality Act 2010 are available on the Gov.uk website, including:

- *Equality Act 2010: What do I need to know? Quick-start guide for businesses who sell goods and services*
- *Equality Act 2010 ban on age discrimination in the provision of services, public functions and associations: A guide for holiday providers, hotels and those letting properties.*

Disabled customers

KEY FACTS

- The **Equality Act 2010** applies to all businesses.
- The Act protects anyone who is disabled, is thought to be disabled or is associated with someone who is disabled.
- The Act gives these people rights of access to goods, facilities and services (including tourist attractions and accommodation) and ensures that they are treated no less favourably than other customers.
- You are also required to make reasonable adjustments to the way you deliver your services and to the physical features of your premises to make it easier for disabled guests to use them.
- It would be unlawful to refuse access to a disabled person accompanied by an assistance dog except in the most exceptional circumstances.

The Equality Act 2010

The **Equality Act 2010** was introduced to consolidate and strengthen all anti-discrimination legislation (including disability discrimination legislation). The Act builds on the Disability Discrimination Act 1995 (DDA) which gives disabled people rights of access to goods, facilities and services, which includes tourist accommodation, by specifically banning discrimination against people associated with disabled people (e.g. carers, friends and family) and people presumed to be disabled. These rights are enforceable by any individual through the Courts, if necessary.

Does the Act apply to me?
Yes: if you provide any sort of goods or services to the public, the Act applies to you.

How is 'disabled' defined?
For the purpose of the law, disabled people are all those whose physical and mental impairments have a substantial and long-term adverse effect on their ability to carry out normal, day-to-day activities.

CUSTOMERS

This includes those who have cancer, HIV and multiple sclerosis, and those who have other progressive conditions likely to result in an impairment which has a substantial adverse effect. These people become covered by the Act from the time they are diagnosed.

Note: a disability may not always be apparent, so it is important not to make assumptions.

Types of discrimination

There are four types of disabled discrimination covered by the Equality Act. They are:
- direct discrimination
- indirect discrimination
- discrimination arising from a disability
- discrimination by association.

Direct discrimination

This is discrimination directly associated with a person's disability. As a 'service provider', you need to make sure you treat disabled customers the same as you treat other customers. You would be treating customers with disabilities less favourably if you:
- refuse to serve them
- offer less favourable terms
- offer a lower standard of service compared with what you normally offer.

It is important to note that the **Equality Act** does not allow any justification for direct discrimination. If you treat someone less favourably, the Act allows them to seek damages from you through the County Court.

Example of unequal treatment: discrimination would occur when a guesthouse or attraction refused access to someone who is mentally impaired on the basis that they felt the person would upset other customers.

Indirect discrimination

This is where a business policy, while applying to all customers, would have a greater impact on disabled customers. Examples could include:
- serving breakfast only in a room that is down a set of stairs
- providing information on an attraction that was only in writing.

The **Equality Act** does allow indirect discrimination if there is 'objective justification'. For example, it may be justified to only allocate loft rooms to people who are not able to move unescorted on the grounds of fire safety. If there is no objective justification (cost is generally not acceptable), then reasonable adjustments (see below) need to be undertaken to adapt to the circumstances of the disabled customer. For example, information in large font sizes or audio tours could be provided.

Discrimination arising from a disability

This is where the discrimination is based on a consequence of the disability rather than the disability itself. Examples would include:
- banning a person with Tourette's syndrome from an event or area because their outbursts may offend other customers
- providing plastic cups and plates to a person with muscular dystrophy because you think that they might break items.

Discrimination by association

This is discrimination against someone associated with a disabled person such as a carer, friend or member of the family. Examples may include:
- refusing the booking of a non-disabled couple because it was known they have a disabled child which they might bring with them
- making the carer of a disabled person sleep in the same room to ensure that they don't disturb other guests.

How does the Act impact on me?

To ensure that you do not discriminate against disabled people or their associates, the law requires you to make reasonable adjustments to both your property and business practices.

Reasonable adjustments

You should make **reasonable** adjustments to the way you deliver your services to make it easier for disabled guests to use them.

The duty is anticipatory, meaning you should consider in advance how to make your services accessible to disabled customers. Waiting for customers to ask you to do something may not be enough.

You should make reasonable adjustments where, if the adjustment were not made, a disabled person would be at a substantial disadvantage compared to people who are not disabled. The question is whether the adjustment is a reasonable one to make in all the circumstances.

The Equality Act 2010 sets out the three requirements for making reasonable adjustments:

CUSTOMERS

1. Adjustments to a policy or procedure

- monitor your policies and procedures to ensure that they are not putting disabled people at a substantial disadvantage in comparison to non-disabled people when accessing goods, facilities and services
- take reasonable steps to ensure that any policies or procedures that put disabled people at a substantial disadvantage are changed or ended.

Note: even if you do not allow animals, you must allow assistance dogs.

2. Adjustments involving the provision of auxiliary aids and services

- anticipate what auxiliary aids or services you need to make available to disabled individuals who would otherwise be at a substantial disadvantage compared to non-disabled people. For example, provide large-print menus for visually-impaired guests or get training in receiving calls via the Next Generation Text Service (NGT), which is a national text to voice service that allows people who can't hear or speak make telephone calls: **ngts.org.uk.**

3. Adjustments to physical features

- you have a duty to take reasonable steps to remove, alter or provide a way of avoiding any physical barriers that make it impossible or unreasonably difficult for disabled people to make full use of facilities. This can include, for example, providing ramp access at steps or a lift if reasonable. If this is not possible, you must look at how the service can be provided by an alternative method.

The need for reasonable adjustments also applies to your website, which may be the first point of contact for a disabled person.

What is reasonable?

Often simple measures can make your facilities more accessible, e.g. taking more time to help disabled guests, letting them know how to ask for help and arranging appropriate training for you and your staff.

You are only required to do what is 'reasonable'. What might be considered reasonable for a national hotel chain may not be so for a small attraction. What is a reasonable step for a particular service provider to have to take depends on all the circumstances of the case. It will vary according to:
- the type of service being provided;

- the nature of the service provider and its size and resources; and
- the effect of the disability on the individual disabled person.

However, without intending to be exhaustive, the following are some of the factors which might be taken into account when considering what is reasonable:
- whether taking any particular steps would be effective in overcoming the substantial disadvantage that disabled people face in accessing the services in question;
- the extent to which it is practicable for the service provider to take the steps;
- the extent of any disruption which taking the steps would cause;
- the extent of the service provider's financial and other resources; and
- the amount of any resources already spent on making adjustments.

The Act permits service providers to justify less favourable treatment (and in some instances failure to make a reasonable adjustment) when there is no possibility to do so, despite the fact that this would mean that a disabled person is treated less favourably. An example is where an historic listed building would have to change the structure of the building to allow step-free access to all floors. Service providers do therefore have flexibility when considering how to make their services accessible to disabled people. In this example, a video tour of the inaccessible floors could be made available as a reasonable adjustment.

Assistance dogs

Assistance dogs are not pets. Thousands of disabled people rely on an assistance dog to help them with day-to-day activities that many people take for granted. It's not only blind people who are helped by assistance dogs. Assistance dogs are also trained to help people with hearing loss, epilepsy, diabetes, physical mobility problems and more. Assistance dogs carry out a variety of practical tasks for people as well as supporting their independence and confidence.

Assistance dog owners are protected by the Act in a number of ways:
1. **Reasonable adjustments** - it will almost always be reasonable not to apply a 'no dogs' policy for assistance dog owners and a failure to do so would amount to unlawful discrimination.

2. **Discrimination arising from disability** – you must not treat a disabled person unfavourably because of something connected to their disability. For example, if a hotel or attraction has a 'no dogs' policy and they bar a disabled person who uses an assistance dog,

not because of their disability but because they have a dog with them, this would be discrimination arising from disability unless the business can objectively justify what it has done.

Guidance by EHRC states 'It would be unlawful to refuse access to a disabled person accompanied by an assistance dog except in the most exceptional circumstances'.

Tourism providers will understandably wish to ensure that only genuine assistance dog users are able to access these rights. However, in determining the legitimacy of assistance dogs providers should note:

- there is no definition of an assistance dog in the Act (other than in relation to carriage of an assistance dog in taxis)
- the Act does not specify acceptable standards of training, behaviour or health. Assistance dogs can be owner-trained
- the Act does not state that assistance dogs have to be registered (there is no regulatory system for the registration of assistance dogs)
- the Act does not state that assistance dogs require any identification documents or an identifying harness or jacket
- there are no blanket exceptions in the Act to cover assistance dogs in food service (or preparation) areas, refusal due to allergies or refusal due to owners' pets
- there is no case law regarding a provider of goods and services refusing to accept/serve a disabled person with an assistance dog. Therefore no clarification can be given on, for example, the appropriateness of requesting proof of training, accepting emotional support dogs or accepting other supporting animals.

Ultimately only a court can determine whether a refusal of service is unlawful and such a determination would be highly dependent on the specific facts and circumstances of the particular case.

Good practice

In terms of what you should do in relation to disabled customers, good practice includes:

- thinking and planning ahead
- not making assumptions based on stereotypes
- asking a disabled person or organisation what is required if you are in doubt
- respecting the dignity of your disabled customer
- establishing a positive policy and practices
- training staff accordingly.

Note: a willingness to help and an attentive ear can help when considering how to make your services accessible to disabled customers. Disabled people will tell you what you need to do to help them best. Also bear in mind that accessibility is often about making compromises, as a feature that will make things easier for one person might make them more difficult for another.

National Accessible Scheme

VisitEngland's National Accessible Scheme (NAS) provides a set of accessibility standards specifically for visitor accommodation in England. The standards booklets are key business support tools in assisting the tourism industry to provide a more accessible environment.

The NAS is a voluntary scheme to which tourism providers can subscribe, in order to accurately promote the facilities they offer to disabled guests. Qualified independent assessors award ratings in line with the robust set of standards, which allow businesses to promote their true level of accessibility. Scheme participation can also demonstrate a commitment to providing accessible experiences for all.

For further information visit the VisitEngland Assessment Services website: **www.visitenglandassessmentservices.com.**

Accessibility Guides

Disabled people, their family and friends need accurate accessibility information in order to make informed decisions as to where to stay and visit in view of their requirements.

Accessibility Guides allow tourism operators to provide a thorough yet concise description of a venue's facilities and services, specifically in relation to individuals with accessibility requirements. They replaced Access Statements in 2017 as an easier format for both operators and consumers to use.

Participants in the VisitEngland quality scheme are required to prepare an Accessibility Guide as part of their quality grading assessment. Participants need to present an Accessibility Guide to the quality assessor at the time of their quality assessment visit.

Businesses can produce an Accessibility Guide on a free website, which also features best practice examples, top tips and frequently asked questions: **www.accessibilityguides.org.**

Further guidance

Equality Act: good practice

More information on the Equality Act and help with good business practice is available on the EHRC website: **www.equalityhumanrights.com**

What the Equality Act means for you

The Government has produced a series of guides to help operators understand what the Act may mean for their business on the Gov.uk website: **www.gov.uk/government/publications/equality-act-guidance**

Make your business accessible

You can find a range of free guidance, tools and resources to help increase engagement with the accessible tourism market in VisitEngland's Business Advice Hub: **www.visitengland.org/access**

Criteria for accessible accommodation

The National Accessible Scheme can help you to develop and certify your accessibility: **www.visitenglandassessmentservices.com/our-schemes/national-accessiblescheme**

Create an Accessibility Guide

Use VisitEngland's free online tool to provide potential customers, including disabled people, with important accessibility information: **www.accessibilityguides.org.**

Luggage and Belongings

KEY FACTS

- If you run a hotel*, you are required by law to take responsibility for the safekeeping of all reasonable items of luggage brought in by guests.
- Hotel* owners have the legal right to detain guests' property until their bill is settled.

Rights and responsibilities

If you operate a hotel* and you accept a guest into your accommodation for at least one night, you are required by law to take responsibility for the safekeeping of all reasonable items of luggage brought in by the guest.

> ***Note: the Hotel Proprietors' Act 1956** defines a hotel as 'an establishment held out by the proprietor as offering food, drink and, if so required, sleeping accommodation, without special contract, to any traveller presenting himself who appears able and willing to pay a reasonable sum for the services and facilities provided and who is in a fit state to be received'. It is worth noting that this definition of a hotel is very old and the Courts are likely to apply the same rights and responsibilities to the operator of any serviced accommodation, even if it does not technically meet the definition.

If a guest's property is lost or damaged, the extent of your liability will vary as follows:

You may not be liable, where the loss or damage to the guest's property is caused by an act of negligence on the part of the guest or by an 'Act of God' (such as a flood).

You may be fully liable, where:
- the loss or damage to the guest's property is caused solely by your negligence or wilful act (or that of your staff), or
- the goods have been entrusted to you for your safekeeping, or
- the goods have been offered to you for safekeeping but refused by you.

You may limit your liability to £50/£100, where the loss or damage to the guest's property does not fit into either of the above categories and you have displayed the statutory notice set out below in a prominent area of your establishment (near the main entrance or reception area). You may then be liable for a minimum amount of £50 per article and £100 maximum per person.

Since the maximum liability has not increased since 1956, many operators now choose to reimburse their clients to a higher level and claim the cost from their hotel insurance.

Note: under the **London Local Authorities Act 2004**, the limits in Greater London are £750 and £1,500 respectively.

The statutory notice is as follows (the second version of the notice is for Greater London only).

NOTICE:
Loss of or damage to guests' property

Under the Hotel Proprietors' Act 1956, a hotel proprietor may in certain circumstances be liable to make good any loss of or damage to a guest's property even though it was not due to any fault of the proprietor or staff of the hotel. This liability however:

- extends only to the property of guests who have engaged sleeping accommodation at the hotel
- is limited to £50 for any one article and a total of £100 in the case of any one guest, except in the case of property which has been deposited, or offered for deposit, for safe custody
- does not cover motor cars or other vehicles of any kind or property lost in them, or horses or other live animals.

This notice does not constitute an admission either that the Act applies to this hotel or that liability thereunder attaches to the proprietor of this hotel in any particular case.

> ## NOTICE:
> ### Loss of or damage to guest's property
> ### (Greater London only)
>
> Under the Hotel Proprietors' Act 1956 and the London Local Authorities Act 2004, a hotel proprietor may in certain circumstances be liable to make good any loss of or damage to a guest's property even though it was not due to any fault of the proprietor or staff of the hotel. This liability however:
>
> - extends only to the property of guests who have engaged sleeping accommodation at the hotel
> - is limited to £750 for any one article and a total of £1500 in the case of any one guest, except in the case of property which has been deposited, or offered for deposit, for safe custody
> - does not cover motor cars or other vehicles of any kind or property lost in them, or horses or other live animals.
>
> *This notice does not constitute an admission either that the Act applies to this hotel or that liability thereunder attaches to the proprietor of this hotel in any particular case.*

What if the guest did not stay overnight?

If you provide serviced accommodation of any kind and the guest did not stay overnight (e.g. they just visited the restaurant or bar), then you will usually be liable for the loss or damage to your guests' property only if you or your staff have been negligent or if the guest handed the property over to you for safekeeping.

It is difficult to be more specific regarding your liability for the loss of guests' property, as each case depends on the circumstances of the loss or damage.

Returning guests' property

If a guest accidentally leaves an item behind, you have both a duty to look after the item (you can be liable for any loss or damage that occurs while it is on your possession) and a duty to reunite the owner with their property. Therefore, you should make every effort to contact the guest to inform them that you have an item belonging to them rather than just putting it in a lost property box.

If you are able to contact the owner, you can mutually agree on what to do with the item (e.g. whether to post it to them, hold it for collection or to simply dispose of the item). You are within your rights to charge the guest for posting the item back, should you wish to do so, as this is an additional service outside the contract you have with them to provide accommodation. However, the charge should be limited to actual justifiable costs.

LICENCES & CONSENTS   MARKETING   CUSTOMERS   FOOD & DRINK   HEALTH & SAFETY   STAFF   BUSINESS MANAGEMENT & TAX   FURTHER INFORMATION

If it is not possible to contact the guest then your actions would depend on the nature of the item. For most relatively low-value items (e.g. clothes) it is sufficient to retain the item for a reasonable period before disposing of it (usually around three months). However, items such as bank cards or driver licences should be handed to the appropriate issuing authority and high-value items should be handed to the police.

Your right to retain a guest's luggage

Hotel owners

Hotel owners (see note above) have the legal right to detain guests' property until they settle their bill. This right does not extend to the guest's car or property left in it, or to the clothes that the guest is wearing.

When the bill is paid, the property must be returned to the guest. No storage charge may be made and you must reimburse the guest accordingly if the property has been damaged while in your possession.

Selling guests' property

If the bill has not been paid in full after six weeks, you may then sell the guest's property. The sale must be by public auction and it must be advertised at least four weeks in advance in both a London and a local newspaper. The adverts must set out your intention to sell the property, give a full description of the goods, name the guest to whom they belonged and give full details of the forthcoming sale.

The proceeds of sale, less the amount owed to you and the costs of the advertisements and organising the auction, must then be returned to the guest on demand.

This right is in addition to any other right that you have, such as that of pursuing a claim for non-payment through the small claims court.

Note: you cannot detain a guest except to await the arrival of the police.

Owners of self-catering accommodation

Operators of self-catering properties have no legal right to detain and sell a guest's property, nor does a proprietor of self-catering accommodation.

If a guest does not pay a bill and further contact or correspondence does not result in payment, then you have the option of pursuing a claim for non-payment through the small claims court (see the *Cancellations and No-shows* section).

Further guidance

Professional legal advice

For more detailed advice, or if a serious claim is made against you, you are advised to obtain professional legal advice.

LICENCES & CONSENTS

MARKETING

CUSTOMERS

FOOD & DRINK

HEALTH & SAFETY

STAFF

BUSINESS MANAGEMENT & TAX

FURTHER INFORMATION

CUSTOMERS

LICENCES & CONSENTS

MARKETING

CUSTOMERS

FOOD & DRINK

HEALTH & SAFETY

STAFF

BUSINESS MANAGEMENT & TAX

FURTHER INFORMATION

LICENCES & CONSENTS

MARKETING

CUSTOMERS

FOOD & DRINK

HEALTH & SAFETY

STAFF

BUSINESS MANAGEMENT & TAX

FURTHER INFORMATION

Childcare

KEY FACTS

- If you regularly provide day care for children under the age of eight for more than two hours in any day, then registration with Ofsted may be necessary.
- The registration process involves filling in an application form and providing details about other people associated with the care.
- Ofsted will need to be satisfied that you are a suitable person, and will expect certain qualifications or recommend some training.

Childcare facilities and the Children Act 1989

Under Part X of the **Children Act 1989**, you are required to register with Ofsted if you are offering certain types of care facilities for children under the age of eight for more than two hours. This applies regardless of whether the child belongs to a member of staff (e.g. a crèche for employees) or a customer (e.g. a childcare service or kids' activity group).

Does this apply to me?
No:
- if the child is over the age of eight, or:
- if the child is in your care for less than two hours.

Yes:
- if the child is between five and eight years old and in your care for more than two hours – you have to be on the **Ofsted Child Care Register**
- if the child is under five years old and in your care for more than two hours – you have to be on the **Ofsted Early Years Register.**

You can apply to join one register or both registers at the same time.

You cannot voluntarily register if you look after each child for under two hours a day – even if your business is open for longer than two hours.

The only exception to this is if you provide before or after-school care for less than two hours a day in total. In this case you can, if you wish, register on the voluntary part of the Childcare Register.

Exemptions

There are various exemptions from the need to register. These include:

1. If you provide tutoring or coaching in either one or two of the following activities to children aged three and over:
- sports
- performing arts
- arts and crafts
- school study support or homework support
- religious, cultural or language studies.

However, you cannot look after children under five for more than four hours in any one day.

2. If you look after children under eight from one place for 14 days or less in any year.

3. If you operate a crèche and all the following apply:
- you look after children under eight for four hours or less each day
- the children's parents plan to stay in the immediate area (close by, where they can be summoned immediately)
- there is no long-term commitment to provide childcare
- this is offered to parents or carers as a short-term convenience, for instance, while they are undertaking an activity.

This is particularly of relevance to activity and holiday centres where care facilities are offered so that parents can undertake an onsite activity.

However, it is important to note that the Act says that you have a duty to ensure that the children are well cared for, even if you are not required to be on a register.

Are baby-sitting and baby listening services covered?

Baby-sitting is not specifically covered by the Act. This is because care that is provided on the parent's own premises is not normally treated as childminding, unless you care for the children of more than two sets of parents in the home of one of them.

Baby-listening services do not come within the scope of the Act. However, if you provide baby-sitting services on a regular basis on particular premises, such as a hotel's baby-sitting service, then you may need to register.

If you need to apply for registration, or are in any doubt as to whether you need to register, you should contact Ofsted.

Registration with Ofsted

In the first instance, you should contact your local authority for information about pre-registration briefings and an application pack. Ofsted recommends a briefing session with your local authority before making your application.

The registration process starts as soon as your form is received by Ofsted. They aim to complete the process within 12 weeks for childminders and 25 weeks for day care providers.

During this time, Ofsted will arrange a registration visit and a 'suitable person' interview with one of their inspectors. They will carry out a number of checks, including with the Criminal Records Bureau, on everyone associated with an application such as the applicant, day care manager or those who live on the premises where the applicant proposes to provide child-minding.

The registration process is explained in the Ofsted leaflets mentioned below in *Further guidance*.

After registration, Ofsted will conduct the first inspection within seven months of starting to care for children. Regular inspections of the quality of care follow this first inspection at least once every three years and, in some cases, more often.

Training

The Department for Education's Early Years Foundation Stage (EYFS) is the statutory framework that sets the standards that all Early Years providers must meet to ensure that children learn and develop well and are kept healthy and safe. This is a comprehensive framework which sets the standards for learning, development and care of children from birth to five and was revised in 2014. All registered early years providers are required to use the EYFS.

Further guidance

Ofsted registration

The Ofsted website gives information on registration for day care providers and childminders: **www.gov.uk/government/ organisations/ofsted**. You can also call their helpline on **0300 123 1231**

Early Years Foundation Stage

The Early Years Foundation Stage handbook can be downloaded from the Foundation Years website: **www.foundationyears.org.uk**.

CUSTOMERS

Alternative Dispute Resolution

KEY FACTS

- If you are unable to resolve a dispute with a customer, you must provide the customer with the name and web address of a certified ADR provider and whether you are willing to use this ADR provider to settle the dispute.
- All businesses must provide an email address for customers on their website.

Note: now the UK has left the EU, businesses are unable to use the EU's Online Dispute Resolution (ODR) Platform and you should remove links any references to the ODR platform from your website.

NEW

Alternative dispute resolution

The traditional means of adjudicating on a dispute between a business and a customer where they have been unable to reach an agreement has been via the court system (usually the small claims court). However, this route can be both expensive and time-consuming.

The **Alternative Dispute Resolution (ADR) Regulations 2015** therefore establish a new low-cost means to resolve these disputes by establishing independent alternative dispute resolution providers that businesses can use to provide adjudication. Although there is no requirement in the regulations that ADR providers need to be certified, it is recommended that you use a certified ADR provider to help ensure the quality of the service.

ADR providers are organisations or individuals who will act as an independent adjudicator and make a decision on the dispute. Normally, before using an ADR provider, you will agree with the customer as to whether the decision will be legally binding. If you sign an agreement that the ADR provider's decision is legally binding, then the decision can be enforced in the same way as adjudicated/arbitrated decisions.

If either you or the customer do not agree to the decision being legally binding, then either side is still able to go to a court or tribunal to seek redress.

While it is not compulsory for businesses to use an ADR provider, all businesses that undertake the sale of goods and services to customers (the regulations do not cover business-to-business transactions) are required to provide customers with information on the ADR.

The dispute resolution process

If you enter into a dispute with a customer, the first course of action is to try to negotiate a resolution that is acceptable to both yourself and the customer. The ADR Regulations only come into effect if your negotiations with the customer have reached an impasse.

At this point, the ADR Regulations require you to inform the customer via a 'durable medium' such as a letter or email (i.e. not verbally) of:

- the name and web address of a certified provider and
- whether you are willing to use this ADR provider to settle the dispute.

> **Note:** if you are a member of a trade association or another organisation that requires members to use an ADR scheme, you must consent to using the ADR provider whose details you provide.

Once you have sent the customer this information, and providing that you have stated that you are willing to use this ADR provider, both sides have 12 months in which to send evidence to the ADR provider.

Within three weeks of receiving the evidence from both sides, the ADR provider will inform both parties as to whether they will adjudicate over the dispute and, if so, will then provide a decision within 90 days.

If you trade online

Up until 1 January 2021, if you traded online, then you were also required to provide a link on your website to the **European Commission's Online Dispute Resolution (ODR)** platform. With the UK now having left the EU, UK businesses no longer have access to the ODR platform and must use a UK based ADR provider instead.

Providing an email address

A final requirement of the ADR Regulations 2015 is for all businesses to provide a contact email address on their website. This means that it's now insufficient to just have an online contact form on your website that does not show the email address.

Further guidance

Alternative Dispute Resolution providers

A list of certified ADR providers, and the sectors they cover, is available from the Trading Standards website: **www.tradingstandards.uk**

Guidance on the Regulations

A copy of the *Alternative Dispute Resolution Regulations 2015 guidance for business* is available on the Business Companion website: **www.businesscompanion.info.**

LICENCES & CONSENTS

MARKETING

CUSTOMERS

FOOD & DRINK

HEALTH & SAFETY

STAFF

BUSINESS MANAGEMENT & TAX

FURTHER INFORMATION

FOOD & DRINK

Food Safety and Hygiene

KEY FACTS

- If you supply food to customers you must comply with the provisions of food safety and hygiene legislation. The word 'food' is defined as including drink.
- You should not provide food that is unsafe (i.e. injurious to health) or unfit for human consumption.
- You must put in place and implement a food safety management system to ensure that the food you provide is safe to eat. These procedures must be based on the Food Standards Agency's Hazard Analysis and Critical Control Point (HACCP) principles.
- You must not keep foods at a temperature that might make them unsafe to eat. There are specified temperatures that different hot or chilled foods must be kept at.
- Registration with the local authority is required for businesses that serve or supply food or drink of any description, including bed and breakfasts.

Food safety legislation

The most important food safety and hygiene legislation applying in the UK comprises:

- the **Food Safety Act 1990**, which provides the framework for food legislation, creates offences in relation to safety, quality and labelling
- the **General Food Law Regulation (EC) No 178/2002**, which creates general principles and requirements of food law (this EU regulation has been transferred into UK law)
- the **Food Safety and Hygiene (England) Regulations 2013**, which revoke and re-enact with some minor changes to the Food Hygiene (England) Regulations 2006 and certain provisions of the General Food Regulations.

Does food safety legislation apply to me?

Yes: if you supply food to customers, you must comply with the provisions of the legislation. The word 'food' is defined as including drink.

Main provisions of the legislation

General Food Law Regulation (EC) 178/2002

Regulation (EC) 178/2002 covers the placing of unsafe or unfit food on the market. You should not place food on the market (that is to sell or supply food, or hold it with intent to supply) which is:

- unsafe (i.e. injurious to health)
- unfit for human consumption, e.g. food that is rotten, 'gone off' or has been subject to considerable contamination would be unfit.

The regulation also covers traceability. You should keep records of businesses which have supplied food to you and any businesses you supply food to. The Food Standards Agency (FSA) guidance says this should include:

- address of customer or supplier
- nature and quantity of products
- date of transaction and delivery.

This is to help when a food manufacturer needs to co-ordinate a withdrawal of unsafe food. There are offences for breaches of these provisions in the **General Food Regulations 2004** (as amended).

Offences under the Food Safety Act 1990

- **Rendering food injurious to health.** Not only is it an offence to place food on the market which is harmful to health, but it is also an offence to do anything which would make food harmful by adding something to it or removing something from it. This may apply even if you did not realise the effect of what you were doing at the time.
- **Selling 'to the purchaser's prejudice' food which is not of the nature, substance or quality demanded.** 'To the purchaser's prejudice' means to his or her disadvantage. This includes things like supplying lemonade when low-calorie lemonade has been requested, or supplying a beef casserole when the customer has ordered lamb casserole.
- **Falsely or misleading describing, advertising, or presenting food.** This offence can be committed when statements or pictures concerning food are untrue. It can also cover statements that are strictly speaking correct but presented in such a way that the customer is led to the wrong conclusion. Bearing this in mind, you should take care with the descriptions of dishes on your menus. There is a similar provision about this in the General Food Law Regulation.

General food hygiene

Do the regulations apply to me?

Yes: if you are a business that supplies food to customers, you must register with your local authority at least 28 days prior to trading and comply with the regulations. It does not matter if you are a small bed and breakfast, a five-star hotel, an attraction or you provide meals in other circumstances. As a food business operator, the onus is on you to make sure you supply safe food.

If you are not sure whether you should register as a food business, you should speak to your local environmental health department for advice.

How do I comply?

Food safety management procedures

You must put in place and implement a food safety management system to ensure that the food you provide is safe to eat. These procedures must be based on the HACCP principles, although they can be proportionate to the nature and size of the business and should not be burdensome on small businesses. HACCP stands for:

- **h**azard
- **a**nalysis
- **c**ritical
- **c**ontrol
- **p**oint.

This means that you must:

- analyse all potential **food hazards** - a hazard is anything that might hurt the consumer
- identify the **points in operation** where hazards might occur
- decide which of the points identified are **critical** to ensuring food safety
- identify and implement effective **control and monitoring** procedures at those critical points
- determine what **corrective actions** must be taken if your procedures are not working
- keep appropriate **records** to show your procedures are working
- **review** all of the above periodically and whenever your food operations change.

Records

The amount of paperwork you will need to keep as part of your safety procedures will also depend on the size and nature of your business. Larger businesses will need to maintain some documented procedures in addition to their records.

FOOD & DRINK

The Food Standards Agency offers a number of models to help you comply with the record-keeping part of the procedures (see *Safer Food, Better Business* in **Further guidance** below.) You can also contact your local authority for advice.

Food premises

As a basic requirement, food premises must comply with the following:
- they must be kept clean, be well maintained and designed to enable good hygiene practices to be adhered to
- they must have adequate hand-washing facilities available, with supplies of hot and cold water, and drying facilities suitably located and designated for cleaning hands. Toilets must not open directly into rooms where food is handled
- they must have adequate means of ventilation, lighting and drainage.

What is adequate in any situation will depend on the nature and size of the business. In addition, the following requirements apply to all rooms, except dining areas, in which food is prepared:
- surface finishes to walls, doors, floors and equipment should be easy to clean and, if necessary, to disinfect
- there must be adequate facilities for cleaning work tools and equipment and for washing food.

Slightly scaled-down, but broadly similar, requirements apply to premises that are only used occasionally for catering purposes.

The full list of requirements are detailed in the *Safer food, better business for caterers* section of the FSA website: www.food.gov.uk/business-guidance/safer-food-better-business-for-caterers.

Domestic premises

Premises 'used primarily as a dwelling house but where foods are regularly prepared' (i.e. this might include some bed and breakfasts) are subject to slightly different requirements with regard to the rooms where food is prepared (**Regulation (EC) 852/2004** Annex II Chapter III). Speak to the environmental health department of your local authority for guidance.

Further requirements

Equipment: all equipment and other items which come into contact with food must be kept clean and well maintained and installed in such a way as to allow adequate cleaning of the surrounding area.

Food waste: waste must not be allowed to accumulate and, as a general rule, must be kept in closed containers which are easy to clean and disinfect. The waste must be eliminated in a hygienic and environmentally-friendly way and must not constitute a direct or indirect source of contamination.

Water supply: there must be an adequate supply of drinking water. Generally, this water supply should be used to make sure that food is not contaminated and any ice should be made from it.

Cleaning agents: cleaning chemicals must not be stored in areas where food is handled..

Personal hygiene: everyone working with food must maintain a high level of personal cleanliness, including clean clothing. You must not allow anyone suffering from an illness which could contaminate food to work in a food handling area. Additionally, staff working in food handling areas are required to report such illnesses to you. You should also ensure that good hand washing routines are maintained.

Raw materials: you should not buy, or supply, any raw material that will not be fit for human consumption.

Protection against contamination: all food must be protected against any form of contamination, including pests, which would make it fail food safety requirements.

Training: all staff handling food must receive training commensurate or appropriate to the work they do. *The Industry Guide to Good Hygiene Practice: Catering Guide* (currently being updated) states that:
- high-risk food handlers, such as those who prepare high-risk foods, should hold a basic or foundation certificate (level 2)
- a waiter/waitress would require hygiene awareness training (level 1)
- the person responsible for implementing the food hygiene management system must have received adequate training to enable them to do this.

The full list of requirements are detailed in the FSA guide pack *Safer Food, better business for caterers*: www.food.gov.uk/business-guidance/safer-food-better-business-for-caterers.

Food and temperature control

The temperature control rules are found in the **Food Hygiene (England) Regulations 2006** (and equivalent legislation in Scotland, Wales and Northern Ireland).

FOOD & DRINK

Do the regulations apply to me?

Yes: if you are a business that offers food to customers, you must comply with the regulations. Just as with the hygiene regulations, it does not matter what type of premises you are – all food operators as defined need to comply with the temperature requirements.

What are the requirements?

You must not keep foods at a temperature that might make them unsafe to eat. Foods which need temperature control for safety must be held either:

- **hot** (at or above a minimum temperature of 63°C) or
- **chilled** (at or below a maximum temperature of 8°C)

In addition to this, foods that are likely to support the growth of harmful bacteria or the formation of toxins should not be kept at temperatures which would result in a risk to health.

Exemptions

Some foods are exempt from the 8°C limit, such as:

- bakery products which are to be used quickly
- most unopened canned foods
- dried foods
- food which is ripening or maturing at room temperature (e.g. soft cheeses)

Serving and display of food

The regulations also have a degree of flexibility in the serving and display of food. For example, food that should normally be kept at or below 8°C may be kept above that temperature for a single period of four hours to allow it to be served or displayed (e.g. food on a buffet table or a cheese trolley). After this period it should either be thrown away or chilled back to 8°C or below until used.

Likewise, food which will be served hot may be kept on display out of temperature control (63°C and above) for a single period of two hours. If any food is left after this time, food should either be discarded, reheated to 63°C or above (in Scotland, food must be reheated to 82°C or above), or cooled as quickly as possible to 8°C or below until final consumption. Guidance on temperature control legislation in the UK is available on the FSA website: www.food.gov.uk.

Handling ready-to-eat foods safely

It is important to handle ready-to-eat foods carefully as they could, if mishandled, lead to cases of food poisoning. They include sandwiches, salads, desserts, cold cooked meats and foods you have cooked in advance to serve cold. The following controls should prevent this from happening:

- check that the temperature of purchased frozen and chilled ready-to-eat foods is correct (under 8°C for chilled foods, -18°C for frozen foods)
- check products are within the date code and that the packaging is not damaged
- do not use products after their 'use by' date
- store ready-to-eat foods separately from raw foods, such as meat, poultry, eggs, etc. Store at the correct temperature and stock rotate
- follow the manufacturer's instructions on storage and preparation
- wash and dry hands before the preparation of ready-to-eat foods
- use clean knives, utensils, and separate boards for the preparation of ready-to-eat foods
- sanitise boards, surfaces and utensils after use
- keep ready-to-eat foods covered after preparation
- once prepared, do not allow ready-to-eat foods to remain at room temperature for any longer than necessary
- buy a thermometer to monitor temperatures.

Enforcement and food hygiene inspections

Local authorities are responsible for enforcing food hygiene laws and authorised enforcement officers have the right to enter and inspect food premises (registered or not) at any reasonable time without having to make an appointment – they will usually come without notice.

They carry out routine inspections and the frequency varies, depending on the degree of risk posed by the business and its previous record. Inspectors may also visit as a result of a complaint.

Inspectors (i.e. 'authorised officers') will look at the way you operate your business to identify any potential hazards and to make sure that you are complying with the law. They will discuss problems with you and advise on possible solutions. They also have the following powers:

- to take samples and photographs and to inspect your records
- to write to you informally, asking you to rectify any problems that they have found. If a breach of the law has been identified, they may serve you with a 'hygiene improvement notice'
- to detain or seize suspect foods
- to recommend a prosecution (although this is normally done only in serious cases)
- to serve 'a hygiene emergency prohibition notice' which forbids the use of the premises or equipment if there is an imminent health risk to the public. Such a notice must be confirmed by the Courts (or a Sheriff in Scotland).

LICENCES & CONSENTS

MARKETING

CUSTOMERS

FOOD & DRINK

HEALTH & SAFETY

STAFF

BUSINESS MANAGEMENT & TAX

FURTHER INFORMATION

FOOD & DRINK

Further guidance on food hygiene inspections can be found on the FSA website: www.food.gov.uk/business-guidance/food-safety-inspections-and-enforcement.

Allergies

A small percentage of the population is allergic to, or intolerant of, certain foods. In the UK, it is estimated that around 2% of the population suffer from food allergies and each year some people become seriously ill and even die from extreme reactions to foods such as peanuts, shellfish and eggs.

Under the **Food Safety Act 1990** and the **General Food Law Regulation 178/2002** you are responsible for ensuring that the food customers eat is safe and the quality is what they expect. This means you should understand exactly what foods can cause problems.

The following is a list of the 14 most common allergens:
- cereals containing gluten, namely: wheat (such as spelt and Khorasan wheat), rye, barley, oats
- crustaceans, for example, prawns, crabs, lobster, crayfish
- eggs
- fish
- peanuts
- soybeans
- milk (including lactose)
- nuts; namely almonds, hazelnuts, walnuts, cashews, pecan nuts, Brazil nuts, pistachio nuts, macadamia (or Queensland) nuts
- celery (including celeriac)
- mustard
- sesame
- sulphur dioxide/sulphites, where added and at a level above 10mg/kg or 10mg/L in the finished product. This can be used as a preservative in dried fruit
- lupin, which includes lupin seeds and flour and can be found in types of bread, pastries and pasta
- molluscs like mussels, whelks, oysters, snails and squid.

You must be aware of any use of these allergens in the food that you prepare and communicate this use to your customers. From October 2021, the way food businesses must provide allergen labelling information for Prepacked for Direct Sale (PPDS) will change. Foods will need to have a label with a full ingredients list with allergenic ingredients emphasised within it. See the *Food labelling* section for more information on your requirement to inform customers of any use of allergens in food you serve customers.

NEW

Food Hygiene Ratings - 'Scores on the Doors'

In 2010, the Food Standards Agency introduced a National Food Hygiene Rating Scheme. This scheme ranks the cleanliness of premises that sell food between '0' (meaning urgent improvement is needed) and '5' (meaning very good and complies with all legal requirements).

The National Food Hygiene Rating Scheme covers all businesses that supply food directly to consumers, so this will include hotels, bed and breakfasts, restaurants, cafés and takeaways and attractions that provide a food offering.

It is not mandatory for you to display the score that you have received if your business is in England (it is a legal requirement to display the rating in Wales and Northern Ireland). However, even if you do not display your rating, it is available to the public on the FSA's searchable online database.

If you believe that the food hygiene rating that you have been given is unfair, you have:
- a right to appeal within 21 days of being notified about your food hygiene rating
- a 'right to reply' which allows you to publish an explanation of any actions you have taken to improve hygiene standards at your premises since your inspection, or to say if there were unusual circumstances at the time of the inspection that might have affected your rating, alongside your rating on the FSA's public database
- an opportunity to request a re-visit when improvements have been made in order to be re-assessed for a 'new' rating.

Note: Food Standards Scotland operates a different Food Hygiene rating scheme in Scotland, which comprises three ratings: Pass, Improvement Required and Exempt Premises.

Further guidance

Your local authority
For information and advice about food safety and hygiene, or food hygiene ratings, contact your local environmental health department: **www.gov.uk/find-local-council**

Food Standards Authority (FSA)
The FSA produces a range of useful publications on their website, including advice on food allergens and food hygiene: **www.food. gov.uk/business-guidance**

FOOD & DRINK

Food hygiene ratings

For more information on the National Food Hygiene Rating Scheme, visit the FSA food ratings website: **ratings.food.gov.uk.**

Food Labelling

KEY FACTS

- If you provide food for customers that contains GM ingredients you need to comply with genetically modified food legislation.
- You need to provide information to customers on 14 allergens that may be used as ingredients in any food you sell.

Pricing food

For details on pricing food, see the *Pricing and charging* section.

Food labelling and genetically modified food

To allow food providers and consumers alike to make informed decisions about the food they use or eat, there are food labelling regulations in place.

The rules covering GM foods are outlined in:
- the **European Regulations (EC) No. 1829/2004, (EC) No. 1830/2004**
- the **GM Food (England) Regulations 2004**
- the **Genetically Modified Organisms (Traceability and Labelling) Regulations 2004** (and equivalent Regulations in Scotland, Wales and Northern Ireland).

Do the regulations apply to me?
No: if there are no ingredients containing, consisting of, or produced from genetically modified organisms in the food you offer to customers, the regulations do not apply to you. Foods produced with the help of GM technology do not have to be labelled. For example, cheese produced with the help of GM enzymes does not need to be labelled as the enzymes are not ingredients in the cheese.

Also, if animals are fed on GM animal feed, the products produced from them (e.g. meat, milk and eggs) do not need to be labelled.

FOOD & DRINK

Yes: if you are providing food for customers that contains ingredients containing, consisting of, or produced from genetically modified organisms, whether or not there is any GM material in the final product (e.g. oil produced from GM soya or maize), you need to comply. Any intentional use of GM must be labelled, but there is a tolerance level (of 0.9%) for the accidental inclusion of EU-authorised GM material. For further information, visit the Food Standards Agency website: www.food.gov.uk/safety-hygiene/genetically-modified-foods.

As any food bought by you to prepare food for customers should be similarly labelled for GM ingredients, you should be able to tell whether or not you need to comply.

What do the regulations require?
The words 'genetically modified' or 'produced from genetically modified [name of organism]' must be displayed on a notice, menu, ticket or label which can be easily read by customers. For example:

Products on the menu marked * contain ingredients produced from genetically modified soya.

Allergies and labelling
It is estimated that around 2% of the population suffer from food allergies and each year some people become seriously ill and even die from extreme reactions to foods such as peanuts, shellfish and eggs.

Under the **Food Safety Act 1990** and the **General Food Law Regulation 178/2002** you are responsible for ensuring that the food that customers eat is safe and the quality is what they expect. This means you should understand exactly what foods can cause problems.

The 14 most common allergens are:
- cereals containing gluten, namely: wheat (such as spelt and Khorasan wheat), rye, barley, oats
- crustaceans, for example, prawns, crabs, lobster, crayfish
- eggs
- fish
- peanuts
- soybeans
- milk (including lactose)
- nuts; namely almonds, hazelnuts, walnuts, cashews, pecan nuts, Brazil nuts, pistachio nuts, macadamia (or Queensland) nuts
- celery (including celeriac)

- mustard
- sesame
- sulphur dioxide/sulphites, where added and at a level above 10mg/kg or 10mg/L in the finished product. This can be used as a preservative in dried fruit
- lupin, which includes lupin seeds and flour and can be found in types of bread, pastries and pasta
- molluscs like mussels, whelks, oysters, snails and squid.

Pre-packaged food

Food labelling requirements for Prepacked for Direct Sale (PPDS) food will change from 1 October 2021 in England, Wales and Northern Ireland as a result of a number of high-profile cases where hypersensitive people have died as a result of inadequate labelling on pre-packaged food.

The new allergen labelling requirements will apply to a category of food called 'prepacked for direct sale'. This is food which is packaged at the same place it is offered to consumers. The food should also be in the packaging before it is ordered or selected.

It includes food that customers select themselves (e.g. packaged sandwiches from a display) and pre-wrapped products kept behind a counter (e.g. bottled drinks or meat and cheese products produced on-site). It can also include some food sold at mobile or temporary outlets.

Prepacked for direct sale food is determined by three criteria:

- **when it is packaged**
  It needs to be packaged before the consumer selects or orders it.
- **where it is packaged**
  It needs to be packaged at the same premises or at the site it is offered or sold to consumers. This includes food packaged by the same business and sold at a temporary or mobile site, such as a food truck or market stall. It also includes making food at home to take to sell a café on the business premises.
- **how it is packaged**
  It needs to be fully or partly enclosed by packaging so that it cannot be altered without opening or changing the packaging in some way. In addition, the food must be ready for final sale to the consumer (e.g. not ingredients that you have packaged to take to a shop or café).

All prepacked for direct sale food that meets the requirements above will need to have a label showing:

- the name of the food
- a full ingredients list with the 14 allergens required to be declared by food law emphasised on the ingredients list (i.e. in capitals or a bold font) if they are present in the food.

LICENCES & CONSENTS

MARKETING

CUSTOMERS

FOOD & DRINK

HEALTH & SAFETY

STAFF

BUSINESS MANAGEMENT & TAX

FURTHER INFORMATION

NEW

FOOD & DRINK

More information on the new requirements and how to comply is available on the FSA website: www.food.gov.uk/business-guidance/allergen-labelling-for-prepacked-for-direct-sale-food.

Unpackaged Food

You need to provide information to customers on any of the 14 allergens used as ingredients in foods sold without packaging or wrapped after ordering. This information could be written down on a chalkboard or menu, or provided orally by a member of staff. Where the specific allergen information is not provided upfront, clear signposting to where this information could be obtained must be provided (i.e. a note on your menu telling customers to ask a waiter regarding the use of allergens in any of the items on the menu).

It is therefore very important that your staff are trained and regularly updated on the use of any allergens in food that you serve.

These rules will only cover information about major allergens intentionally used as ingredients. They do not cover allergens present following accidental contact.

Further guidance

Allergen guidance for businesses
Further information on GM foods, food allergies and intolerance is available from the FSA website: **www.food.gov.uk/business-guidance/allergen-guidance-for-food-businesses**

Guidance on the new packaged food labelling requirements is also available on the FSA website: **www.food.gov.uk/business-guidance/allergen-labelling-for-prepacked-for-direct-sale-food**

Your local authority
Contact your Trading Standards department at your local authority for more information on food labelling: **www.gov.uk/find-local-council.**

Single-Use Plastics

KEY FACTS

● New legislation on single-use plastics makes it illegal to provide plastic drink stirrers and cotton buds to customers and puts significant restrictions on providing customers with plastic straws.

To reduce the level of plastic waste, the Government has introduced the **Environmental Protection (Plastic Straws, Cotton Buds and Stirrers) (England) Regulations 2020**, which came into effect on 1 October 2020.

These regulations make it an offence to provide customers with three different types of single-use plastic products – straws, cotton buds and drink stirrers. The Regulations treat these different products in slightly different ways.

Plastic drink stirrers
It is an offence to sell or supply drink stirrers to end-users and businesses in England. This means it is an offence for you to be sold plastic drink stirrers by a supplier and for you to supply them to your customers.

Plastic cotton buds
It is an offence to sell or supply plastic cotton buds to end-users in England, but they can still be supplied to businesses. This means that you will be able to purchase plastic cotton buds if you need them for a purpose such as cleaning fixtures and fittings, but it will be an offence for you to provide them to your customers.

Plastic straws
It is an offence to sell or supply plastic straws to end-users in England but they can still be supplied to businesses.

LICENCES & CONSENTS   MARKETING   CUSTOMERS   FOOD & DRINK   HEALTH & SAFETY   STAFF   BUSINESS MANAGEMENT & TAX   FURTHER INFORMATION

NEW

However, there is an exemption to this Regulation for catering establishments, which includes restaurants, pubs, bars, cafés and hotel dining rooms. If you are providing food and/or drink for immediate consumption, you will be allowed to continue to provide customers with single-use plastic straws, provided that:

- the straws are not kept in a place where they are visible to customers;
- the straws are not kept in a place where customers have access to them, and
- the straws are not offered or provided to customers unless requested by the customer.

This means that you can provide a plastic straw to a customer if they specifically ask for one. You cannot serve a drink with a plastic straw in it or put a box of straws on a counter for customers to help themselves.

If you sell products such as cartons of drink with straws attached, you can continue to display and sell these products with the straws attached until 3 July 2021.

The Regulations are enforced by local authorities, who can inspect premises to make sure that businesses are complying and are able to levy fines on businesses that are found to be in breach of the Regulations.

Further guidance

Single-use plastics

Guidance on the new Regulations for single-use plastics is available on the Gov.uk website: **www.gov.uk/guidance/straws-cotton-buds-and-drink-stirrers-ban-rules-for-businesses-in-england.**

HEALTH & SAFETY

Health and Safety at Work Act

KEY FACTS

- **The Health and Safety at Work etc. Act (HSWA)** places general duties and responsibilities on all people at work, including employers, employees and the self-employed.
- You are responsible for ensuring, so far as is reasonably practicable, the health, safety and welfare of all your employees at work plus anyone else who could be affected by your work activities, e.g. customers, casual workers, and contractors.
- You are required to consult with employees, or their representative, on issues that may affect their safety.
- Your employees also have a responsibility to take reasonable care of their own health and safety.
- If you employ more than five people you must have a written health and safety policy.
- You must carry out a risk assessment to identify and manage any risks.

Your responsibilities as an employer to employees and others

It is your duty to protect the health, safety and welfare of your employees and other people who might be affected by your business, including customers and contractors who enter the premises to undertake work for you such as cleaners and people undertaking maintenance work. You are required to do whatever is reasonably practicable to achieve this.

The Health and Safety at Work Act etc.1974 (HSWA) sets the framework for health and safety regulations in the workplace. The Act places general duties and responsibilities on all people at work, including employers, employees and the self-employed. There are two important responsibilities for an employer:

LICENCES & CONSENTS

MARKETING

CUSTOMERS

FOOD & DRINK

HEALTH & SAFETY

STAFF

BUSINESS MANAGEMENT & TAX

FURTHER INFORMATION

NEW

HEALTH & SAFETY

- you are responsible for ensuring, so far as is reasonably practicable, the health, safety and welfare of all your employees at work (your employees also have a responsibility to take reasonable care of their own health and safety)
- you have a wider responsibility to ensure, again so far as is reasonably practicable, the safety of other people who are affected by your business, for example, customers, casual workers and contractors.

All the health and safety legislation covered in this section relates to employers, employees, the self-employed and the workplace.

Health and safety law seldom prescribes specific rules for you to follow. Rather, it requires you to undertake whatever measures are necessary to manage safety on your business premises. There are severe penalties for not doing so, which include the possibility of a jail sentence. It is mandatory that you devote time and careful attention to the management of safety in your business; this is at the heart of the law and you cannot fulfil your legal duties by form-filling or cursory treatment of the topic.

It is important to note that under the **Safety Representatives and Safety Committees Regulations 1977** and the **Health and Safety (Consultation with Employees) Regulations 1996**, you have a duty to consult with your employees, or their representatives, on health and safety matters. You must consult on:

- the introduction of any measure which may substantially affect their health and safety at work, e.g. the introduction of new equipment or new systems of work
- arrangements for getting competent people to help them comply with health and safety laws (a competent person is someone who has the necessary knowledge, skills and experience to help an employer meet the requirements of health and safety law)
- the information you must give your employees on the risks and dangers arising from their work, measures to reduce or get rid of these risks and what employees should do if they are exposed to a risk
- the planning and organisation of health and safety training
- the health and safety consequences of introducing new technology.

Further information on your requirements regarding consulting employees can be found on the HSE website: www.hse.gov.uk.

Additional health and safety legislation

Other health and safety legislation supplements the HSWA's general responsibilities with specific requirements. The key regulations are covered in the following sections:

- *Fire Safety (General)*
- *Fire Safety of Furniture And Furnishings*
- *Safety Management*
- *Hazards in the Workplace*
- *Hazards from Work Activities*
- *Swimming, Gym and Outdoor Safety.*

Policy statement and risk assessment

At the heart of health and safety legislation is the requirement for you to undertake a health and safety assessment of your premises, identifying:

- any significant health and safety risks
- any group of employees identified as being especially at risk.

On the basis of this assessment, you must develop and implement a safety policy to manage any risks that you identify.

If you employ five or more people, your health and safety policy must be written down, including the arrangements for the management of safety in your business.

Even if you do not employ five people, it is still good practice to make a written record of your assessment and policy statement. If you do not, it may later be difficult to demonstrate that you have fulfilled your duties under the Health and Safety at Work Act.

For information about how to do a risk assessment see the *Safety management* section.

Health and safety notices

If you employ anyone, you are required by the **Health and Safety Information for Employees Regulations 1989** to display the HSE-approved Health and Safety Law poster.

Alternatively, you can provide your employees with individual copies of the same information in a leaflet entitled *Your Health, Your Safety - A Guide for Workers*.

Mental health

Under the Health and Safety at Work Act, you also have a legal duty to assess risks related to work-related stress and to adopt practices aimed at safeguarding the mental health of your staff. There are six

LICENCES & CONSENTS   MARKETING   CUSTOMERS   FOOD & DRINK   HEALTH & SAFETY   STAFF   BUSINESS MANAGEMENT & TAX   FURTHER INFORMATION

UPDATED

LICENCES & CONSENTS

MARKETING

CUSTOMERS

FOOD & DRINK

HEALTH & SAFETY

STAFF

BUSINESS MANAGEMENT & TAX

FURTHER INFORMATION

main areas where all employers need to assess the impact on the mental health of their employees, to ensure that they are fulfilling their duty of care:

Demands on employees

This means assessing each employee's workload, target setting, work requirements and the workplace environment to make sure that they are not causing undue stress.

Control

This means assessing how much control staff feel they have over the way they work and their work environment.

Relationships

This means promoting a positive working environment that avoids conflict or harassment, either between employees or between employees and customers or contractors. It must be remembered that one person's "jokes" or "banter" is another person's harassment.

Support

This means that if an employee does encounter a problem, the organisation will provide support either through procedures or at least by having an environment where they feel that they can voice their concerns and that these concerns will be treated seriously.

Role

This means ensuring that employees have the confidence to know what their role is and the training to successfully fulfil it, as well as knowing the roles of the other employees so that conflict is avoided.

Change

This means having management, communication and support plans in place when the business is going through change (e.g. redundancies, expansion or being sold) and that staff understand their individual situation and can plan accordingly.

To help managers undertake this assessment, the Health and Safety Executive have produced a publication called *Tackling work-related stress using the Management Standards approach: A step-by-step workbook*.

Enforcement

Local Environmental Health Officers (EHOs) are responsible for enforcing health and safety in all business premises.

Further guidance

Guidance from the Health and Safety Executive (HSE)

The Health and Safety Executive website (www.hse.gov.uk) has a range of guidance publications, including:

- *Consulting employees on health and safety: A brief guide to the law*
- *Tackling work-related stress using the Management Standards approach: A step-by-step workbook.*

On the website, you can also find a toolkit to help you write a health & safety policy, control risks and provide the right facilities (**www.hse.gov.uk/simple-health-safety**), as well as an online toolbox to help you control the risks in the workplace (**www.hse. gov.uk/toolbox**)

Contact your local authority

Contact the environmental health department of your local authority for further assistance: **www.gov.uk/find-local-council**.

LICENCES & CONSENTS

MARKETING

CUSTOMERS

FOOD & DRINK

HEALTH & SAFETY

STAFF

BUSINESS MANAGEMENT & TAX

FURTHER INFORMATION

HEALTH & SAFETY

LICENCES & CONSENTS

MARKETING

CUSTOMERS

FOOD & DRINK

HEALTH & SAFETY

STAFF

BUSINESS MANAGEMENT & TAX

FURTHER INFORMATION

Health and Safety Liabilities

KEY FACTS

- If you have control over your premises, the **Occupier's Liability Acts 1957 and 1984** apply to you.
- The person who controls the premises (the 'occupier') is liable for the physical safety of everyone who comes onto the premises.
- Under the **Employers' Liability (Compulsory Insurance) Act 1969**, employers must have insurance to cover their liability for any harm suffered by an employee at work.
- Public liability insurance is not compulsory but is strongly recommended for all businesses.

Your liability to guests and the public

Under the **Occupiers' Liability Act 1957** and **Occupiers' Liability Act 1984**, the person who controls the premises (the 'occupier') is liable for the physical safety of everyone who comes onto the premises. In some cases, this liability also extends to trespassers and other 'uninvited' guests.

Occupiers have what is known as a 'duty of care' to customers and other visitors, and must make sure that the premises are reasonably safe for the purpose for which customers were invited to use them. If there is a specific danger on the premises, then this danger must be highlighted to all visitors. This could include ponds, wells or areas where machinery is operating.

Does the legislation apply to me?
Yes: if you have control over your business premises, either through ownership, rental or leasing arrangement.

These Acts create a liability, i.e. you can be sued for compensation. You cannot be prosecuted and fined, sent to jail or receive a criminal record under this legislation, but you could be prosecuted under other legislation if you do not take proper precautions.

UPDATED

What does this mean in practice?

You must make sure that the premises are 'reasonably safe.' For example, you should ensure:

- floors, walkways and paved areas are not slippery
- passageways are clear
- cables are tucked away
- furniture and wall fixtures are secure
- equipment (e.g. playground equipment) is well maintained and serviced
- any outdoor structures are sound
- trees on the property are well maintained
- customers are acquainted with emergency procedures and the layout of the premises.

> **Note:** special attention needs to be taken to make sure your premises are safe for disabled people and children.

Duty of care

Your duty of care in relation to customers does not normally extend to parts of your premises that are clearly marked as being out of bounds (such as the kitchens, machine operating plants, or electrical control rooms).

Generally, you are also liable for accidents caused as a result of the actions of your staff or other visitors. For example, if a member of staff leaves a bucket on the stairs, or if a visitor leaves the gate to a swimming pool open, you may be held responsible.

No matter how many notices you put up to the contrary and whatever your booking conditions, or conditions of entry, may say, the law does not allow you to exclude or restrict your liability for death and injuries to customers arising from your negligence (or that of your staff or agents). However, you can take out insurance to cover your liability.

You will not normally be liable for customers who injure themselves while involved in an activity that is not something they might reasonably have been expected to do on the premises, such as trying to jump from the roof of a building into the swimming pool.

Each customer has a duty to take care of his or her own safety. If the guest's own negligence led to an accident, this would reduce, or could even override, any liability that you would otherwise have.

The transportation of customers

If you transport customers, even if this is only occasionally picking up or dropping someone off at the station, there are three issues that need consideration:

- whether a licence is required
- what insurance is required
- health and safety considerations.

Occasional transport

At the lowest level, you do not need a licence for occasional transport if:

- you very occasionally help out a customer by providing a lift
- you do not charge for this, and
- your vehicle has no more than eight seats.

However, you will need to ensure that you have business insurance for your vehicle as, regardless of the lack of payment from the customer, you are still undertaking a business activity.

You should also undertake a quick health and safety assessment prior to transporting the customer– i.e. is the car roadworthy at the time, has the customer put on a seatbelt and is any luggage stowed safely.

Regular transport

If you are providing a lift for your customers to and from their point of arrival as a regular or standard service (e.g. running a shuttle service from a local railway station), then regardless of whether there is a separate charge for this service, you will require a special operating licence and appropriate vehicle insurance.

In this case, you will need a Passenger Service Vehicle (PSV) licence. There are two forms of this licence – restricted and full.

Restricted PSV licence

A restricted licence allows you to operate up to two vehicles that have up to 16 seats, provided that you do not use them as part of a passenger transport business, or you are operating your vehicles as part of your accommodation business and that it is not your main occupation. To gain a licence you will have to provide evidence that you:

- have sufficient money to undertake a passenger service business
- have no convictions
- have a maintenance and safety programme in place for your vehicle
- understand the legislation relating to the maximum hours that you can work driving the vehicle
- have the relevant category of driving licence for the vehicle.

For each vehicle with more than nine seats, you will also need a Certificate of Initial Fitness for the vehicle to prove that the vehicle was properly constructed for the purpose of transporting passengers. You will require this even if you buy the vehicle second-hand.

Separately from the requirements for the PSV licence, you will also need to undertake a written health and safety assessment of the operation and keep this updated.

> **Note:** the Government is reviewing the requirement for accommodation and attraction operators to gain a restricted PSV licence in order to transport customers to or from their premises. However, any review will not remove the requirement for operators to gain a Certificate of Initial Fitness, have appropriate insurance for their vehicle or to undertake a health and safety assessment.

Full PSV licence
If you wish to operate more than two vehicles or a vehicle of more than 16 seats, you will require a Full or Standard PSV licence. In addition to the requirements for a restricted PSV licence, you will also need a certificate of professional competence.

On-demand transport
If you wish to provide customers with an 'on-demand' service that transports them to wherever they request to go, you will require either a Taxi or Private Hire Licence. This is an expensive and time-consuming process requiring, among other things, a Criminal Records Bureau check, a knowledge test of roads and destinations in the area, a medical examination and special insurance.

The costs and stringent requirements associated with this form of licence mean that it is not generally recommended for accommodation providers.

Your liability to employees

Under the **Employers' Liability (Compulsory Insurance) Act 1969**, every employer must have insurance to cover their liability for any bodily injury or disease sustained by an employee at work. Failure to do this is a criminal offence.

How does this apply to me?
If you employ at least one person, you are required to take out and maintain employers' liability insurance cover with a minimum of £5 million for any one claim (most policies available offer £10 million cover).

You must display a copy of the certificate of insurance at your place(s) of business so that it can be seen and read by all your employees. The policy document, or a copy of it, must also be kept available for inspection by Health and Safety Executive inspectors or Environmental Health Officers and, for future reference, all policy documents should be retained permanently.

Operating a business at home
If you start operating a business at your home, whether it be serviced, self-catering or caravan accommodation, or you are thinking of opening a visitor centre or museum in your garage, you need to consider whether you have appropriate and adequate insurance to cover, for example, your potential liability under the Occupiers' and Employers' Liability Acts.

Most household policies will not cover:
- your use of the premises for business purposes
- your legal ability to employees or paying guests
- any theft or damage to your property by guests.

In any event, you should contact your existing insurers as soon as possible.

Public liability insurance
One type of insurance cover you should consider, particularly as the public becomes increasingly claims-conscious, is public liability insurance. This covers your liability to customers and other people such as contractors and business visitors for injury, loss or damage sustained while on your premises (e.g. under the Occupiers' Liability Acts).

There is no legal requirement to take out public liability insurance, but it is strongly recommended that you have this type of cover as injury claims can be extremely high. Having public liability insurance is also a requirement for participation in all VisitEngland Quality Assessment Schemes.

Public liability insurance must not be confused with employers' liability insurance. It also does not cover any loss or damage that occurs to your property and is therefore not a substitute for business, property and contents insurance.

Taking out insurance
Most insurance brokers have special business insurance packages available that will protect you against losses suffered in the course of normal business activities, particularly when the business faces a compensation claim. These business insurance packages generally include:

HEALTH & SAFETY

- public liability insurance
- employers' liability insurance
- property and contents insurance.

A broker will be able to advise you on these types of comprehensive packages or about adding extra cover to an existing policy.

Your local destination management organisation may be able to recommend local insurance brokers who have specific experience in arranging cover for accommodation and attraction operators. Insurance brokers should be registered with and regulated by the Financial Conduct Authority and you can check brokers on their website: www.fca.org.uk.

Insurance for transporting guests

Ensure that you have adequate insurance cover for your vehicle if you transport guests for any reason. See *The transportation of guests* above for more details.

Legionnaires' disease

Information on your legal obligations in minimising the risk of Legionnaires' disease can be found in the *Legionnaires' disease* section.

Further guidance

Seek professional legal advice

If anyone makes a claim against you, you should seek legal advice immediately

Understand Employer Liability Insurance

You can download *A brief guide to the Employers' Liability (Compulsory Insurance) Act* from the HSE website: **www.hse.gov.uk**

Contact your local authority

For Taxi and Hackney Carriage information, contact your local authority: **www.gov.uk/find-local-council.**

Safety Management

KEY FACTS

- The **Management of Health and Safety at Work Regulations 1999** place general duties and responsibilities on all employers at work.

- Employers must carry out a 'suitable and sufficient' assessment of the health and safety risks to employees and others arising out of work activities.

- If you have five or more employees, you must keep a record of any significant findings of the assessment and your health and safety arrangements.

- Employers, the self-employed and those in control of work premises must report certain work-related accidents, diseases and dangerous occurrences.

- Employers must provide first aid equipment and facilities appropriate to the circumstances in the workplace.

Main provisions of the regulations

The **Management of Health and Safety at Work Regulations 1999** follow on from the general responsibilities outlined in the Health and Safety at Work Act 1974, by covering in more detail how an employer should manage health and safety at work in order to avoid accidents and ill-health.

Risk assessment is the key to effective management of health and safety and is a legal requirement. The main requirements relating to an accommodation employer are as follows:

Carry out a risk assessment

Employers must carry out a 'suitable and sufficient' assessment of the health and safety risks to employees at work, and any other people, arising out of work activities. The assessment allows you to identify any extra measures that you need to take.

Doing a risk assessment

A risk assessment is nothing more than a careful examination of what, on your premises, could cause harm to people, so that you can weigh up whether you have taken enough precautions or should do more to prevent harm. You also have to do a risk assessment for fire safety (see the 'Fire Safety (General)' section), and it is acceptable to combine the fire risk assessment into the general one. There are five basic steps:

- **Step 1: Look** for the hazards, i.e. anything that can cause harm. For most accommodation premises the hazards are few and simple but assessing them thoroughly is a necessity. You probably know already if, for example, you have steps that are awkward or kitchen furniture that is unstable. Always consider electricity, gas, carbon monoxide poisoning and falls especially carefully, as these are potential causes of serious injury or even death. Do not neglect the garden or grounds
- **Step 2: Decide** who may be harmed and how, including those especially at risk (see the section below)
- **Step 3: Evaluate** the risks - consider in particular:
  - how likely a mishap is to happen, and
  - how serious the consequences might be. The more likely and the more serious the potential accident, the higher the risk and the more you need to do to prevent it. Decide whether the existing precautions are adequate or whether more should be done. The test of whether you should do more is whether it is 'reasonably practicable' (see section below) to carry out the possible additional measure
- **Step 4: Record** your findings
- **Step 5: Review** your assessment and revise it if necessary.

You don't need to overcomplicate the process. Check that you have taken the precautions you can to avoid injury. You can probably do the assessment yourself. If you get stuck you can contact your local environmental health officer for further advice, although they cannot do the assessment for you.

Consider those especially at risk

You must take into consideration visitors and members of the public who might be affected by your work. You also need to give special consideration to:

- workers who are young
- workers who are inexperienced or new to a particular job
- trainees doing work experience
- disabled workers
- customers who are children, elderly, or disabled.

Members of staff at special risk

If you have members of staff at special risk, any risk assessment and health and safety arrangements need to deal specifically with them.

- **Disabled staff:** if you have disabled staff you must make sure you undertake a risk assessment that takes into account their impairment and, as well as undertaking any adjustments, ensure that you have systems and emergency procedures in place that do not expose them to undue risk
- **Staff with poor English:** if you have staff whose first language is not English, you must make sure they understand, for example, all the preventative health and safety measures, signs and emergency procedures
- **Young people:** there are special requirements covering young people (under the age of 18), which require employers to do a specific risk assessment and give specific information to the young person and their parents or guardians (see the *Employing Under 18s* section)
- **New and expectant mothers:** again, there are special requirements and considerations that are explained in the HSE guide *New and Expectant Mothers who Work* - see *Further guidance* below.

Reasonably practicable

This is a balance between the cost and inconvenience of undertaking actions to reduce risk and the benefits of improved safety.

For example, if the cost of repairing a loose carpet is small, and the risk of tripping or falling down stairs is high, then you must make the repair. At the other extreme if the removal of an awkward step would involve rebuilding part of the house, and the consequences of any foreseeable trip are minor, it wouldn't be reasonably practicable to do it (although, of course, warnings might well be needed).

Health and safety arrangements

You must put into place any extra measures identified in the assessment, along with arrangements for:

- organising health and safety in the workplace
- ensuring safety procedures are followed
- reviewing and updating the measures and procedures.

Health surveillance

Health surveillance is a system of ongoing health checks which are required if you have employees who are exposed to noise or vibration, ionising radiation, solvents, fumes, dusts, biological agents and other hazardous substances. If you have employees who are exposed to hazardous substances, you must provide health surveillance, appropriate to the risks identified in the assessment.

Competent person

Employers must appoint a competent person, preferably a member of staff with the necessary training or experience, to assist in health and safety matters.

Recording

If you have five or more employees, you must keep a record of:
- any 'significant findings' of your assessment
- your health and safety arrangements (best included in your overall 'health and safety policy statement' - a template form for you to use is available on the HSE website: www.hse.gov.uk).

Even if you have fewer than five employees, it is still sensible to keep a record. This will give you increased protection if there is an accident.

Emergency procedures

Employers must draw up procedures for dealing with emergencies and establishing contact with the emergency services (such as fire and medical care).

Information, instruction and training

You must give your employees information on the risks, the preventative measures and the emergency procedures so they can understand them.

You need to consult with your employees on these and any other key health and safety issues.

You also need to make sure that when a new employee starts you give them sufficient health and safety training so that they can go about their work safely. For example, if you have a new cleaner starting, you need to explain how to use all the different cleaning agents safely.

The staff training needs to be repeated or updated as appropriate; it should take place during working hours and must not be paid for by employees.

Agency workers

If you hire agency workers, you must tell the employment agency about:
- risks to the worker's health and safety and steps you have taken to control them

- any necessary legal or professional qualifications or skills
- any necessary health surveillance.

Temporary staff

Employers must give temporary staff information, before they start, on any special qualifications or skills required to do the work safely, and any health surveillance you are required to provide.

Employees' duties

Employees have a duty to follow health and safety instructions and to report dangers.

Accident reporting

If you are an employer, self-employed or in control of work premises, you are required by law to report certain work-related accidents, diseases and dangerous occurrences. Details of the types of accidents that you need to report can be found at the RIDDOR website: www.hse.gov.uk/riddor.

All incidents can be reported online but a telephone service remains for reporting fatal and major injuries only - call the Incident Contact Centre on 0845 300 9923.

You will be sent a copy of the final report for your own records - this meets your statutory obligation to keep records of all reportable incidents for inspection and also allows you to correct any error or omission.

First aid

Employers must provide first-aid equipment and facilities appropriate to the circumstances in the workplace. The minimum would be a suitably stocked first-aid box and a person appointed to take charge of first-aid arrangements.

First-aid provision should be part of your risk assessment process under the Management of Health and Safety at Work Regulations (see *Carry out a risk assessment* section above).

You have no responsibility for administering first aid to guests or the public at large, although you should be familiar with local medical facilities.

Other regulations

Other health and safety legislation supplements these general responsibilities with specific requirements. The key regulations are covered in this service – see the following sections:

- *Fire Safety (General)*
- *Fire Safety of Furniture And Furnishings*

- *Hazards in the Workplace*
- *Hazards from Work Activities*
- *Swimming, Gym and Outdoor Safety.*

Further guidance

Guidance from the Health and Safety Executive (HSE)

The Health and Safety Executive website (**www.hse.gov.uk**) has a range of guidance publications, including:

- *Plan, Do, Check, Act: an introduction to managing health and safety*
- *Risk Assessment: a brief guide to controlling risks in the workplace*
- *Basic Advice on First Aid at Work.*

The website also has dedicated sections, including:

- A toolkit to help you write a health & safety policy: **www.hse.gov. uk/simple-health-safety**
- Example health & safety policies and guided templates: **www. hse.gov.uk/simple-health-safety/policy/index.htm**
- Guidance for the catering industry: **www.hse.gov.uk/catering/ guidance.htm**
- Detailed advice if you employ new or expectant mothers: **www. hse.gov.uk/mothers**
- Detailed advice if you employ young people: **www.hse.gov.uk/ youngpeople**
- Guidance on reporting an accident: **www.hse.gov.uk/riddor.**

Hazards from Work Activities

KEY FACTS

- All employers must consider the risks to staff arising from the hazards associated with work activities. A hazard is something with the potential to cause harm.

- Any work equipment must be suitable for the job and safe, as required by the **Provision and Use of Work Equipment Regulations 1998**.

- If staff habitually use computers or other kinds of display screen equipment, the **Health and Safety (Display Screen Equipment) Regulations 1992** (as amended) apply.

- If staff lift and carry objects, the **Manual Handling Operations Regulations 1992** (as amended) apply.

- Under the **Work at Height Regulations 2005** (as amended), employers are required to avoid work at height where possible, or, where it cannot be avoided, to take measures to ensure that the person working at height does not fall.

- If you are an employer you must assess all hazardous substances.

- These are the main regulations to be aware of, but other health and safety legislation may apply, depending on the work activity being done.

Work equipment

The Provision and Use of Work Equipment Regulations 1998 cover the safety of work equipment (including an employee's own equipment and equipment used by a self-employed person, e.g. a self-employed cleaner who works on your premises).

The general duties of an employer include:
- making sure that equipment is suitable - select the right equipment for the job
- making sure equipment is properly installed and safe to operate
- giving proper training and instructions on the use of the equipment and follow manufacturers' or suppliers' instructions

- making sure equipment is maintained and in good repair through regular maintenance, inspection and, if appropriate, thorough examination
- providing equipment that conforms to any relevant product safety standard.

Display screens

The **Health and Safety (Display Screen Equipment) Regulations 1992** apply where staff habitually use computers or other kinds of display screen equipment (also known as visual display units or VDUs) as part of their normal work.

Employers have to:
- analyse workstations, and assess and reduce risks
- ensure workstations meet minimum requirements set out in the regulations
- plan VDU work so that staff have breaks or changes of activity
- provide eye and eyesight tests for VDU users who request them, and provide spectacles if special ones are needed
- provide health and safety training and information for VDU users.

Safe manual handling

More than a third of all 'over three day' injuries reported each year to HSE and local authorities are the result of manual handling. In the catering industry alone it is the second most common cause of injury.

As seen in the *Safety management* section, the **Management of Health and Safety at Work Regulations 1999** require an employer to assess the risks in any work activity and take the appropriate precautions.

In addition, the **Manual Handling Operations Regulations 1992** require an employer to:
- ensure, so far as it is reasonably practicable, that employees are not required to undertake any manual handling operations at work if there is a risk of them being injured
- if any hazardous operations cannot be avoided, thoroughly assess the risks and take steps to minimise the risks of injury as far as reasonably practicable.

Work at height

Falls from a height account for around 30 fatalities each year and account for around a quarter of all worker deaths. One of the main causes is falls from ladders.

The regulations and types of work at height

Work at height means working where a person could fall and be injured. It therefore includes working at ground level next to a well or cellar opening, etc. There is no fixed height that is considered dangerous. This depends partly on where the person might land (e.g. on grass or concrete).

The **Work at Height Regulations 2005** require employers to avoid work at height where possible, or, where it cannot be avoided, to take measures to ensure that the person working at height does not fall. There must be a risk assessment carried out before a person works at a height.

Light work of short duration may be carried out using ladders if conditions are suitable, there are adequate hand-holds and the ladder can be secured.

People involved in working at a height must be competent and adequately trained and supervised.

You must:
- avoid work at height if you can
- use equipment or take other measures to prevent a fall if you can't avoid work at height
- as a last resort, if no more can be done to prevent a fall, take measures to minimise the consequences of a fall.

Window cleaning and painting are common reasons for working at height. Although very common, window cleaning using ladders has led to many deaths in the past. A ladder is not usually a safe way to clean first-floor windows and above. If you decide to have work done by a person standing on a ladder, you must ensure you have measures in place to prevent him or her from falling off, or the ladder from slipping. There are alternatives, such as:
- water-fed hose cleaning
- the installation of interior eye bolts by a specialist company, that enables windows to be cleaned using a harness.

Things to consider
To ascertain the risk of falling from height, consider these questions:
- how far would a person fall?
- are there adequate hand-holds?
- are there any fragile surfaces (e.g. roof lights) involved?
- where might the person land? (e.g. on grass, concrete, spiked railings)

- what is the nature of the work to be done? (consider especially any leaning, stretching, or carrying that might increase the risk of falling)
- is the ladder or other equipment secured, top and bottom, to prevent it slipping?

Falling off a ladder carries a significant risk of severe injury or death. Ladders are best regarded as a means of access and not as a place from which to do work.

Reducing risks from working at height

To help prevent falls from a height you should assess and reduce the risks to all your workers and ensure they are:

- trained and have suitable and safe equipment for the task(s)
- properly managed and supervised
- provided with sufficient protection measures (e.g. suitable and sufficient personal protective equipment) while they are working at height.

Hazardous substances

Hazardous substances can generally be identified from the product label. In most small businesses only domestic cleaning materials will be used, but some products used for drain cleaning, pest control, gardening, cleaning pools or hot-tubs or other purposes may also be hazardous. For larger businesses, more concentrated commercial cleaning products are likely to be used and these will pose a greater hazard to staff and customers.

COSHH assessment

If you are an employer you must assess all hazardous substances under the **Control of Substances Hazardous to Health Regulations 2002** (COSHH). The employer has a duty to remove employees' exposure to hazardous substances, e.g. powerful commercial cleaning agents or, where this is not possible, to adequately control it.

To help with the assessment, you may need to obtain a safety data sheet (SDS) from the supplier or manufacturer of the hazardous substance. (This will not be necessary for very common products like household bleach, for which plenty of information is readily available.) The SDS describes the substance and the dangers it may pose. You will only then be in a position to plan the measures that you will need to take to control the substance and prevent harm. It will usually be best to keep it in a secure location, especially if there are children on the premises.

COSHH Essentials

By logging on to COSHH Essentials on the Health and Safety Executive website you can carry out a free, quick and simple risk assessment (COSHH Essentials is also available in a paper version which you can buy from HSE Books): www.hse.gov.uk/coshh/essentials/index.htm.

You will need to enter some very basic information about the chemicals or products that you use and the system will automatically work out the correct control procedures for you. Alternatively, for some tasks such as cleaning, you can simply go directly to the control advice.

Other legislation

The regulations already mentioned are the main ones to be aware of, but other health and safety legislation may apply, depending on the work activity.

Further guidance

Guidance from the Health and Safety Executive

A wide range of guidance documents on how to mitigate the risks associated with various activities are available on the Health and Safety Executive Website: **www.hse.gov.uk/guidance/index.htm**. These include the following guides:

- *Providing and using work equipment safely: A brief guide*
- *Working with display screen equipment (DSE): A brief guide*
- *Working at height: A brief guide*
- *Safe use of ladders and stepladders: A brief guide*
- *Lifting equipment at work: A brief guide*
- *Working with substances hazardous to health: A brief guide to COSHH*
- *Preventing manual handling injuries to catering staff information sheet*

Safety relating to musculoskeletal disorders

Find up-to-date information on health and safety relating to musculoskeletal disorders e.g. back pain and repetitive strain injury on the Health and Safety Executive website: **www.hse.gov.uk/msd**.

LICENCES & CONSENTS

MARKETING

CUSTOMERS

FOOD & DRINK

HEALTH & SAFETY

STAFF

BUSINESS MANAGEMENT & TAX

FURTHER INFORMATION

Legionnaires' disease

KEY FACTS

- Legionella is classified as a 'hazardous substance' and you are required to undertake a risk assessment, and any subsequent remedial actions, in order to protect both your staff and customers.
- If you have five or more employees, you need to record both what assessment and actions you undertook.

Note: the risk of Legionella bacteria breeding in a property's water system increases significantly if the property remains unused for a prolonged period. Therefore, if your property was required to close due to COVID-19 restrictions, it is recommended that you either drain the water system or flush the system prior to reopening.

Legionnaires' disease is a potentially fatal form of pneumonia caused by Legionella bacteria. While these bacteria are common in natural water systems, they usually occur in numbers too small to cause health problems. However, in the right conditions these bacteria can multiply quickly and cause a significant health risk.

These conditions are where water is maintained between 20–45C, is stored or recirculated, where there is a source of nutrients in the water (including rust or scale) and where there are aerial water droplets. This means that water tanks, spas or hot tubs, air conditioning units and showers are the most common places for the bacteria to breed.

Legionella is classified as a 'hazardous substance' and, therefore, you are required to undertake a risk assessment, and any subsequent remedial actions, in order to protect both your staff and customers.

If you have five or more employees, you need to record both what assessment and what actions you undertook. While it is not a legal requirement to record the assessment and actions if you have fewer than five employees, it is always recommended that you do so in case you are challenged at a later date.

If you have self-catering property or a B&B with a normal residential water system, this risk assessment will be straight forward as the risk of Legionnaires' Disease should not be high. A full specialist assessment is generally only needed if you have a large commercial property or you are uncertain of the property's water system.

The main things to check for are:
- make sure that any debris is not getting into the system (e.g. ensure any water tanks have a tight-fitting lid)
- make sure that the Hot Water Cylinder is set on at least 60°C
- make sure there is no redundant pipework in which water could become stagnant
- make sure showerheads are regularly cleaned and disinfected.

If you have machinery that contains water, such as air conditioning units or a spa/hot tub, then special attention needs to be made to ensure that this is regularly serviced and cleaned.

If you operate a property where the water system is not in regular use (e.g. a self-catering property that has long void periods or closes over winter) then additional precautions need to be undertaken to make sure that the water in the system does not stagnate. If your property is going to be vacant for a significant period, you should either drain or flush the system before the guests arrive.

Further information on Legionella and how to control it in water systems is available on the Health and Safety Executive website: **www.hse.gov.uk/legionnaires/index.htm**.

Further guidance

Legionnaires' disease: a brief guide
You can download *Legionnaires' disease: a brief guide* from the HSE website: **www.hse.gov.uk**

How to control Legionella
You can download the approved code of practice and guidance *Legionnaires' disease: The control of legionella bacteria in water systems* from the HSE website: **www.hse.gov.uk**.

Hazards in the Workplace

KEY FACTS

- All employers must consider the risks to staff arising from the hazards associated with aspects of the workplace. A hazard is something with the potential to cause harm.
- The working environment must be suitable, at a reasonable temperature, have adequate lighting and ventilation and include sufficient rest facilities.
- Employers should reduce the risk of slips, trips and falls by cleaning spillages, keeping walkways clear and organising work better.
- All electrical systems in places of work must be maintained 'so far as is reasonably practicable' to avoid danger to all who use the premises (including customers).
- Although Health and Safety can be a complex area of legislation, there are two main sets of regulations that you need to be aware of: the **Workplace (Health, Safety and Welfare) Regulations 1992** and the **Management of Health and Safety at Work Regulations 1999**.

The Workplace (Health, Safety and Welfare) Regulations 1992

The **Workplace (Health, Safety and Welfare) Regulations 1992** cover your employees' working environment, setting out the requirements in respect of:
- the quality of the working environment (e.g. reasonable temperature, lighting and ventilation)
- suitability of the environment (e.g. room dimensions, space, passageways and windows)
- the facilities for your employees (e.g. toilets, washing and eating facilities, drinking water, changing and rest areas and rest facilities for pregnant women)
- the maintenance and cleanliness of the workplace, equipment and facilities.

The Management of Health and Safety at Work Regulations 1999

The main requirement of the **Management of Health and Safety at Work Regulations 1999** is that employers must carry out risk assessments to eliminate or reduce risks. Employers with five or more employees need to record the significant findings of a risk assessment - it is not necessary to record risk assessments for trivial or insignificant risks. In addition, employers also need to:

- make arrangements for implementing the health and safety measures identified as necessary by risk assessments
- monitor and review those arrangements
- appoint people with sufficient knowledge, skills, experience and training to help them implement these arrangements
- set up emergency procedures and provide information about them to employees
- provide clear information, supervision and training for employees and ensure that suitably competent people are appointed who are capable of carrying out the tasks entrusted to them
- work together with any other employer(s) operating from the same workplace, sharing information on the risks that other staff may be exposed to, e.g. cleaning, catering or maintenance contractors
- take particular account of risks to new and expectant mothers.

Use of safety glass

The **Workplace (Health, Safety and Welfare) Regulations 1992** include the use of safety glass or materials in the workplace.

Always be sure that the glass used in your premises is adequate for the use to which it is being put.

If there is a large pane of glass, especially if it extends to below waist height, you need to consider the risk of it being broken or walked into. If the circumstances lead to the conclusion that there is no risk, no action needs to be taken, but if there is a risk of it being broken it should be glazed with safety glass and also marked so that it is obviously present (e.g. with an etched design).

What glass is covered by the regulations?

It is not the case that the regulations apply to all glazing. In the past, a number of glaziers have misrepresented these regulations in attempts to persuade businesses to replace or modify all windows, glazed doors, walls or partitions. The actual requirement is as follows.

Windows and transparent or translucent doors, gates and walls

Every window or other transparent or translucent surface in a wall or partition, and every transparent or translucent surface in a door or gate shall, where necessary for reasons of health or safety:

- be of safety material or be protected against breakage of the transparent or translucent material
- be appropriately marked or incorporate features so as, in either case, to make it apparent.

General guidance to the regulations then adds that transparent or translucent surfaces in doors, gates, walls and partitions should be of a safety material or be adequately protected against breakage in the following cases:

- in doors and gates, and door and gate side panels, where any part of the transparent or translucent surface is at shoulder level or below
- in windows, walls and partitions, where any part of the transparent or translucent surface is at waist level or below, except in glasshouses where people will likely be aware of the presence of glazing and avoid contact.

Safety glass or materials are only necessary in certain cases where a particular need or risk has been identified. Indeed, the chances are that it will already have been fitted as a matter of routine. Wholesale replacement of windows and glazed doors or partitions is not implied by the regulations.

Slips and trips

Accidents as a result of a slip or trip are the most common cause of injuries at work. Resulting falls can be serious. They can happen in all kinds of businesses, but sectors such as the food and catering industry report a higher than average number of incidents and it is a particularly important subject if members of the public use your premises.

What are the chances of slips and trips at your workplace?

To identify problems and prevent accidents happening, consider the following questions:

- do you have outside paths, walkways or paved areas that can be slippery if wet, grow moss or have ice form on them?
- do you have floors that are, or can become, slippery e.g. when wet?
- does spillage or contamination occur and is it dealt with quickly?
- do people use unlit areas, such as paths or yards, in the dark?
- might temporary work such as maintenance or alterations take place? It could introduce slipping and tripping hazards, such as trailing cables

- do you use floor-cleaning materials anywhere?
- are the right methods and materials being used?

Reducing risk

Effective solutions are often simple, cheap and lead to other benefits. You should ensure that you:

- clean up spillages, organise work better, and keep walkways clear
- 'design-in' safety equipment and materials
- regularly clean and maintain walkways and have steps in place to mitigate risks due to natural events such as rain and ice
- obtain help and advice, e.g. from the Health and Safety Executive, publications and guidance, or your local environmental health officer.

Electricity at work

The **Electricity at Work Regulations 1989** are wide-ranging. Business operators should be aware of one objective in particular: that all electrical systems in places of work must be maintained 'so far as is reasonably practicable' to avoid danger to all who use the premises (including customers).

For self-catering operators, these regulations only apply if you have one or more employees working on the premises (although it is important to remember that this includes cleaners and people undertaking maintenance and that your general duties under the Health and Safety at Work Act include ensuring that guests are protected from electrical hazards).

The safety of electrical equipment in self-catering accommodation is also covered in the *Product safety* section.

Which electrical equipment is affected?

All electrical systems are covered by the regulations, whether they are used solely by:

- you and your staff
- you, your staff and customers
- your customers.

'Electrical systems' means the mains wiring and all mains-powered electric equipment.

Electrical equipment brought in by guests is not affected by these regulations, which are restricted to matters within your control.

Testing and maintenance

There is no specific requirement for the regular routine testing of systems. Nevertheless, you do have a duty of maintenance under the

LICENCES & CONSENTS

MARKETING

CUSTOMERS

FOOD & DRINK

HEALTH & SAFETY

STAFF

BUSINESS MANAGEMENT & TAX

FURTHER INFORMATION

regulations and regular testing is the only practical way for you to be sure that you are complying with this duty.

- The **fixed wiring installation** should be tested every few years - exactly how often will depend on its age and the likelihood that it has been damaged. It is important to remember that whilst there are no specific rules requiring testing every so often, if you never have it tested you will most probably not be carrying out your general duties to ensure the safety of your guests.
- You will often be able to tell from a quick visual inspection whether a piece of **portable equipment** is faulty or damaged. Regular visual inspection is the most important measure you can take. This will detect a large proportion of common faults such as damaged plugs, frayed or damaged cables, or cracks in a casing.

If you wish to have your electrical systems tested professionally, you should ensure that those doing the work are competent. This can be done by using electrical contractors who belong to either the Electrical Contractors' Association or to the National Inspection Council for Electrical Installation Contracting (NICEIC). However, portable appliance testing can be carried out by a trained, competent person who need not be a qualified electrician.

Records of testing and maintenance
Keep a record of all the testing and maintenance that has been carried out. In the event of an accident involving the electrical systems on your premises, this record should enable you to demonstrate that you have complied with your duty of maintenance under the regulations.

Cold callers
Health and safety legislation is an area that has been targeted by disreputable firms trying to sell products and services. Do not be intimidated by salespeople who may be misrepresenting the regulations in an attempt to win your custom. Remember, in particular, that the regulations do not generally specify what materials you must use, what tests you should undertake or how often you should undertake them.

Work equipment and machinery
Key legislation covering the safety of work equipment includes the **Provision and Use of Work Equipment Regulations 1998 (PUWER)**, which requires employers to ensure work equipment is safe for its intended use. These regulations are extremely broad in their application and cover any machinery, appliance, apparatus, tool or installation used on work premises or taken by employees or

LICENCES & CONSENTS   MARKETING   CUSTOMERS   FOOD & DRINK   HEALTH & SAFETY   STAFF   BUSINESS MANAGEMENT & TAX   FURTHER INFORMATION

NEW

customers for use off-site. It also includes machinery and equipment that is used by customers including, for example, go-carts, fairground rides and steam engines.

Complying with the PUWER means ensuring that:
- equipment is suitable for the intended process and conditions of use
- equipment is safe for the intended use, e.g. regular maintenance must occur and safety inspections must be carried out as required
- the person who is to use the equipment has received suitable health and safety training and information about the equipment's operation
- equipment is fitted with appropriate warning signs, marks, safety bars or guards.

To comply with these requirements you must, among other things:
- ensure the equipment is constructed or adapted to be suitable for the purpose it is used or provided for
- take account of the working conditions and health and safety risks in the workplace when selecting work equipment
- ensure the equipment is only used for suitable purposes
- ensure equipment is maintained in an efficient state, in efficient working order and in good repair
- where a machine has a maintenance log, keep this up to date
- where the safety of work equipment depends on the manner of installation, it must be inspected after installation and before being put into use
- where work equipment is exposed to deteriorating conditions liable to result in dangerous situations (e.g. equipment that is left outside), it must be inspected to ensure faults are detected in good time so the risk to health and safety is managed
- ensure that all people using, supervising or managing the use of work equipment, including customers, are provided with adequate, clear health and safety information. This will include, where necessary, written instructions on its use and suitable equipment markings and warnings
- ensure that all people who use, supervise or manage the use of work equipment have received adequate training, which should include the correct use of the equipment, the risks that may arise from its use and the precautions to take
- where the use of work equipment is likely to involve a specific risk to health and safety (e.g. woodworking machinery), ensure that the use of the equipment is restricted to those people trained and appointed to use it.

The Health and Safety Executive provides a range of guidance on how to fulfil your obligations under these regulations on their website: www.hse.gov.uk. Foremost among these is the *Provision and Use of Work Equipment Regulations 1998: Approved Code of Practice and guidance* which sets out what you need to do to comply with the regulations.

Fairgrounds and amusement parks

Because of the unique health and safety issues associated with fairground attractions and amusement park rides, the Health and Safety Executive has separate guidance for operators of these attractions. The publication *Fairgrounds and amusement parks: Guidance on safe practice* provides guidance for businesses involved in the organisation, operation and management of fairgrounds and theme parks. While the guidance is aimed at ride controllers, ride operators and fair organisers, it is also useful for event organisers and employees, the self-employed and contractors working in the fairground and amusement park sector.

Further guidance

Guidance from the Health and Safety Executive (HSE)

The Health and Safety Executive website (**www.hse.gov.uk**) has a range of guidance publications, including:

- *Workplace Health, Safety and Welfare: A Short Guide for Managers*
- *Welfare at Work: Guidance for Employers on Welfare Provisions*
- *Preventing Slips and Trips at Work*
- *Maintaining Portable Electrical Equipment in Low-risk Environments*
- *Electrical Safety and You*
- *Provision and Use of Work Equipment Regulations 1998: Approved Code of Practice and guidance*
- *Fairgrounds and amusement parks: Guidance on safe practice.*

HEALTH & SAFETY

Product Safety

KEY FACTS

- Business operators have a responsibility for ensuring that gas appliances and flues in the premises are safely maintained and checked. All safety checks must be carried out by a Gas Safe registered engineer.

- Electrical equipment safety regulations require that all electrical equipment supplied 'in the course of business' is safe. There is no specific requirement for annual maintenance, but to ensure electrical equipment remains safe, you are strongly advised to have it checked and serviced regularly by a registered electrician.

- The essential requirements are to ensure that you supply only safe products to your customers, and to ensure that a product remains safe throughout its period of use. The general product safety regulations also apply if you provide self-catering accommodation.

Gas safety

Installing and maintaining gas appliances

Each year there are fatalities from carbon monoxide poisoning caused by poorly installed or badly maintained gas boilers, appliances and flues. The **Gas Safety (Installation and Use) Regulations 1998** are there to protect your staff and your customers.

They supplement any responsibilities you may have under the **Health and Safety at Work, etc Act 1974** and the **Management of Health and Safety at Work Regulations 1999**.

Registration schemes for gas engineers

The CORGI registration scheme for gas engineers ended on 1 April 2009 and has been replaced by the Gas Safe registration scheme. It is illegal for any engineer to undertake work under the **Gas Safety (Installation and Use) Regulations 1998** unless they are Gas Safe registered.

What do the gas safety regulations cover?

- The regulations specifically deal with the installation, maintenance and use of gas appliances and fittings and flues in domestic, residential and commercial premises
- The regulations place duties on a wide range of people, including gas suppliers and those installing and working on gas equipment
- The regulations include extensive duties on business operators for ensuring appliances and flues in their premises are safely maintained and checked.

What types of premises are affected?

The premises affected include all attractions and tourist accommodation including:

- commercial installations generally
- self-catering properties
- hotels, guesthouses, hostels and bed and breakfasts
- permanently sited caravans
- touring caravans and inland waterway boats hired out in the course of business.

What are my main duties?

Duties as a business operator

You are required to:

- ensure all gas fittings and flues are maintained in a safe condition
- ensure an annual safety check is carried out on each gas appliance/flue by a Gas Safe registered engineer (see *Registration schemes for gas engineers* above for more details)
- keep a written record of the inspection for two years, containing information such as the following:
  - the date of check
  - location and details of the appliance/flue
  - any defects found and action taken
  - a confirmation that the check was made in accordance with the regulations.
- for accommodation, issue a copy of the record to any person staying for more than 28 days, or if the premises is let for 28 days or less, display a copy of the record prominently in the premises.

Duties as an employer

You have a duty to ensure that gas appliances under your control are

LICENCES & CONSENTS   MARKETING   CUSTOMERS   FOOD & DRINK   HEALTH & SAFETY   STAFF   BUSINESS MANAGEMENT & TAX   FURTHER INFORMATION

'maintained in a safe condition so as to prevent injury to any person'. This includes staff or people that you contract to work on your premises (e.g. security guards and cleaners).

Other important provisions
Other important provisions include the following:
- anyone carrying out work on gas appliances or fittings not as part of their business (e.g. as a favour to you) must still be competent (do-it-yourself work can be dangerous and illegal)

Note: employers can only use Gas Safe engineers (see *Registration schemes for gas engineers* below for more details).

- you must not use any gas appliance or fitting you know or suspect to be unsafe
- with the exception of 'room-sealed' appliances, there are restrictions on the installation of gas appliances in sleeping areas fitted after 1 January 1996
- it is illegal to install instantaneous water heaters that are not room-sealed or fitted with a safety device which automatically turns off the gas supply before a dangerous level of poisonous fumes builds up.

Additional precautions
The Health and Safety Executive highlights additional precautions:
- whenever draught exclusion, double glazing or a conservatory extension is fitted to a room containing a gas appliance, the appliance should subsequently be checked for safety
- never block or obstruct any fixed ventilation grilles or air bricks
- never block or cover outside flues.

While there is no legal requirement to install a carbon monoxide detector, their use is a requirement of the VisitEngland National Quality Assessment Scheme and is considered best practice for properties which have a gas supply.

Your liabilities and those of your agent or landlord
IMPORTANT: if you use an agent to manage your properties (e.g. self-catering accommodation) or you rent your premises, you should ensure that the management contract or rental agreement specifies who is responsible for the maintenance of gas appliances and for keeping records to indicate when this maintenance has been carried out.

The liability of purely marketing and booking agencies (rather than managing agencies) under these regulations is unclear. Some agencies therefore seek to exclude themselves from liability by inserting into their contracts with owners a clause which commits those owners to ensuring that their property complies at all times with the gas safety requirements.

Electrical equipment

What do the regulations cover?

The **Electrical Equipment (Safety) Regulations 1994** require, among other things, that all electrical equipment supplied 'in the course of business' is safe. This applies equally to new and second-hand equipment.

Do the regulations apply to me?

The regulations apply to everyone who supplies electrical equipment to customers in the course of their business, regardless of whether or not their business is actually the supply of electrical equipment. The regulations are particularly relevant to self-catering accommodation, as equipment in these premises may not be covered by the Electricity at Work Regulations, which covers fixtures and fitting on the premises (see the *Hazards in the workplace* section for more details).

What does safe mean?

For electrical equipment to be regarded as safe, there should be no risk (or only a minimal risk) that the equipment will in any way cause death or injury to any person or domestic animal, or cause damage to property.

If you are buying any new electrical equipment in the UK, it should be 'safe' as manufacturers and suppliers are bound by the same regulations. It should also carry a CE marking (indicating that the manufacturer believes the product complies with all relevant European Directives and safety standards). If you are buying second-hand electrical equipment from a professional dealer (or auction house) it should likewise be 'safe', although it does not have to carry a CE marking.

Do I need to maintain electrical equipment?

Although these regulations require electrical equipment to be safe, unlike for gas appliances there is no specific requirement for annual maintenance. However, to be sure that the electrical equipment in your accommodation remains safe, you are strongly advised to have it checked and serviced regularly by a registered electrician.

The Health and Safety Executive (HSE) provide a free guidance publication *Electrical Safety and You* which you can download from the HSE website: www.hse.gov.uk. This provides useful information about checking electrical equipment.

Note: letting agents and landlords can also be held responsible for the safety of the electrical equipment in premises they let or rent, depending on the terms of their management or rental agreements. Check your agreement and speak with your agent/landlord to ensure you both understand who is responsible for the safety of electrical products.

General product safety

The **General Product Safety Regulations 2005** are aimed at making sure that all products supplied to customers are safe in their normal or reasonably foreseeable usage.

The regulations cover products made available to consumers for their use in the course of a delivery of a service (e.g. the provision of a hairdryer in a hotel room, a riding helmet provided to someone pony trekking or a cot for customers who have a baby).

Where a product is already subject to other existing regulations then those regulations will still apply to that product. The **General Product Safety Regulations** will also apply where they go further than the existing regulations.

Do the regulations apply to me?

Yes: if you are providing equipment for the use of customers.

Note: letting agents can be held responsible for product safety in self-catering accommodation, depending on the terms of their agreement with the property owners.

How do I comply with the regulations?

The essential requirements are to ensure that you supply only safe products to your customers, and take steps (where appropriate) to help ensure that a product remains safe throughout its period of use.

A safe product is defined as 'any product which under normal or reasonably foreseeable conditions of use presents no risk or only the minimum risk compatible with the product's use and which is consistent with a high level of protection for consumers'.

You are required to provide customers with all relevant information, warnings, and instructions for the safe operation and use of products.

You are also required to keep yourself informed about possible risks.

General precautions

The regulations require no formal testing of products and, as you can see from the examples below, it is really just a matter of common sense and routine checking.

- if instructions are needed to operate a piece of equipment, make sure that they are provided
- if a piece of equipment provided is damaged, repair it, e.g. an ironing board with loose or fragile legs
- if an item of furniture or equipment can be damaged and made dangerous, make sure your customers know this.

Requirements as a 'distributor' of products

As a 'distributor' of products, you are also required, 'within the limits of your activity', to participate in monitoring the safety of products that you supply and to pass on information on product risks. In practice this means:

- passing on to customers information provided by producers about a product's risks
- passing back to producers safety complaints, information and experiences on safety-related matters obtained from customers
- co-operating with the authorities and others in the supply chain in taking action to avoid or remove those risks.

Note: if you discover that you have provided an unsafe product for your customers to use, you are obliged to notify your local authority of the fact and what action you have taken to remove the risks to your customers.

Enforcement

The Trading Standards department of your local authority is responsible for enforcing the regulations mentioned above (except for the **Electrical Equipment Regulations**).

Further guidance

Gas safety

Visit the Gas Safe Register website (**www.gassaferegister.co.uk**) or call the gas safety advice line on 0800 300 363

Guidance from the Health and Safety Executive (HSE)

The Health and Safety Executive website (**www.hse.gov.uk**) has a range of guidance publications, including:

- *Gas Appliances. Get Them Checked, Keep Them Safe*
- *Landlords, A Guide to Landlords' Duties: Gas Safety (Installation and Use)*
- *Electrical safety and you: A brief guide*

Contact your local authority

Further advice is available from the Trading Standards department of your local authority, who enforce most of the regulations: **www.gov.uk/find-local-council**

General product safety

You can download the *Chartered Trading Standards Institute guidance on general product safety in rented accommodation* from the Business Companion website: **www.businesscompanion.info.**

LICENCES & CONSENTS

MARKETING

CUSTOMERS

FOOD & DRINK

HEALTH & SAFETY

STAFF

BUSINESS MANAGEMENT & TAX

FURTHER INFORMATION

Swimming, Gym and Outdoor Safety

KEY FACTS

- There are no specific regulations on swimming pool or gym safety, but you must manage these activities so they comply with health and safety legislation.
- Anyone who sells adventure activities intended for young people under 18 must be inspected and licensed under the **Adventure Activities Licensing Regulations 2004**.

Swimming and gym safety

Drownings in swimming pools in the UK are rare. However, this does not mean that you should not pay particular attention to the safety of customers and staff around pool areas.

General legislation that applies

Currently, there is no specific legislation on swimming pool or gym safety. These are covered by general health and safety regulations. Your main responsibility as a pool or gym operator, in relation to the safety of your guests or clients, is to be found in the **Health and Safety at Work, etc Act 1974** and the **Management of Health and Safety at Work Regulations 1999**. See the sections on the *Health and Safety at Work Act* and *Safety management* for more information.

Safety in swimming pools is a complex subject and should be studied closely by those who manage them. A thorough risk assessment should be carried out, and, amongst other things, this will determine whether constant supervision is needed. This risk assessment should include topics such as:

- slipping and tripping
- signage
- water depth and any changes of level
- water clarity

LICENCES & CONSENTS

MARKETING

CUSTOMERS

FOOD & DRINK

HEALTH & SAFETY

STAFF

BUSINESS MANAGEMENT & TAX

FURTHER INFORMATION

- the availability of alcohol or likelihood of swimming after drinking
- child protection issues
- unsupervised children
- hazards in changing areas
- life-saving equipment
- rescue and emergency arrangements.

Guidance on swimming pools

The Health and Safety Executive (HSE) has published a very useful guide, *Managing Health and Safety in Swimming Pools*, which provides detailed guidance on the risks associated with swimming pool operation and the precautions which may be taken to help achieve a safer environment. It also covers supervision and signage: www.hse.gov.uk.

The guide draws on legislation from the **Health and Safety at Work, etc Act 1974**, the **Management of Health and Safety at Work Regulations 1999**, the **Workplace Health and Safety Regulations 1992** and the **Provision and Use of Work Equipment Regulations 1998**.

Outdoor activity safety measures

Anyone who sells adventure activities intended for young people under 18 must be inspected and licensed under the **Adventure Activities Licensing Regulations 2004**.

Do I need an inspection and licence?

Yes: if you provide, in return for payment, any of the activities listed below to young people under 18 unaccompanied by a parent or guardian.

Activities covered by the inspection and licensing scheme

The scheme covers 26 main activities under the following four specified adventure activity groups:

- **caving:** underground exploration in natural caves and mines including pot-holing, cave diving and mine exploration
- **climbing:** climbing, traversing, abseiling and scrambling activities, except on purpose-designed climbing walls or abseiling towers
- **trekking:** walking, running, pony trekking, mountain biking, off-piste skiing, and related activities when done in moor or mountain country which is remote (i.e. over 30 minutes' travelling time from the nearest road or refuge)
- **water sports:** canoeing, rafting, sailing and related activities when done on the sea, tidal waters or inland waters which are more than 100m across or are turbulent.

The scheme does not cover:
- activities that are offered to young people who are accompanied by their parents or guardians
- activities offered by voluntary associations to their members or by schools to their pupils.

Note: in 2018, the HSE undertook a review and public consultation regarding the delivery and scope of AALA to ensure that the provision of licensing of adventure activities is delivered in a sensible, proportionate and cost-effective manner, and encourages the participation by young people in adventure activities. At time of print, the outcome of the review has not been published.

The activity provider's duty under the regulations
The primary duty of the activity provider is to ensure the safety of young people using activity facilities. To be able to comply with this duty, providers must have in place a safety management system that involves a systematic approach to recognising risks and making sure something is done to control them.

Important factors include:
- the risk assessment process
- the number of competent instructors
- the suitability and maintenance of equipment
- emergency procedures.

The inspection/licensing process
The HSE currently has responsibility for the Adventure Activities Licensing Authority (AALA) and has enforcement responsibility for the 2004 regulations.

All the inspections and most of the administration work that the AALA carried out have been taken over by Tourism Quality Services Ltd (TQS) under contract. TQS is operating under the name Adventure Activities Licensing Service (AALS).

Applications, inspections and licensing are handled by TQS. Inspections are rigorous. Licences will only be granted if the licensing authority is satisfied that the applicant meets management safety requirements.

Further guidance
Managing Health and Safety in Swimming Pools
The guide *Managing Health and Safety in Swimming Pools* can be downloaded from the HSE website: **www.hse.gov.uk**

HEALTH & SAFETY

Contact your local authority

Health and safety standards for private pools are enforced by the Environmental Health department of your local authority: **www.gov.uk/find-local-council**

Adventure activities licensing

Information on adventure activities and the change from licensing to Codes of Practice is available on the HSE website: **www.hse.gov.uk/aala.**

Fire Safety (General)

KEY FACTS

- Fire safety legislation applies to virtually all workplaces including attractions, hotels, B&Bs and self-catering properties.

- A 'suitable and sufficient' fire risk assessment must be carried out, and where there are five or more employees, the assessment should be recorded.

- There should be one person responsible for the fire risk assessment and ensuring that fire protection and prevention measures are observed and maintained.

- An emergency plan should be drawn up. It should be displayed in the form of a fire action notice in guest rooms and adjacent to the fire alarm call points in the staff and common areas.

Fire safety

The **Regulatory Reform (Fire Safety) Order 2005** requires the 'responsible person' in virtually all workplaces, including attractions, hotels, B&Bs and self-catering properties, to adopt a self-assessment approach to fire safety in the workplace.

The **Regulatory Reform (Fire Safety) Order 2005** applies to England and Wales, but there is equivalent legislation in Scotland and Northern Ireland.
- In Scotland the Fire (Scotland) Act 2005 and the Fire Safety (Scotland) Regulations 2006 apply
- In Northern Ireland the relevant legislation is the Fire and Rescue Services (Northern Ireland) Order 2006.

Do the regulations apply to me?

Yes: the regulations apply to all attractions and accommodation premises, including self-catering accommodation.

Houses in multiple occupation

Properties defined as Houses in Multiple Occupation (HMOs) are subject to the **Regulatory Reform (Fire Safety) Order 2005** in that the common areas that may be visited by the landlord or others are subject to a suitable and sufficient Fire Risk Assessment. The individual residential areas are not subject to this requirement. HMOs are still subject to the fire safety requirements imposed by the **Housing Act 2004**.

How do I comply?

The **Regulatory Reform (Fire Safety) Order 2005** requires every business to nominate a person to take responsibility for carrying out a Fire Risk Assessment of the premises and ensure that fire protection and prevention measures are observed and maintained.

Although not a legal requirement, it is advisable to identify the nominated responsible person on the assessment document and make that person known to all staff.

If you have five or more employees, the Fire Risk Assessment must be recorded. However, it is strongly recommended that even if you do not employ five or more people, you should keep a record in case any issues arise concerning your fire safety provisions. A record will also prove that you have undertaken an assessment.

> **Note:** it is a requirement of VisitEngland's National Quality Assessment Scheme for accommodation that you demonstrate to the assessor that you have carried out your Fire Risk Assessment. In addition, for any business your public liability insurance provider will also require proof that you have undertaken an assessment.

What is a Fire Risk Assessment?

A Fire Risk Assessment is a structured consideration of the fire hazards and management of fire in the premises. It can be undertaken in five steps:

- identify the fire hazards
- identify the people at risk
- evaluate, remove, reduce and protect from risk
- record, plan, inform, instruct and train
- review the assessment periodically.

Remember: you know your premises best, so follow the guidance and assess how your staff and customers would escape from the building quickly if a fire started (under 2.5 minutes is the target time).

Think about how they would be alerted and how easily they would find their way out. After all, customer safety is the most important thing to consider - and yours too if you live on the premises.

Identify the fire hazards

- **potential sources of ignition, e.g.:**
  - cooking equipment
  - lighting
  - electrical apparatus
  - machinery
  - display screen equipment, e.g. computer screens
- **combustible materials that may burn, e.g.:**
  - the furnishings and furniture
  - parts of the building such as panelling and curtains
  - combustible linings on escape routes
  - displays
- **flammable liquids and gases e.g.:**
  - products used for cleaning or maintenance purposes, including those used to clean swimming pools and hot tubs
  - fuel storage areas.

Identify the people at risk

The people at risk include:

- customers
- staff
- contractors
- other visitors
- people outside the property, e.g. neighbours and passers-by.

Particular note should be made of the number of people likely to be on the premises, where they could be on the premises if a fire occurs and any persons - staff or customers - who may require additional assistance in the event of an evacuation e.g. disabled people.

Evaluate, remove, reduce and protect from risk

This step involves evaluating the hazards and taking measures to eliminate these where possible. The prohibition of smoking on the premises or replacing candles on dinner tables with an alternative without an open flame, and the regular removal of rubbish from bins and storage areas, for example, will help to reduce the hazards.

Particular care should be taken when selecting curtains and display materials, especially temporary decorations used for specific events or to celebrate public holidays and festivals.

Any simple changes should be made straight away, such as clearing obstacles and removing flammable items from escape routes. If you identify something that would be too expensive or cause too much disruption to rectify straight away, make a note of the work and when you intend to carry it out. Out of season is always a good time to catch-up on such work.

Record, plan, inform and train

Where there are five or more staff, the Fire Risk Assessment must be recorded. In other cases (e.g. small attractions, B&Bs and self-catering accommodation) it is good practice to record the assessment anyway to demonstrate compliance with the law. The log book should contain details of maintenance and servicing to fire protection measures. It should also include details about alarms, detectors and fire extinguishers.

An emergency plan should be drawn up to indicate the actions that should be taken by staff, as well as customers and others, in case of a fire on the premises. This is particularly important for attractions where the customers are in enclosed spaces and/or in large groups (e.g. escape rooms and theatres).

The plan, in the form of a Fire Action Notice, should be displayed adjacent to the fire alarm call points in the staff and public areas. For accommodation businesses, it should also be displayed in guest bedrooms.

These actions should include the measures that would be taken to identify and assist disabled people to leave the premises safely.

Staff should be trained in the actions that they would be expected to take in an emergency and this should include all staff participating in periodic fire drills at least once, and preferably twice, a year. Where staff do not speak fluent English, special attention should be given to ensuring that instructions are fully understood by the staff concerned.

Where an attraction or hotel is part of a complex of buildings (such as a shopping centre) or parts of the buildings are occupied by franchise holders, then the responsible person should liaise with the appropriate staff in these areas.

Review the assessment periodically

The Fire Risk Assessment for the premises should be reviewed periodically and when:
- alterations are made to the structure or layout of the premises
- there are changes in the use of an area of the building

LICENCES & CONSENTS   MARKETING   CUSTOMERS   FOOD & DRINK   HEALTH & SAFETY   STAFF   BUSINESS MANAGEMENT & TAX   FURTHER INFORMATION

UPDATED

- there are significant changes to the number or location of the visitors or staff
- there is a significant change in the mobility level or other factors influencing the response of visitors or staff in an emergency
- there are changes in the management of the building.

There are no prescribed times for the reviews, but many businesses choose to review their assessment annually.

How do I know what fire precautions I need?

It is up to the nominated person to determine the appropriate fire precautions as a result of their Fire Risk Assessment.

For **accommodation businesses**, the guidance publication *Do You Have Paying Guests?* is available on the Gov.uk website: www. gov.uk/government/publications/do-you-have-paying-guests. It provides advice tailored specifically to B&Bs, guest houses and self-catering properties. It is designed to encourage compliance, by giving businesses practical advice on reducing fire risks in their establishments. It explains the risk assessment process, sets out sources of further advice and guidance and offers some practical information for owners on what may represent appropriate and proportionate fire safety measures in these types of premises.

For **attractions**, the Home Office produces two publications: *Fire safety risk assessment: small and medium places of assembly*, which is targeted at places that accommodate up to 60 people (small) and up to 300 people (medium), and *Fire safety risk assessment: large places of assembly*, for premises that hold over 300 people.

There is also separate guidance for:
- outdoor attractions and events - *Fire safety risk assessment: open-air events and venues*
- theatres and music halls - *Fire safety risk assessment: theatres, cinemas and similar premises*
- zoos and farm parks - *Fire safety risk assessment: animal premises and stables*.

These guidance documents contain detailed information on how to undertake a Fire Risk Assessment related to different business types, as well as templates for the assessment and fire safety maintenance checklists. There are also sections in the guidance documents on how to adapt fire precautions for historic buildings.

The most important factor is fire prevention. Staff should be made aware of fire hazards and safe working practices in order to prevent

NEW

LICENCES & CONSENTS

MARKETING

CUSTOMERS

FOOD & DRINK

HEALTH & SAFETY

STAFF

BUSINESS MANAGEMENT & TAX

FURTHER INFORMATION

a fire breaking out. There should be an emergency plan drawn up so that all staff know what actions they should take in the event of a fire.

The fire protection provisions will vary according to the particular premises but should include the following:

- **means of escape:** in all premises it is important that there are adequate means of escape. In all but the smallest guesthouses there should normally be at least two escape routes from all parts of the building and these should be available for use and free of obstructions at all times
- **fire alarm:** there should be a means of alerting people to a fire, should it break out. See below for more details
- **emergency lighting:** in order for everyone to find their way out of the building safely there should be automatic emergency escape lighting. In some very small guesthouses there may be sufficient 'borrowed light' from street lights outside but this is not often the case
- **signs:** these should be prominently displayed to guide customers to the fire exits with which they will not be familiar
- **fire fighting equipment:** a suitable number of appropriate fire extinguishers should be provided and at least some staff should be instructed in their use.

Which alarm system?

Since the interpretation of the Order may vary with each fire service around the country, it is difficult to advise businesses in a general way on exactly what type of alarm system they should fit.

The types of system required will, however, depend on the level of the risk - a very sophisticated system would not be necessary in small premises. Whatever system is used should take into account disabled people (e.g. those with hearing loss), so that their safety is not compromised.

The **Regulatory Reform (Fire Safety) Order 2005** requires that premises are provided with suitable and sufficient means of detecting fire and giving warning in the event of a fire. For small buildings this may be linked mains-powered smoke and heat alarms that both sound in the event of fire.

Guidelines for small premises are that they can install simple systems - LD2 or LD3 - that comprise mains-operated smoke and heat alarms with battery back-up. Current legislation defines a 'small' property as being up to two storeys high (from the ground) with no floor more than 200 square metres in total. This equates to a floor with eight to ten en-suite double rooms.

LD2 properties must have alarms in corridors and all rooms leading off the main escape route, while LD3 properties require them only in the corridor, landing and hallway of the main escape route. These LD3 alarms are the same as those required in all new homes. If the property was built after 1990, it is likely to comply already.

Larger properties may be expected to install more sophisticated detectors and alarms, which are classed as L2 systems.

Note: the Home Office is currently revising the guidance publication *Do You Have Paying Guests?*, which may provide updated information on the types of recommended alarm systems for accommodation businesses. Download the guide from Gov.uk to check the latest version.

How do I undertake the assessment?

Guidance on undertaking a Fire Risk Assessment is set out on Gov. uk: https://www.gov.uk/workplace-fire-safety-your-responsibilities/fire-risk-assessments.

Further advice can be gained from a fire safety consultant or your local fire authority.

Fire risk assessment template for small accommodation businesses

VisitEngland provides a free downloadable Fire Risk Assessment template for smaller domestic-type accommodation: www.visitbritain.org/business-advice/complete-your-fire-risk-assessment.

How do I record the Fire Risk Assessment?

The legislation does not prescribe a specific format for the assessment but you do have to record the **significant findings** and the **persons especially at risk** from fire. The significant findings are a list of the actions that should be taken to reduce the fire hazards to a minimum.

You should also record any shortcomings that are identified in the management of the general fire precautions. A note should be kept of the remedial actions that are taken to demonstrate to the fire brigade, should they visit, that you are taking steps to address these matters.

Is the assessment a one-off exercise?

No: you are required to keep your assessment under review and update it when necessary. A new assessment should always be undertaken whenever a property is renovated or structurally altered.

Who enforces the legislation?

The **Regulatory Reform (Fire Safety) Order 2005** is enforced by the local fire and rescue service. Fire Safety Officers will make periodic visits to the premises and will ask to see the fire risk assessment to ensure that it is 'suitable and sufficient'.

What do Fire Safety Officers look at?

As well as inspecting the means of escape and other fire precautions, the Fire Safety Officer may ask to see the fire log book containing the records of the servicing and maintenance of the fire protection measures (e.g. the automatic fire detection and alarm system and the emergency lighting).

The officer may also ask to see the record of false fire alarms in the premises so these should also be kept up-to-date.

Notices

If your premises does not meet the Order, the Fire Safety Officer will provide practical advice or, if the risk is serious or if the Officer is not satisfied, you may be issued with one of the following.

- **an alterations notice:** this does not require alterations to be made to the premises. It is served when the enforcing authority believes that there will be a serious risk to people in the building if a change is made to any particular part of the premises or their use
- **an enforcement notice:** this requires certain measures to be taken within a specified timeframe
- **a prohibition notice:** this requires the business to cease trading immediately until certain remedial action has been taken.

In all cases, you will have a right of appeal, both informally and formally. An informal appeal can sometimes identify a different way of meeting the Order which satisfies both parties.

The fire authority will work with you to achieve a satisfactory level of fire safety.

Further guidance

Fire safety for accommodation businesses

The guide *Do you have Paying Guests?* is designed to provide advice on fire safety to small accommodation businesses: **www.gov.uk/ government/publications/do-you-have-paying-guests**

Making your premises safe from fire

The guide *Regulatory Reform (Fire Safety) Order 2005 - A short guide to making your premises safe from fire* can be downloaded from Gov.uk: **https://www.gov.uk/government/publications/ making-your-premises-safe-from-fire**

How to complete a fire risk assessment: accommodation

Download the guide *Fire Risk Assessment for sleeping accommodation* from the Gov.uk website: **www.gov.uk/government/publications/ fire-safety-risk-assessment-sleeping-accommodation**

How to complete a fire risk assessment: attractions

The general guidance document on how to complete a fire risk assessment, *Fire Safety in the Workplace*, is available on the Gov.uk website: *www.gov.uk/workplace-fire-safety-your-responsibilities/ fire-risk-assessments*

Fire evacuation for disabled guests

Download the guide *Fire Safety Risk Assessment - Means of Escape for Disabled People* from the Gov.uk website: **www.gov.uk/ government/publications/fire-safety-risk-assessment-means-of- escape-for-disabled-people**.

HEALTH & SAFETY

HEALTH & SAFETY

LICENCES & CONSENTS

MARKETING

CUSTOMERS

FOOD & DRINK

HEALTH & SAFETY

STAFF

BUSINESS MANAGEMENT & TAX

FURTHER INFORMATION

Fire Safety of Furniture and Furnishings

KEY FACTS

- If you provide hotel or B&B accommodation or operate a pub, restaurant or medium hazard attraction, which includes indoor premises where public entertainment is provided, you need to purchase furniture and furnishings that comply with commercial fire safety standards.

- If you provide self-catering accommodation or have a low hazard attraction, such as a museum or exhibition that contains upholstered furniture, you need to comply with the Furniture and Furnishings (Fire) (Safety) Regulations 1988.

- All furniture (new and second-hand) in self-catering accommodation or low hazard attractions that is covered by the regulations must comply with certain safety tests.

- An agency's liability for the fire safety of the furniture in the properties it handles depends on the terms of its arrangement with the accommodation owner.

The Fire Safety Order requires you to undertake a fire safety assessment of your property, identifying risks and taking practical steps to mitigate these risks. This assessment includes whether the fire safety characteristics of the furniture and furnishings in your property are appropriate to the level of fire risk.

Fire safety of furniture in all premises

The British Standards Institute (BSI) defines four categories of fire risk for all premises – low hazard, medium hazard, high hazard and very high hazard. Residential properties and self-catering properties, along with attractions such as museums and exhibitions, are deemed to be low hazard, while B&Bs, hotels, places of public entertainment, casinos, pubs and restaurants are deemed to be medium hazard because they are generally larger and occupied by more than one party.

For low hazard properties, you are able to use furniture and furnishings that meet fire safety standards for domestic properties. As such, you are able to use any new product from a reputable supplier because this is the minimum standard for all manufacturers and retailers. However, you are still required to comply with the **Furniture and Furnishings (Fire) (Safety) Regulations 1988**, which cover domestic furniture and furnishings.

For medium hazard properties, BSI states that furniture and furnishings should comply with standards BS 7176 (upholstered furniture), BS 7177 (bed bases and mattresses) and BS 5867 (curtains and drapes), which provide greater fire protection than domestic products. This commercial or contract furniture should meet CRIB 5/Ignition Source 5 standards, which means it has been tested for fire safety and is often sold by specialist companies. When ordering furniture for medium hazard premises, it is important to ensure that it complies with these standards. Your local fire safety officer will be able to advise.

The Furniture and Furnishings (Fire) (Safety) Regulations 1988

The Furniture and Furnishings (Fire) (Safety) Regulations 1988 (as amended) set fire resistance standards for upholstered furniture in domestic use (new and second-hand).

Do the Furniture and Furnishings (Fire) (Safety) Regulations apply to me?
Yes: if you are providing self-catering accommodation that contains upholstered furniture or have an attraction that is deemed to be low hazard.

What do the regulations cover?
The Furniture and Furnishings (Fire) (Safety) Regulations 1988 (as amended) set fire resistance standards for upholstered furniture in domestic use (new and second-hand).

The regulations apply only to upholstered furniture supplied for domestic use, a type of use that implies a low fire hazard. Most holiday lets are regarded as constituting domestic use and, therefore, are covered by the regulations.

Furniture designed to cope with a greater fire hazard (e.g. hotel beds and chairs) is available and may be offered to you by some retailers. When re-equipping your self-catering property, it will normally be for you to decide whether or not you require the new furniture to meet these higher fire resistance standards. If in any doubt, check with your local fire authority.

For simplicity's sake in the information that follows, furniture and furnishings is referred to as 'furniture'.

What furniture is affected?
To come within the scope of the regulations, furniture must be upholstered. Such furniture would include:
- domestic furniture, including children's furniture
- beds and divans (including their bases and headboards), mattresses of any size
- sofa beds, futons and other convertibles
- nursery furniture (e.g. highchairs, cots and playpens)
- domestic garden furniture
- scatter cushions and seat pads
- pillows
- furniture in new caravans.

The regulations also apply to loose and stretch covers for furniture.

What furniture is not affected?
The regulations do not apply to:
- bedclothes (including duvets)
- loose covers for mattresses
- pillowcases
- curtains
- carpets
- sleeping bags
- goods made before 1 January 1950 and the materials used to re-upholster them.

Main provisions of the regulations
All furniture (new and second-hand) in self-catering accommodation or low hazard attractions that are covered by the regulations must comply with certain safety tests. These are very broadly as follows:
- upholstered furniture must pass a prescribed cigarette resistance test
- cover fabric, whether for use in permanent or loose covers, will normally have to pass a match resistance test
- filling materials for all furniture must pass ignitability tests as specified in the regulations
- all new upholstered furniture (except mattresses and bedding) and loose and stretch covers for furniture must carry a permanent label detailing compliance with fire safety requirements. Always look for these labels before buying any upholstered furniture for your property.

HEALTH & SAFETY

If you are having items re-upholstered, make sure that the materials used comply with the regulations. However, remember that the regulations do not apply to materials used to re-upholster furniture made before 1950, unless that furniture is being significantly reworked and upholstered.

Can I use fire-inhibiting sprays to increase the life of my existing furniture?

These sprays are available from a number of companies who will treat the furniture for you. However, the Local Government Association and the Department for Business, Energy and Industrial Strategy (BEIS) advise operators to exercise extreme caution in using them because of issues relating to their durability. The treatment may, for example, be rendered ineffective by laundering.

Before deciding to have your furniture treated, you should:
- remember that the regulations apply both to covers and to filling materials
- make absolutely sure that the spray on offer is appropriate for the covers and filling materials used in your furniture
- be sure that the spray will not be affected by previous treatments (e.g. waterproofing) carried out on the furniture
- bear in mind that some sprays are not water-resistant and will wash out, even when fluids, such as tea, are spilled on the treated fabric
- ask the company to provide strong evidence and guarantees that the spray does do what it is supposed to do.

If the furniture which you have had treated is subsequently found not to meet the fire resistance standards specified in the regulations, it will be you (as the supplier of the furniture), and not the supplier or manufacturer of the spray, who is held responsible under this legislation.

Are letting agencies caught by the regulations?

Possibly. Whether or not an agency is liable for the fire safety of the furniture in the properties it handles will depend on the terms of its arrangement with you, the owner of the accommodation.

It seems that agencies that do no more than market your property and take bookings are unlikely to be liable. However, agencies that also manage and maintain properties on an owner's behalf could possibly be liable.

As this is something of a grey area, some marketing/booking agencies cover themselves by including a clause in their contracts with owners which commits those owners to ensuring that their property complies at all times with these regulations (and others).

Expect any prospective agency to ask about the fire resistance standards of your furniture before it agrees to take your property on to its books.

Review of the Regulations

In 2016 the Department for Business, Energy and Industrial Strategy (BEIS) undertook a review of the Furniture and Furnishing (Fire) (Safety) Regulations. The Government's response to the review was published in July 2019 and stated that new legislation would be developed to replace these regulations, It is uncertain as to when this new legislation will be introduced, but the new legislation will probably only affect materials that can be used in the manufacture of furniture and furnishings and safety tests conducted on them, rather than affecting the responsibilities of businesses using either domestic or commercial furniture.

Further guidance

Your local authority

For further assistance, contact the Trading Standards department of your local authority: **www.gov.uk/find-local-council.**

HEALTH & SAFETY

LICENCES & CONSENTS

MARKETING

CUSTOMERS

FOOD & DRINK

HEALTH & SAFETY

STAFF

BUSINESS MANAGEMENT & TAX

FURTHER INFORMATION

Smoking in Public Places

KEY FACTS

- Smoking is banned in enclosed public spaces and places of work, with some exemptions.
- There is a legal duty for you to display a legible no-smoking sign where it can be seen by customers and staff.
- There is a legal duty on any person who owns or manages smoke-free premises to ensure that customers, visitors and staff do not smoke on the premises.

Smoking ban

There has been a ban on smoking in enclosed public spaces and places of work (with some exemptions) since 1 July 2007, when the **Health Act 2006** came into force.

Does the Act apply to me?

Yes: if you own or manage enclosed or substantially enclosed premises that are open to the public or are used as a place of work by more than one person or where members of the public might visit to receive or provide goods or services.

> **Note:** while the areas of premises to which the ban applies, definitions and exemptions are the same in Wales, the signage requirement is different.

Definitions

Enclosed places: premises are considered to be enclosed if they have a ceiling or roof and, except for doors, windows or passageways, are wholly enclosed, whether on a permanent or temporary basis.

Substantially enclosed areas - the 50% rule: substantially enclosed premises are defined as those that have a ceiling or roof (including retractable roofs such as awnings), but have permanent openings in the walls, not including doors or windows, which are less than half of the total area of the walls. Walls include fixed or retractable structures that serve the purpose of walls and constitute the perimeter of premises (e.g. windbreaks). Temporary structures such as tents, marquees or similar will be classified as enclosed premises if they fall within the definition.

Exemptions

While smoking is banned from all the indoor public and communal areas of attractions, hotels and guesthouses, there are a number of exemptions:

- **self-contained short-term rental accommodation** (holiday cottages/flats/caravans) are not required to be smoke-free but you retain the right to determine whether to allow smoking in your property
- the **private areas of bed and breakfasts and guesthouses** are not covered by the ban, provided that the areas are not used by any staff (i.e. the laundry may be out of bounds for customers but if a cleaner has to use it, it is covered by the ban)
- **designated bedrooms** in hotels, guesthouses and bed and breakfasts. To qualify, a designated bedroom must:
  - be designated in writing by the person in charge of the premises as being a smoking room
  - be completely enclosed except for doors and windows
  - have a ventilation system that must not discharge into any non-smoking part of the premises
  - have doors to smoke-free parts of the premises that shut mechanically after use
  - be clearly marked as a room in which smoking is permitted.

It should be noted that there is no legal requirement for an accommodation owner to provide designated smoking bedrooms. Providing such rooms is purely at the discretion of the owner.

Signage

The **Smoke-free (Signs) Regulations 2012** (England only) require you to display at least one legible no-smoking sign. There is no requirement on the location or size of the sign, provided that it is able to be seen by customers and staff.

Enforcement and penalties

Enforcement is the responsibility of local authorities. Environmental health officers have the power to enter all 'no-smoking premises' in order to establish that the smoke-free legislation is being enforced in accordance with the law.

Failure to display appropriate non-smoking signage may result in a fine, and the legislation also places a legal duty on any person who owns or manages smoke-free premises to ensure that customers and staff do not smoke on the premises.

Owners or managers who are found not to have taken reasonable steps to stop people smoking on their premises will be liable to a fine of up to £2500 on conviction.

Vaping

The ban on smoking in enclosed public spaces and places of work does not apply to the use of e-cigarettes or vaping. It is therefore up to operators to determine whether vaping is allowed anywhere on the premises, restricted to only certain areas or prohibited in any part of the premises.

Further guidance

Guidance on smoke-free legislation

A checklist and information for employers and businesses on the Smoke-Free England website: **www.smokefreeengland.co.uk/ what-do-i-do/business**.

STAFF

LICENCES & CONSENTS

MARKETING

CUSTOMERS

FOOD & DRINK

HEALTH & SAFETY

STAFF

BUSINESS MANAGEMENT & TAX

FURTHER INFORMATION

STAFF

Working Hours

KEY FACTS

- The **Working Time Regulations 1998** (as amended) apply to all businesses that have employees.
- You must take reasonable steps to ensure that employees do not work more than an average of 48 hours a week (excluding lunch breaks).
- Employees are entitled to 5.6 weeks' paid leave a year and rest periods of a specified length in each working day and in each seven day period.
- You need to keep sufficient records to show that you are complying with the regulations.

Working time regulations

Are the regulations relevant to me?

The **Working Time Regulations 1998** (as amended) apply to any business that has employees, however small the business.

What employees are covered by the regulations?

Anyone who is working for you including trainees and young workers (those aged 16 and 17), but excluding the genuinely self-employed.

What are the requirements?

Working time

You are responsible for taking reasonable steps to ensure that employees do not work more than an average of 48 hours a week, excluding lunch breaks. (The number of hours worked each week should be averaged out over 17 weeks).

- Employees can choose to work longer, but the agreement must be in writing and signed by the worker. This is known as a Working Time Regulations Opt-Out Agreement.
- Young workers may not ordinarily work more than eight hours a day or **40 hours a week**. There is no opt-out possible from the young workers' limitations.

Night-time workers

You are also responsible for taking reasonable steps to ensure that any night workers do not work on average more than eight hours in 24. There is no opt-out from the night work limits. Night workers are those who normally work at least three hours between 23:00 and 06:00.

- You must offer a free health assessment to a night worker before they start working nights and on a regular basis to ensure they are fit for night work
- Young workers may not ordinarily work between 22:00 and 07:00
- However, they may work between 22:00 and 0:00 and between 04:00 and 07:00 in certain special circumstances (e.g. working in a hotel, restaurant or pub, in catering and in retail).

Child Employment

There are separate restrictions for employing children under the age of 16. These restrictions mean that children cannot be employed:

- before 07:00 or after 19:00
- during school hours
- for more than an hour before school
- in any job harmful to their health or wellbeing
- for more than four hours without a one hour break.

There are also restrictions on the length of time that children can work during term time and during holiday periods. There may also be local authority restrictions on employing children in your area. More information on employing children is available on Gov.uk: www.gov.uk/child-employment/restrictions-on-child-employment.

See the *Employing Under 18s* Section for more information.

Paid annual leave

Employees, whether full-time or part-time, are entitled to 5.6 weeks' paid leave a year, starting on the first day of employment. A 'week's leave' is the equivalent of the time normally worked in a week. This should be applied pro-rata for part-time employees. For example, if a worker normally works five days a week, 5.6 weeks' paid leave equates to 28 working days a year and for a Saturday worker, this equates to 5.6 days a year.

You must set out an employee's paid holiday entitlement in their 'written statement of employment'. This should enable them to work out their entitlement and pay for any untaken holiday if they leave.

Note: the holiday entitlement can include bank holidays, provided that you pay them for those days.

Rolled-up Holiday Pay

Rolled-up Holiday Pay is where businesses pay employees an additional amount on top of their normal wages over the course of the year as holiday pay instead of paying it as a lump sum when the holiday is taken. ACAS advice is that this practice is **not** legal.

Further information, including a template for a 'written statement of employment' is available on the ACAS website: www.acas.org.uk.

Rest periods

Employees have the right to:
- at least a 20-minute break if they will work longer than six hours. However, organisations often allow longer and/or more frequent breaks
- not work on average more than 48 hours per week. Individuals may choose to work longer by 'opting out' (see below)
- 11 consecutive hours' rest in any 24 hour period
- one day off each week or two consecutive days off in a fortnight
- a limit on the normal working hours of an average eight hours in any 24 hours period
- young workers are entitled to 12 hours' rest for each working day and two day's rest for every seven-day period.

Special circumstances

For night workers' rest periods and in-work rest breaks there are exceptions to the regulations, e.g. during busy peak periods, but workers must normally be given equivalent rest periods in compensation.

Records

You need to keep sufficient records in each case to show that you are complying with the regulations.

Further guidance

Working Time Regulations

Visit the ACAS website: **www.acas.org.uk**. You can also call the ACAS national helpline on 0300 123 1100

Zero-hours contracts

Guidance on zero-hours contracts can be found on Gov.uk: **www.gov.uk/government/publications/zero-hours-contracts-guidance-for-employers**

Working time and health assessments

Guidance on matters to do with weekly and night working time limits and health assessments is available from the Health and Safety Executive website: **www.hse.gov.uk**.

National Minimum Wage

KEY FACTS

There are five rates of National Minimum Wage
(as of 1 April 2021):
- for workers 23 and over – The National Living Wage – £8.91 per hour
- for workers aged 21-22 - £8.36 per hour
- for workers aged between 18-20 - £6.56 per hour
- for workers under 18 - £4.62 per hour
- for apprentices - £4.30 per hour.

Is this relevant to me?

The National Minimum Wage came into effect on 1 April 1999. It is relevant to all businesses that have employees, regardless of the size of the business. The National Minimum Wage is enforceable by HM Revenue and Customs (HMRC).

If HMRC finds that you have underpaid any of your staff, they can issue a Notice of Underpayment requiring you to repay arrears to your staff (paid at the current minimum wage rate) and pay a penalty to the Government. The penalty is 200% of the total underpayment, with a maximum of £20,000 per worker.

Who is entitled to the National Minimum Wage?

Anyone working for you (including part-time and casual staff) is entitled to receive the National Minimum Wage **except**:
- anyone 'genuinely self-employed' (e.g. someone who controls their own time, what work they do, and invoices you rather than receiving wages)
- voluntary workers
- workers who are based permanently outside the UK or who are based in the Channel Islands or the Isle of Man.

LICENCES & CONSENTS · MARKETING · CUSTOMERS · FOOD & DRINK · HEALTH & SAFETY · STAFF · BUSINESS MANAGEMENT & TAX · FURTHER INFORMATION

What is the National Minimum Wage?

There are five rates of the National Minimum Wage. Rates as of 1 April 2021 are:

- **£8.91 per hour** for employees aged 23 and over (National Living Wage)
- **£8.36 per hour** for employees aged 21 -22
- **£6.56 per hour** for employees aged 18-20
- **£4.62 per hour** for employees aged under 18
- **£4.30 per hour** for apprentices aged under 19 or those in the first year of their apprenticeship.

Further information on the National Minimum Wage, including current rates, can be found on the Gov.uk website at www.gov.uk/national-minimum-wage-rates.

What counts as part of a wage?

Included: in addition to basic pay, certain other payments may count towards the National Minimum Wage, including:

- bonuses
- incentives
- accommodation
- money for items such as clothing and shoes, where the worker can decide where to buy the items.

Excluded: other additional payments are excluded, including:

- premium payments for overtime of shift work
- special allowances
- expenses
- tips, service charges or any other type of gratuity (see *Tips and service charges* below)
- expenditure on items such as clothing and tools related to work
- all benefits in kind, including meals, except accommodation. Benefits in kind do not count towards minimum wage pay, even if they have a monetary value. However, there are special rules where you provide a worker with accommodation.

Accommodation offset

If you provide accommodation to a member of staff, you are entitled to offset an amount for this against the National Minimum Wage. If the accommodation is provided free of charge, the daily accommodation offset rate is £8.36 and the weekly offset rate is £58.52 from 1 April 2021. For more details see the Gov.uk website at www.gov.uk/national-minimum-wage-accommodation.

Does the National Minimum Wage apply to rest breaks, sick time and holidays?

There are four main types of work and each can apply in the tourism sector:

- **time work:** when you pay the worker according to the number of hours he/she works
- **salaried hours work:** when the workers have a contract to work a set number of basic ascertainable hours each year in return for an annual salary paid in instalments
- **output:** paid by the piece - the number of things they make, or tasks they complete
- **unmeasured:** paid in other ways.

The different types of work give rise to varied ways of determining entitlements. For more information, go to Gov.uk at www.gov.uk/minimum-wage-different-types-work.

Regardless of the contract type, the determination of work hours does not include rest breaks, sick time, or holidays.

What is the National Living Wage and how does it affect me?

The National Living Wage does not replace the National Minimum Wage. Rather, it is a premium to be paid on top of the National Minimum Wage to employees aged 25 (now 23) and over in order for those employees to receive an income that is 60% of median earnings by 2020.

When it was introduced on 1 April 2016, the National Living Wage increased the minimum wage that must be paid to employees aged 25 and over. From April 2021, the rate is £8.91 per hour and must be paid to employees aged 23 and over. Those employees aged between 21 and 22 are not eligible for the premium and therefore remain on £8.35 per hour, while the other three National Minimum Wage rates (for those aged 18-20, under 18 and apprentices aged under 19) are unaffected by the National Living Wage.

As with the National Minimum Wage, the National Living Wage premium is set annually by the independent Low Pay Commission. Both rates will apply from 1 April each year.

Further information on the National Living Wage is available online at www.gov.uk/national-minimum-wage-rates.

UPDATED

Tips and service charges

You are not allowed to use tips and service charges to form part of the National Minimum Wage. This means that employees must receive at least the National Minimum Wage as base pay, with any income from tips or service charges being additional. This is regardless of whether the gratuity is paid directly by the customer to the employee (e.g. a cash tip left on the table in a restaurant) or through the payroll (e.g. a discretionary service charge added to the customer's bill).

The Department for Business, Energy and Industrial Strategy (BEIS) has produced a code of practice for the treatment of tips and service charges by businesses: *A Code of Best Practice on Service Charges, Tips, Gratuities and Cover Charges*. This code has been endorsed by UKHospitality, the Trade Union Congress and the Confederation of British Industry (CBI) and is based on four principles:

1. That businesses clearly display their policy on tips and service charges for customers.
2. That businesses have a process in place for explaining to customers how charges are distributed and what, if any, deductions are made.
3. That businesses should ensure that staff understand the policy and are able to explain it to customers.
4. That staff are fully informed of the distribution of tips and service charges and any deductions and are consulted on any changes.

Note: the Employment (Allocation of Tips) Bill 2019-20 was announced in the Queen's Speech on 14 October 2019 with the aim of ensuring that all tips must go to the staff providing the service, but at time of publication the Bill has not yet gained Parliamentary time due to the COVID-19 outbreak.

How should cash tips be dealt with?

Cash tips are payments given directly by customers to individual employees, not to the business. Any arrangement for sharing cash tips among employees should be in accordance with their wishes. The business owner will not be involved in this process. It is the responsibility of the employees receiving such cash tips to make proper disclosure to HM Revenue and Customs and to account for Income Tax in respect of these earnings.

How should service charges be dealt with?

For gratuities, such as service charges that are incorporated into the billing system, the business can deduct costs incurred in handling and distributing these payments to employees. Such deductions would cover credit card and banking charges, payroll processing costs, and the average costs of credit card fraud.

Businesses are also able to make deductions associated with other costs including breakages, till shortages and customers leaving without paying. While the level of these costs will vary depending on the nature of the business, the Department for Business, Energy and Industrial Strategy guidance suggests that total deductions should not be more than 30% of gratuities received.

These deductions should be revealed to customers as part of the disclosure process.

Where discretionary service charges and non-cash tips are paid to employees by the business, they should be paid from the company bank account, with Income Tax deducted under PAYE. The broad process for distribution of these amounts should be revealed to customers as part of the disclosure process (see below).

What disclosure should be made?
Businesses should disclose to customers how they deal with service charges and non-cash tips, at least by a written note available for inspection at each restaurant and on the company website, if there is one. The disclosure should cover:
- whether an amount is deducted for handling costs (and how much)
- how the remainder is shared between the business and the employees
- the broad process for distribution, e.g. that they are shared between the employees in the business through a system controlled by a representative of the employees.

Records
- You are required to keep sufficient records to prove you are paying the National Minimum Wage
- You must allow workers to see their record within 14 days if they make a request in writing.

Further guidance
National Minimum Wage and National Living Wage
The ACAS helpline on 0300 123 1100 gives free advice on National Minimum Wage issues. You can also visit Gov.uk for more information: **www.gov.uk/browse/working/tax-minimum-wage**

Calculating the National Minimum Wage

The Department for Business, Energy & Industrial Strategy has published guidance on calculating the minimum wage to help employers: **www.gov.uk/government/publications/calculating-the-minimum-wage**

Tipping policies

The Code of Best Practice on Service Charges, Tips, Gratuities and Cover Charges is available on **Gov.uk.**

Discrimination

KEY FACTS

- Discrimination laws apply to all businesses.
- It is unlawful to discriminate directly against anyone.
- It is unlawful to discriminate indirectly against anyone.

The Equality Act 2010

The **Equality Act 2010** consolidated nine pieces of existing anti-discrimination legislation into one single Act. In doing so, it also simplifies and strengthens the existing legislation in order to reduce discrimination and inequality.

Under the Act, it is unlawful to discriminate against any employee or customer (that is to treat them less favourably) on the basis of nine protected characteristics:

- disability
- gender reassignment
- pregnancy and maternity
- marriage and civil partnership
- race - this includes ethnic or national origins, colour and nationality
- religion or belief
- sex
- sexual orientation
- age - this applies to those aged 18 or above.

It should be noted that amendments to the legislation clarify and strengthen the protection afforded to women undertaking breastfeeding under pregnancy and maternity, making it illegal to ask a woman to stop breastfeeding in a public place.

The protections afforded also apply where a person is unfairly treated because they are wrongly perceived to have a particular characteristic (or are treated as though they do), or because they associate with someone who has the characteristic. For example, the protection extends to the carer, partner or family of a person discriminated against.

STAFF

As it applies to employees

You are required to treat all employees or job applicants the same. This covers all areas of employment, including recruitment, terms and conditions, promotion and transfers, training and development, and the dismissal process. This requirement applies to all employers regardless of the size of the business.

There are rules against employers asking job applicants disability-related questions and you are required to make reasonable adjustments to help disabled people fulfil the job they are employed to undertake or are applying for. For example, you would not be allowed to reject an applicant who uses a wheelchair for a receptionist position on the grounds that the reception desk was too high. Rather, you are required to make modifications to the desk to enable them to undertake this role.

Harassment

You are required to protect your staff from harassment at all times. This means taking steps to protect staff from harassment by other staff members, suppliers and customers. Further, an employee may claim harassment even if they are not the person that is being harassed. This can happen, for example:

- where witnessing the harassment of another employee results in the creation of an intimidating environment for the witness
- where an employer has been informed that an employee has been harassed on two or more occasions by a third party, such as a customer or supplier, and does nothing to prevent further harassment
- where unwanted conduct relates to the sex of a person, even if it is not prompted by the complainant's sex.

Employers face unlimited fines under the legislation if they are found not to be protecting staff from harassment or treating them in a discriminatory manner. For more details and guidance on discrimination legislation, go to the Gov.uk website.

As it applies to customers

As with employment, it is illegal to discriminate on the basis of the nine protected characteristics when providing goods and services to customers, unless there is objective justification for doing so. This means that there have to be valid, justifiable reasons why a service cannot be provided to certain groups. For example, there may be medical reasons for not providing certain goods or services.

The **Equality Act 2010** makes it easier for customers to require you to make reasonable adjustments in the way that you provide goods or service. For example, making sure that there are suitable options on the menu for people who do not eat certain foods for religious beliefs. The test will be whether the way that you provide goods or services places a person with a protected characteristic at a substantial disadvantage to other customers.

However, the Act does enable businesses to undertake positive action to target their goods, facilities or services to a particular group that is either disadvantaged or currently under-represented in their consumer base, or that has particular needs. For example, discounts could be given to disabled customers or their carers.

Note: even if you do not allow customers to bring their pets to your premises, you **must** allow people who need to use assistance dogs (such as visually impaired people) to be accompanied by their dogs.

Age discrimination
In 2012 the Government introduced age discrimination. This makes it illegal to provide a different product or service, charge a different price, or to apply different terms and conditions to any customer over 18 years old on the basis of age unless:

- there is an 'Objective Justification'. Objective Justification means that there is a valid objective reason for doing so (for example, charging different premiums for travel insurance could be justified on the basis of different levels of risk)
- the discrimination is beneficial: this means that offering discounts to people that allow them improved access to goods and services would be acceptable (for example, discounts for retired people would be acceptable as it would increase social inclusion).

Further guidance

Equality Act 2010
Further information on discrimination and the Equality Act 2010 is available on the Equality and Human Rights Commission website: **https://www.equalityhumanrights.com/en/advice-and-guidance/guidance-employers.**

LICENCES & CONSENTS

MARKETING

CUSTOMERS

FOOD & DRINK

HEALTH & SAFETY

STAFF

BUSINESS MANAGEMENT & TAX

FURTHER INFORMATION

STAFF

Time Off for Parents

KEY FACTS

- All employers are required to comply with legislation related to family-friendly working.
- Employees' rights in this area include maternity and paternity rights, adoption leave, flexible working and parental leave.

Family-friendly working

There are laws that support working parents in combining work with looking after their children. As well as your legal duty to uphold these rights, it is also good practice to support family-friendly working and flexible working arrangements for all types of employees.

Maternity rights

Regardless of how long they have worked for you, all pregnant employees, (i.e. those working under a contract of employment) are entitled to take up to 52 weeks' statutory maternity leave (SML). This comprises:

- **26 weeks Ordinary Maternity Leave**
- **26 weeks Additional Maternity Leave**

Additional Maternity Leave starts immediately after Ordinary Maternity Leave.

Statutory maternity pay

To qualify for Statutory Maternity Pay (SMP) an employee must have been:

- employed continuously (some breaks do not interrupt continuous employment) for at least 26 weeks into the 15th week before the due date
- earning an average of at least £120 a week (before tax).

UPDATED

STAFF

Statutory Maternity Pay is paid for up to 39 weeks with employees receiving:

- 90% of their average weekly earnings (before tax) for the first 6 weeks
- £151.20 or 90% of their average weekly earnings (whichever is lower) for the next 33 weeks.

SMP is to be paid in the same way as the employee receives their normal wages (e.g. monthly or weekly).

Employees can choose when SMP will start, although this will normally coincide with their taking Ordinary Maternity Leave. SMP starts automatically if the employee is off work for a pregnancy-related illness in the four weeks before the week that the baby is due. The earliest SMP can start is 11 weeks before the due date. Employees entitled to SMP are entitled to receive it even if they decide to leave before they start receiving SMP. They do not have to repay it if they decide not to go back to work or leave their job whilst getting SMP.

Paternity rights

Paternity leave

Employees who have 26 weeks' service by the 15th week before the Expected Week of Childbirth are entitled to two weeks' paternity leave at or around the date the child is born. Employees may also take paternity leave if:

- they are not the biological father, but are the biological mother's partner
- they expect to have responsibility for the child's upbringing
- they have adopted the child or are the partner of the person who has adopted.

Ordinary Paternity Leave is for a period of one or two weeks which must be taken consecutively.

Statutory paternity pay

Similarly to maternity pay, the statutory weekly rate of Ordinary Paternity Pay and Additional Paternity Pay is £151.20, or 90% of average weekly earnings (whichever is lower).

Note: maternity and paternity leave and pay requirements also apply to same-sex couples.

Shared parental leave and pay

Traditionally, it has only been an option for a mother to take paid time off work to look after a new-born or adopted child. Shared Parental Leave allows most couples who are in paid work and bringing up a child together the option of sharing the leave entitlement following the birth or adoption of their child.

An employee may be eligible for Shared Parental Leave (SPL) and Statutory Shared Parental Pay (ShPP). To quality for SPL, your employee must share responsibility for the child with one of the following:
- their husband, wife, civil partner or joint adopter
- the child's other parent
- their parent (if they live with them).

Your employee or their partner must be eligible for maternity pay or leave, adoption pay or leave of Maternity Allowance.

They must also:
- have worked for you continuously for at least 26 weeks by the end of the 15th week before the due date (or the date they are matched with their adopted child)
- still be employed by you while taking SPL
- give you the correct notice including a declaration that their partner meets the employment and income requirements which allow them to get SPL.

They can also get ShPP if they're a worker and they're eligible for SMP or SPP.

Under Shared Parental Leave, parents can share up to 50 weeks of leave and up to 37 weeks of pay and choose to take the leave and pay in a more flexible way (each parent can take up to three blocks of leave, more if their employer allows, interspersed with periods of work).

Eligible parents can be off work together for up to six months or alternatively stagger their leave and pay so that one of them is always at home with their baby in the first year.

ShPP is paid at the rate of £151.20 a week or 90% of an employee's average weekly earnings, whichever is lower.

Adoption leave

Employees who are newly matched with a child for adoption and who have 26 weeks' service when this happens are entitled to up to 26 weeks' Ordinary Adoption Leave, and up to a further 26 weeks'

Additional Adoption Leave.

Employees who adopt individually are entitled to adoption leave and pay and where a couple adopt together, one member of the couple is entitled to adoption leave and pay. The couple can decide which partner will take adoption leave.

Employees don't qualify for Statutory Adoption Leave or Pay if they:
- arrange a private adoption
- become a special guardian or kinship carer
- adopt a stepchild
- have a child through surrogacy
- adopt a family member

Statutory adoption pay
Statutory adoption pay is 90% of their gross average weekly earnings for the first six weeks and then £151.20 or 90% of average weekly earnings before tax (whichever is lower) is payable for the next 33 weeks.

Reclaiming Statutory Maternity, Paternity and Adoption Pay
You can usually reclaim 92% of employees' Statutory Maternity (SMP), Paternity and Adoption Pay. You can reclaim 103% if your business qualifies for Small Employers' Relief. You get this if you paid less than £45,000 in Class 1 National Insurance in the last complete tax year before the qualifying or matching week.

Flexible working
Introducing flexible working practices can benefit everyone in your business. Many employers believe flexible working makes good business sense and brings about a range of improvements, including greater cost-efficiencies and better staff morale.

There are many different forms of flexible working. Flexible working can include:
- part-time working
- flexi-time
- job-sharing
- working from home
- term-time working
- staggered hours.

As an employer, you have a duty to consider any request for flexible working seriously and you must have a sound business reason for rejecting a request from an employee. It should be noted that employees can only make one flexible working request in any 12 month period.

Information on making and assessing an application for flexible working is available from the ACAS website: www.acas.org.uk/making-a-flexible-working-request.

Unpaid Parental Leave

Unpaid Parental Leave is a right for parents to take time off work to look after a child or make arrangements for the child's welfare, which may include:

- spending more time with their children
- looking at new schools
- settling children into new childcare arrangements
- spending more time with family, such as visiting grandparents.

Which staff can claim it?

Employees who have, or expect to have, parental responsibility for a child and have been employed for at least a year.

What are the main provisions?

- Each parent is entitled to **18 weeks' unpaid parental leave** for each child, which can be taken up until the child's fifth birthday (or, the end of the fifth year after adoption, or the child's 18th birthday if that is sooner)
- The leave should be taken in blocks of one week, up to a maximum of 4 weeks a year for each child (greater flexibility is allowed if the employee receives a disability living allowance or personal independence payment for their child)
- At the end of parental leave, the employee is entitled to return to the same job if the leave was for four weeks or less. If it was for longer, the employee is **entitled to return to the same job**, or if that is not reasonably practicable, a similar job
- You can reach your **own agreement** with an employee about the practicalities. If you do not, there are fall back provisions (21 days' notice; minimum of one week blocks; maximum of four weeks a year for each child; the employer can postpone the leave for up to six months when particularly disruptive to the business, except for leave requested immediately after the child is born/adopted)
- You do not have to keep **records**, but you can be asked by a subsequent employer about how much leave an employee has taken (you can also ask a previous employer)
- You are entitled to ask to see **evidence** to confirm that an employee is the parent or the person legally responsible for the child
- There are additional entitlements for parents of disabled children.

> **Note:** employees also have the right to take a reasonable period off work to deal with an emergency involving a dependent.

Further guidance

Your rights and responsibilities

The ACAS website has a useful range of online guides to maternity, paternity, adoption and flexible working policies: **www.acas.org.uk/advice.** You can also call their helpline on 0300 123 1100.

Migrant Workers

KEY FACTS

- To be entitled to work in the UK, a foreign national must provide you with the necessary documentation.
- You should check any documentation provided to ensure, to the best of your ability, that those documents are genuine and that the potential employee is entitled to work in the UK.
- Generally, to employ someone living outside the UK, including the European Union:
  - they need to pass a points-based assessment before they are given permission to enter or remain in the United Kingdom
  - you need to have a sponsor licence from the Home Office.

Important note regarding right to work checks (March 2021)

Due to the COVID-19 (coronavirus) pandemic, the Government has temporarily adjusted right to work checks to make it easier for employers to carry them out. For more information see www.gov.uk/guidance/coronavirus-covid-19-right-to-work-checks.

Employers' responsibilities

It is important that you are aware of your responsibilities when employing foreign nationals. The legislation that applies to migrant workers is the **UK Borders Act 2007**. The Act covers all aspects of immigration, from asylum seekers through to permanent migration, including the right to work and study in the UK.

On the basis of this legislation, the Home Office develops and implements the UK's immigration rules, which provide the detail as to how the Act is implemented. The rules are available online at www.gov.uk/check-job-applicant-right-to-work. These rules are updated on a regular basis, so it is worthwhile checking the site regularly for any changes relating to employing foreign workers.

If you employ, or plan to employ, people from outside the UK, you need to make sure that they have permission to work here before they start working for you.

Proof of entitlement to work in the UK

There are different types of documents that employers should check to ensure that their foreign employees are entitled to work in the UK. Employers who do not undertake these checks are liable to prosecution if they are found to be employing foreign nationals who are not entitled to work in the UK.

To be entitled to work in the UK, a foreign national must provide you with one of the following:

- a passport showing that the holder, or a person named in the passport as the child of the holder, is a British citizen or a citizen of the United Kingdom and Colonies having the right of abode in the United Kingdom
- a residence permit, registration certificate or document certifying or indicating permanent residence issued by the Home Office or the Border and Immigration Agency to a national of a European Economic Area country or Switzerland
- a permanent residence card issued by the Home Office or the Border and Immigration Agency to the family member of a national of a European Economic Area country or Switzerland
- a Biometric Immigration Document issued by the Border and Immigration Agency to the holder, which indicates that the person named in it is allowed to stay indefinitely in the United Kingdom, or has no time limit on their stay in the United Kingdom
- a passport or other travel document endorsed to show that the holder is exempt from immigration control, is allowed to stay indefinitely in the United Kingdom, has the right of abode in the United Kingdom, or has no time limit on their stay in the United Kingdom
- an Immigration Status Document, issued by the Home Office or the Border and Immigration Agency, with an endorsement indicating that the person named in it is allowed to stay indefinitely in the United Kingdom or has no time limit on their stay in the United Kingdom, when produced in combination with an official document giving the person's permanent National Insurance Number and their name issued by a Government agency or a previous employer
- a full birth certificate issued in the United Kingdom which includes the name(s) of at least one of the holder's parents, when produced in combination with an official document giving the person's permanent National Insurance Number and their name

issued by a Government agency or a previous employer
- a full adoption certificate issued in the United Kingdom, which includes the name(s) of at least one of the holder's adoptive parents, when produced in combination with an official document giving the person's permanent National Insurance Number and their name issued by a Government agency or a previous employer
- a birth certificate issued in the Channel Islands, the Isle of Man or Ireland, when produced in combination with an official document giving the person's permanent National Insurance Number and their name issued by a Government agency or a previous employer
- an adoption certificate issued in the Channel Islands, the Isle of Man or Ireland, when produced in combination with an official document giving the person's permanent National Insurance Number and their name issued by a Government agency or a previous employer
- a certificate of registration or naturalisation as a British citizen, when produced in combination with an official document giving the person's permanent National Insurance Number and their name issued by a Government agency or a previous employer
- a letter issued by the Home Office or the Border and Immigration Agency to the holder which indicates that the person named in it is allowed to stay indefinitely in the United Kingdom, when produced in combination with an official document giving the person's permanent National Insurance Number and their name issued by a Government agency or a previous employer
- a document from the Home Office to show that the person has been granted 'Settled' or 'Pre-Settled' Status under the EU Settlement Scheme.

All the documents that potential employees provide must be originals – photocopies, printouts or other copies are not acceptable. The process of checking that a worker is entitled to work in the UK is outlined in more detail in the Home Office publication *Prevention of Illegal Working* which can be downloaded from www.gov.uk/government/publications/preventing-illegal-working.

EU Settlement Scheme
EU, EEA or Swiss nationals who started living in the UK prior to 1 January 2021 can apply to continue to live and work in the UK through the EU Settlement Scheme after 30 June 2021. The deadline for applications is 30 June 2021.
- Applicants that have been living continuously in the UK for 5 years prior to 1 January 2021 will be granted 'Settled Status', which allows them to remain and work in the UK indefinitely.

STAFF

- Applicants that have not been living continuously in the UK for 5 years prior to 1 January 2021 will be granted 'Pre-Settled Status', which allows them to remain and work in the UK for a further five years, after which they can apply for 'Settled Status'.

> **Note:** EU nationals that are Irish citizens or already have indefinite leave to remain do not have to apply for the right to remain in the UK through the EU Settlement Scheme.

Checking employees' documentation

It is your responsibility to look carefully at the documents that candidates provide and to ensure that, to the best of your ability, these documents are genuine and that the potential employee is entitled to work in the UK.

Care should be taken over the following aspects of the documentation provided.

- **Photographs** - does the person look like the photographs on their documents?
- **Date of birth** - is the date consistent with the appearance of the candidate?
- **Expiry dates** - are the documents still valid?
- **Stamps and endorsements** - do the passport stamps allow your job applicant to do the type of work you are offering?
- **Name** - is the same name used on all the documents?

When you have checked the candidate's documents and you are satisfied that they are genuine, you will need to save copies of them for your records either by photocopying or scanning the documents onto your computer.

The Public Register of Authentic Identification and Travel Documents Online (PRADO) can help you ascertain the authenticity of a document.

Penalties for non-compliance

Penalties include:

- civil penalties for employers who employ illegal migrant workers
- a criminal offence for knowingly employing illegal migrant workers, which carries a maximum two-year prison sentence and/ or an unlimited fine
- employers' continuing responsibility for checking the ongoing entitlement to work in the UK of migrant workers with a time-limited immigration status.

To avoid a civil penalty, you should check prospective employees' documents and undertake repeat document checks at least once a year for those employees who have limited leave to enter or remain in the United Kingdom.

Points-based migration system

The Government has introduced a points-based migration system for people living overseas wanting to live and work in the UK. Migrants need to pass a points-based assessment before they are given permission to enter or remain in the United Kingdom.

Under the points-based scheme, applicants are required to score 70 points.

To achieve the 70 points, the applicants must meet three mandatory requirements which provide 50 points:
- they have a job offer from a Home Office licensed sponsor
- the job offer is at the required skill level – RQF 3 or above (A-Level and equivalent)
- they speak English to the required standard.

To gain the additional 20 points, the job offer must meet the applicable minimum salary threshold (£25,600, or the specific salary requirement for their occupation, known as the "going rate").

Alternatively, the job offer may be as low as £20,480, provided that the applicant can gain 20 points by:
- filling a job in an occupation where the Migration Advisory Committee has designated a skills shortage
- having a PhD in a relevant subject
- having a PhD in a STEM subject where they will be able to trade characteristics, such as their qualifications, against a lower salary to get the required number of points.

If the job offer is less than the minimum salary requirement, but no less than £20,480, an applicant may still be eligible if they have:
- a job offer in a specific shortage occupation
- a PhD relevant to the job

Characteristics	Mandatory/ Tradeable	Points
Offer of job by approved sponsor	Mandatory	20
Job at appropriate skill level	Mandatory	20
Speaks English at required level	Mandatory	10
Salary of £20,480 to £23,039 or at least 80% of the going rate for the profession (whichever is higher)	Tradeable	0
Salary of £23,040 to £25,599 or at least 90% of the going rate for the profession (whichever is higher)	Tradeable	10
Salary of £25,600 or above or at least the going rate for the profession (whichever is higher)	Tradeable	20
Job on a shortage occupation as designated by the Migration Advisory Committee	Tradeable	20
Education qualification: PhD in a subject relevant to the job	Tradeable	20
Education qualification: PhD in a STEM subject relevant to the job	Tradeable	20

Note: There are different salary rules for 'new entrants' at the start of their careers.

Sponsoring overseas workers

If you aim to employ someone from overseas, you have to have a sponsorship licence. Applications for a licence can be made online and the licence lasts for four years. The licence fee is £536 for businesses with fewer than 50 employees, and £1,476 for businesses with over 50 employees. (The fee is per business rather than per employee). See www.gov.uk/uk-visa-sponsorship-employers for more information.

Further guidance

Employing foreign nationals

More information on employing foreign nationals can be found on Gov.uk: www.gov.uk/browse/visas-immigration. Alternatively, you can call the UK Visa and Immigration helpline: 0300 123 4699

Preventing illegal working

The process of checking that a worker is entitled to work in the UK is outlined in more detail in the Home Office publication *Prevention of Illegal Working*, which can be downloaded from **www.gov.uk/government/publications/preventing-illegal-working**.

STAFF

LICENCES & CONSENTS

MARKETING

CUSTOMERS

FOOD & DRINK

HEALTH & SAFETY

STAFF

BUSINESS MANAGEMENT & TAX

FURTHER INFORMATION

Employing under 18s

KEY FACTS

- There are special requirements that you must comply with if you are employing children under the age of 18.
- It is illegal to employ anyone under the age of 13 and children can only undertake full-time employment once they reach school-leaving age.
- Unless the child is a family member, you must undertake a separate Health and Safety assessment of their position that takes into consideration their age and lack of experience.
- Children aged 16 and 17 are able to serve alcohol in a dining room or restaurant without supervision or behind a bar if each individual sale is approved by a responsible person.

The **Children (Protection at Work) Regulations 2000** were introduced to help ensure that children are protected in the workplace and that employers pay special attention to their safety and well-being.

Does this apply to me?

Yes: although there are some exemptions if you are employing a family member on an occasional or short-term basis.

Employing children

It is not uncommon for small businesses to provide part-time or occasional employment to the children of friends and family. However, you need to be aware that it is illegal to employ children under the age of 13 to do any type of work (regardless of whether the work is part-time, full-time or the payment is monetary or in-kind) and that there are a number of legal requirements and restrictions that govern the employment of children until they become adult workers at the age of 18.

Employing children aged 13-16

Children between the ages of 13 and 16 can only work part-time. There are considerable restrictions on the times at which they can work, the length of time they can work, the places where they can work and the type of work they can undertake. In general, it is illegal to employ children in any work that may be harmful to their health, well-being or education.

While some of these restrictions are set nationally (see www.gov.uk/child-employment/restrictions-on-child-employment for restrictions on child employment) there are also local bylaws that restrict the employment of children.

Most local councils also require businesses intending to employ school-aged children to apply for a child employment permit, so it is important that you contact your local council to check the rules in your area.

Employing children aged 16-18

Children can only start full-time work once they've reached the minimum school leaving age of 16. However, they must be employed as part of an apprenticeship or traineeship scheme.

There are also specific requirements relating to their hours of work. These employees must not work more than eight hours a day (or more than 40 hours a week) and there must be at least twelve hours' rest between each working day and 48 hours' rest per working week. You must also provide a 30-minute rest break when they work longer than four and a half hours.

See the *Working Hours* section for more information.

Minimum pay

There is no minimum pay for children under the age of 16. Children under 16 also do not pay National Insurance, so you only need to include them on your payroll if their total income is over their Personal Allowance.

Children aged 16 and 17 are entitled to at least £4.55 per hour and, if they earn more than £120 a week, you will need to register them as an employee and operate PAYE.

Health and safety

A child under 18 cannot be employed for work that:
- is beyond the child's physical or psychological capacity
- involves harmful exposure to toxic or carcinogenic substances
- involves harmful exposure to radiation
- involves a risk which cannot be recognised or avoided by young persons because of their lack of attention to safety or lack of experience or training (this is likely to mean that any employment in kitchens involving the use of sharp knives or slicers will be prohibited)
- involves a risk to health from extreme cold or heat, noise or vibration.

If you are employing someone under 18, you must undertake a separate Health and Safety assessment, paying particular attention to their age and lack of experience. This does not apply if the child is a family member undertaking short-term or occasional work.

If the child is under 16, you must also tell one of their parents the results of the assessment. This must include any risks identified and any measures you are putting in place to protect their health and safety at work.

Serving alcohol

Under 18s can work in restaurants, dining rooms and even pubs, where they can wait on tables, collect glasses, clear tables and take orders from customers.

Children aged 16 or 17 are allowed to sell or serve alcohol in a restaurant without supervision provided that:
- it is sold or supplied to be drunk with a table meal, and that
- it is served in a part of the premises used only for that purpose.

This means that a child aged 16 or 17 can work as a waiter or waitress in a dining room and serve alcohol without supervision.

Children can also work in a bar serving alcohol, as long as each individual sale has been specifically approved by a responsible person. The responsible person is either the holder of the Premises Licence, the Designated Premises Supervisor (DPS) or anyone aged 18 or over who has been authorised by the Premises Licence Holder or the DPS to authorise sales made by under 18s.

Note: you need to check whether your local authority has any by-laws that restrict people aged under 18 selling alcohol. It is known that some local authorities prevent children under 18 selling alcohol that is not in a sealed container (e.g. unopened bottles or cans).

Further guidance

Guidance on the employment of children
The guide *Guidance on the employment of children* can be downloaded from the Gov.uk website: **www.gov.uk/child-employment**

ACAS guidance on employing younger workers
ACAS have also produced guidance on employing younger workers: **www.acas.org.uk/young-workers-apprentices-and-work-experience.**

Workplace Pensions

KEY FACTS

- If you have employees, you must implement a Workplace Pension Scheme.
- You must notify all employees to explain why they either have or have not been included in your Workplace Pension Scheme.
- Those employees not eligible to be included in a scheme must be allowed the opportunity to join the scheme.
- The minimum contributions that both you and your employees have to contribute to the scheme are determined by law.
- Three years after setting up a Workplace Pension Scheme, you must undertake 'Re-enrolment'.

Background

Under the **Pensions Act 2008**, every employer in the UK must put certain staff into a pension scheme and contribute towards it. The pension scheme is called a "Workplace Pension" and the process by which you put eligible staff into the scheme is called 'Automatic Enrolment'.

Do the regulations apply to me?

Yes: if you employ at least one person, either full-time, part-time or on a casual basis provided that:

- they earn over £10,000 per annum
- they are aged between 22 and the state pension age.

The usual determinant of whether you have staff is whether you decide the work that the person does, tell them how they are to do it, provide the equipment, pay them for the hours that they undertake the work (rather than a fixed price for the work) and the person is entitled to benefits such as holiday pay or sick pay.

Maybe: if you employ someone outside the criteria above and they ask to join a Workplace Pension Scheme.

No: if you have no staff.

Note: if you have staff who are not eligible, you still have other tasks to carry out in order to meet your legal duties, including writing to these staff to tell them how automatic enrolment applies to them.

Four steps to set up a Workplace Pension Scheme

1. Choose a pension scheme
Your first task is to choose the pension scheme that you will use to provide your workplace pension. If you have an existing pension scheme, you can use this or you can seek advice from a pension advisor. Alternatively, you can use the National Employment Savings Trust (NEST), which is a pension scheme provider that has been set up by Government and must accept all employers that apply to use it for automatic enrolment.

2. Determine who to include in the pension scheme
You are required to determine who to include in the pension scheme and to provide information on these employees to your pension provider. You must include any of your staff who are aged between 22 and the state pension age and earn over £10,000 per year (or £833 per month or £192 per week) who are not already enrolled in a company pension scheme. Employees who fall outside this requirement only need to be included if they specifically ask to be included.

3. Write to inform your staff
Within six weeks of your workplace pension starting, you must write to all your staff individually and tell them how the workplace pension applies to them. That means writing to those who have been enrolled to tell them that they are in the pension scheme and to those who have not been enrolled to explain why, as well as let them know that they can be enrolled if they request to be included.

4. Declaration of compliance
Finally, within five months of setting-up your Workplace Pension Scheme, you must complete an online declaration to confirm that you have met your legal duties.

Note: even if you do not have any employees, you still need to complete a Declaration of Compliance to say your business has complied with the legislation. This can be completed online at www.autoenrol.tpr.gov.uk.

Contributions

While there is no maximum level for contributions to a Workplace Pension Scheme, the Government has introduced a minimum contribution level. The minimum employee contribution is 5% and the minimum employer contribution is 3%, making the total minimum contribution 8%.

Re-enrolment

Every three years you must put certain staff back into a pension scheme. This is called 're-enrolment'. Your re-enrolment duties must be carried out approximately three years after your automatic enrolment staging date. Your duties will vary depending on whether you identify that you have staff to re-enrol, or whether you have no staff to re-enrol. Either way, you will need to complete a re-declaration of compliance.

As with setting up a Workplace Pension, Re-enrolment is a four-step process.

1. Choose your re-enrolment date

First, you need to choose your re-enrolment date from within a six-month window, which starts three months before the third anniversary of your automatic enrolment staging date and ends three months after it.

2. Assess your staff

On your chosen re-enrolment date, you'll need to assess certain staff to determine whether you need to put them back into your pension scheme.

3. Write to the staff you have re-enrolled

You then need to write to staff to tell them that you have put them back into a pension scheme.

4. Complete a re-declaration of compliance

You must again complete an online declaration stating that you have complied with the legislation by undertaking re-enrolment.

Re-enrolment tool

The Pensions Regulator has a free re-enrolment tool to help you meet your re-enrolment date at www.thepensionsregulator.gov.uk/en/ employers/re-enrolment.

Ongoing duties

Monitor the ages and earnings of your staff

You must monitor your employees' ages and pay. If any staff reach the criteria of being aged 22 and earning over £10,000 per annum, you must put them into a pension scheme and write to them within six weeks from the day they meet the age or earnings criteria.

Manage requests to join or leave your scheme

If an employee writes to you asking to join your scheme, you must put them into it within a month of receiving their request.

You will have to pay into the pension scheme if they are:

- aged 16-74
- **and** earn at least £520 a month or £120 per week.

To find out how much you will need to pay, you should ask your pension scheme provider.

Employees can choose to leave the pension scheme. If they ask to leave within one month of being put into a scheme, this is known as opting out. Many pension providers will manage the opt-out process on your behalf. If an employee opts out, you need to stop taking money out of their pay and arrange a full refund of what has been paid to date. This must happen within one month of their request.

For more information on your ongoing duties with regards to workplace pensions, see www.thepensionsregulator.gov.uk.

Further guidance

Pensions Regulator

For more detailed information on the process and the rules surrounding it, refer to the Pensions Regulator website: **www.thepensionsregulator.gov.uk/en/employers.**

BUSINESS MANAGEMENT & TAX

Legal Form of Business, VAT and Tax

KEY FACTS

- You must establish your income tax position and whether you are claiming all the expenses and capital allowances you are entitled to.
- There are different tax and legal implications, depending on whether you operate your business as a sole trader, a limited company, a partnership or a charity.
- Tax and VAT are very large and complex areas of legislation that are constantly being revised and amended. For this reason, it is advisable to contact your accountant or financial advisor to discuss all related issues.

Income tax

It is important that you establish your income tax position and whether you are claiming all the expenses and capital allowances you are entitled to claim.

You must keep records of your business income and expenses for your tax return if you are self-employed as a:
- sole trader
- partner in a business partnership (if you're the nominated partner in a partnership, you must also keep records for the partnership)
- charity.

There are different rules on keeping records for limited companies and you are advised to consult an accountant for advice if your business is structured as a limited company.

Regardless of whether you are a sole trader, a partner in a business partnership or run your business as a limited company, you will need to keep records of your personal income.

Many businesses use traditional accounting where you record income and expenses by the date you were invoiced or billed. However, there is an option of using cash accounting if you are a small business.

Cash basis accounting

The Government has introduced a 'cash basis' tax scheme for self-employed individuals or partnerships carrying on the smallest trading businesses.

You can use cash accounting if:
- you run a small, self-employed business as a sole trader or partnership (you cannot use the scheme if your business in is a limited company)
- you have a turnover of £150,000 or less a year.

You can stay in the scheme up to a total business turnover of £300,000 per year. Above that, you'll need to use traditional accounting for your next tax return.

VAT Cash Accounting Scheme
In addition to the cash accounting scheme, there is also the VAT Cash Accounting Scheme. Under this scheme, you:
- pay VAT on your sales when customers pay you
- reclaim VAT on your purchases when you have paid your supplier.

To join the scheme, your VAT taxable turnover must be £1.35 million or less.

Further information is available on the Gov.uk website: www.gov.uk/simpler-income-tax-cash-basis.

You can speak to an accountant or a financial advisor, or visit the HM Revenue & Customs (HMRC) website, which has a range of helpful information and contact numbers: www.gov.uk/government/organisations/hm-revenue-customs.

VAT

VAT threshold
You do not have to register for VAT if your turnover for the previous 12 months is less than £85,000 (2020/21). This figure is known as the VAT registration threshold. The Government adjusts this figure regularly so it is important to check on the HMRC website to find the current level.

You must also register for VAT if:
- you think your VAT taxable turnover may go over the threshold in the next 30 days alone
- you take over a VAT-registered business as a going concern.

VAT deregistration threshold
The deregistration threshold is £83,000 (2020/21). If your VAT taxable turnover for the year falls below £83,000, or you expect it to fall below £83,000 in the next 12 months, you can ask to be deregistered for VAT.

Flat Rate VAT Scheme
If your VAT taxable turnover is less than £150,000, you can simplify your VAT accounting by calculating your VAT payments as a percentage of your total VAT-inclusive turnover. The current flat-rate VAT percentage for accommodation businesses is 10.5% and the rate for museums and cultural activities is 9.5% of your VAT-inclusive turnover. Once you join the scheme you can stay in it until your total business income is more than £230,000.

In 2017 the Government introduced changes to the Flat Rate Scheme for businesses with a very low-cost base. These businesses are now called 'limited cost traders'.

A limited cost trader is defined as one that spends less than 2% of its sales on goods (not services) in an accounting period. The amount spent on goods cannot include purchases of:
- capital goods (such as new equipment used in a business)
- food and drink (such as lunches for staff)
- vehicles or parts for vehicles (unless running a vehicle hiring business).

A firm can also be a limited cost trader if it spends less than £1,000 a year, even if this is more than 2% of the firm's turnover on goods.

Limited cost traders can still use the Flat Rate Scheme, but their percentage is 16.5% rather than 10.5%.

It is recommended that you talk to your accountant as to whether joining the Flat Rate Scheme would be beneficial for your business.

For information go to The VAT Guide or contact the HMRC's National Advice Service on 0845 010 9000, which is available from Monday to Friday, 8:00am to 6:00pm.

LICENCES & CONSENTS   MARKETING   CUSTOMERS   FOOD & DRINK   HEALTH & SAFETY   STAFF   **BUSINESS MANAGEMENT & TAX**   FURTHER INFORMATION

Setting Up a Charity

Some businesses, especially historic, cultural or environmental attractions, can be established as a charity. Charities don't pay tax on most types of income as long as they use the money for charitable purposes. Charitable purposes that help the public can include:

- education
- religion
- community development
- the arts
- the protection of the environment
- animal welfare.

However, you may need to pay tax if you have:

- received income that doesn't qualify for tax relief
- spent any of your income on non-charitable purposes.

Charities can also claim back tax that has been deducted e.g. on bank interest and donations (this is known as Gift Aid).

There are six steps to setting up a charity:

1. Find trustees for your charity - you usually need at least three.
2. Make sure the charity has a 'charitable purpose for the public benefit'.
3. Choose a name for your charity.
4. Choose a structure for your charity. There are four different structures that have different responsibilities and obligations.
5. Create a 'governing document'.
6. Register as a charity with the Charity Commission. You need to do this if your annual income is over £5,000, if you set up a charitable incorporated organisation (CIO) and if you want to get tax relief from HMRC.

Detailed information on how to set up a charity is available from the Charity Commission: www.gov.uk/government/organisations/charity-commission.

Gift Aid

Gift Aid is a scheme whereby charities can claim an extra 25p for every £1 visitors donate.

To claim Gift Aid on donations from individuals, the donor must:

- have paid the same amount or more in Income Tax or Capital Gains Tax in the UK during that tax year
- make a Gift Aid declaration that gives you permission to claim it.

This means that Gift Aid cannot be claimed for overseas visitors or donations by businesses.

NEW

There are special rules if you want to claim Gift Aid on your entrance fees. Generally, entrance fees to visit and view your charity property do not qualify for Gift Aid because they are not a gift. But a voluntary donation that allows visitors to view your property do qualify for Gift Aid if they:

- are 10% or more than the normal admission fee
- allow admission for at least 12 months.

There are also special rules for:

- funds from sponsored challenges, for example, overseas treks or marathons
- charity membership fees
- charity auctions
- charity events
- volunteer expenses donated back to your charity or CASC.

More information on how to claim Gift Aid can be found on Gov.uk: www.gov.uk/claim-gift-aid.

Tax and your staff

For information on PAYE, National Insurance, download the *Employer Further Guide to PAYE and National Insurance Contributions* from Gov.uk.

There is a range of guidance available from HMRC's website and you can also contact their helpline: 0300 200 3200. You will need your employer reference number or accounts office reference number when you call.

Legal form of the business

There are different tax and legal implications depending on whether you operate your business as a sole trader, a limited company or a partnership. There are advantages and disadvantages for each category. You need to seek professional advice from lawyers or independent financial advisors.

Legal advisors

The Law Society is able to provide you with a list of solicitors within your area. Your local destination organisation may also be able to give you names of suitable local firms: solicitors.lawsociety.org.uk.

Independent financial advisors

The IFA consumer website allows you to find a list of independent financial advisors, accountants or solicitor in your area: www. unbiased.co.uk.

Making Tax Digital

Making Tax Digital is a major HMRC initiative to move all business accounting to a digital format. This is a staged process over the next five years.

The first component of Making Tax Digital is VAT payments. All VAT-registered businesses with a taxable turnover above the VAT threshold (£85,000) are now required to follow the Making Tax Digital rules by keeping digital records and using software to submit their VAT returns to HMRC.

If you are below the VAT threshold, you can voluntarily join the Making Tax Digital service now but you will be required to follow Making Tax Digital rules for your first return starting on or after April 2022.

The next stage of Making Tax Digital is to require self-employed businesses with an annual business or property income above £10,000 to follow the rules for Income Tax from their next accounting period starting on or after 6 April 2023.

For Corporation Tax, the Government has started to provide businesses with an opportunity to take part in a pilot 'Making Tax Digital for Corporation Tax' scheme and will not mandate its usage before 2026.

Further guidance

HMRC
For further information on income tax, PAYE for employers, VAT and more visit the HMRC website: **www.gov.uk/government/organisations/hm-revenue-customs**

Making Tax Digital
HMRC provides a wide range of support to help you comply with the Making Tax Digital requirements: **www.gov.uk/government/publications/making-tax-digital/overview-of-making-tax-digital**

Establishing a charity
The Charity Commission provides a wide range of advice and guidance on establishing a charity:**www.gov.uk/government/organisations/charity-commission**

Gift Aid
More information on Gift Aid can be found on Gov.uk: **www.gov.uk/claim-gift-aid.**

Tax Status of Self-Catering Businesses

KEY FACTS

- In terms of taxation, there is a fundamental difference between the way HM Revenue & Customs (HMRC) treats self-catering accommodation and residential rental properties.
- Having your self-catering property treated as a trade business, rather than a rental property, carries a number of advantages.
- To comply with the Furnished Holiday Letting (FHL) Rules, a property must be available for at least 210 days a year, let for at least 105 days and operated in a commercial manner.

Rental and trade businesses

In terms of taxation, there is a fundamental difference between the way HM Revenue & Customs (HMRC) treats holiday accommodation and residential rental properties.
- Residential rental properties are treated as property investment businesses.
- Hotels, guesthouses and B&Bs are treated as trading businesses.
- Self-catering accommodation can be treated as a trading business provided that the conditions of the 'Furnished Holiday Letting Rules' are met.

Having your self-catering property treated as a trading business carries the following advantages:
- it ensures that income, net of allowable expenses, is treated as earned income. This means that capital allowances can be claimed in respect of all furniture and equipment used in the business. This compares favourably with the treatment of residential rental properties, where losses can only be offset against future income, you cannot claim capital allowances in respect to any new furniture and equipment and only part of the interest on mortgage payments can be off-set against income
- trading businesses are treated as a business asset for the purposes of determining Capital Gains Tax, which gives you far greater

allowances than you get for residential rental properties
- for Inheritance Tax purposes, the property is also deemed to be a business asset and can be passed on tax-free.

Note: HMRC has successfully challenged the Inheritance Tax exemption of a self-catering property by arguing the level of service provided to guests was not sufficient for it to be deemed a trading business for the purposes of Inheritance Tax. You should therefore seek professional advice as to whether your property is exempt from Inheritance Tax.

Furnished Holiday Letting Rules (FHL)
In order for your self-catering property to qualify as a trading business the following conditions need to be met:
1. **Commercial operation**: the business must be carried on commercially, with a view to making a profit.
2. **Pattern of occupation**: total periods of longer-term occupation must not exceed 155 days (approx. five months) during the relevant period. A period of longer-term occupation is a letting to the same person for longer than 31 continuous days.
3. **Availability**: the property must be available for commercial letting as holiday accommodation to the public for at least 210 days (approx. seven months) during the relevant period.
4. **Letting**: the property must be commercially let as holiday accommodation to members of the public for at least 105 days during the relevant period. A letting for a period of longer-term occupation is not a letting as holiday accommodation for the purposes of this condition.

The reason for these conditions is to prevent people from trying to gain trade business status and the associated benefits, for either their home or their holiday home, when they have no intention of operating them as a commercially viable B&B or self-catering operation.

Note: it is important to note that if you operate a self-catering property, you are unable to claim sideways loss relief against other income. Also, regardless of complying with the FHL Rules, HMRC may deem your self-catering property to be subject to Capital Gains Tax and Inheritance Tax, if it is determined that you do not provide a sufficient level of service to demonstrate that it is trading businesses. It is therefore important to gain advice from an accountant who understands the taxation rules for self-catering businesses.

Further guidance

Professional legal advice

Tax rules relating to holiday accommodation are complex, so it is best to seek advice from a professional tax consultant.

LICENCES & CONSENTS

MARKETING

CUSTOMERS

FOOD & DRINK

HEALTH & SAFETY

STAFF

BUSINESS MANAGEMENT & TAX

FURTHER INFORMATION

LICENCES & CONSENTS

MARKETING

CUSTOMERS

FOOD & DRINK

HEALTH & SAFETY

STAFF

BUSINESS MANAGEMENT & TAX

FURTHER INFORMATION

Business Rates

KEY FACTS

- Business rates generally apply to bed and breakfast establishments **unless** the business does not intend to offer short-stay accommodation to more than six people simultaneously **and** you occupy part of the property as your only or main home **and** letting out the rooms is subsidiary to the use of the rest of the house as your home.

- Business rates apply to a self-catering establishment unless you offer short-term lets for fewer than 140 days a year.

- Only the part of the property used for business purposes is subject to business rates.

- Business rates apply to visitor attractions. Those that are operated by charities are entitled to a mandatory 80% reduction in business rates.

- Your local authority will calculate the business rates for your property based on its 'rateable value'.

Do I need to pay business rates?

Yes: if you are a visitor attraction or providing serviced or self-catering accommodation, unless:

- you qualify for Small Business Rate Relief, or
- for **bed and breakfast**:

    -you do not intend to offer short-stay accommodation to more than six people simultaneously, and;

    -you (the owner) occupy part of the property as your only or main home, and;

    - letting out the rooms is subsidiary to the use of the rest of the house as your home ('subsidiary' is based on factors such as the length of your season, the scale of modifications undertaken for guests and the proportion of the house you occupy). For example, if you only let two of six bedrooms in your property as a bed and breakfast, business rates are unlikely to apply.

However, if you let four of your six bedrooms, you will probably have to pay business rates. Your local authority will be able to advise you.

Note: if you have to pay business rates, but use your property for business and domestic purposes (a composite hereditament), it is only the part you use for business purposes that is subject to business rates. The domestic accommodation is liable to council tax. Where parts of a house have a shared use, such as a kitchen or dining room, the Valuation Officer will visit the property and assess the amount to be paid (see below).

- For **self-catering**:
  -you offer short-period lets for fewer than 140 days a year. It is important to note that this is the period of the year when the property is available to be let, NOT the period over the year that it is let.

Note: the Government is currently consulting on the criteria under which self-catering and holiday lets become chargeable to business rates rather than council tax. The reason for this consultation is to ensure that owners of holiday homes are not claiming to be self-catering operators in order to avoid paying council tax.

Small Business Rate Relief

Small Business Rate Relief is available to businesses where the rateable value of the property is less than £15,000. Businesses with a rateable value of up to £12,000 receive 100% relief, while businesses with a rateable value between £12,000 and £15,000 receive tapered relief.

If you have a second property, you'll keep getting any existing relief on your main property for 12 months. You can still get Small Business Rate relief on your main property after this if both of the following apply:

- none of your properties have a rateable value above £2,899
- the total rateable value of all your properties is less than £20,000 (£28,000 in London).

If your property has a rateable value of more than £15,000 but less than £51,000, your bill will be calculated using the small business multiplier, which is lower than the standard multiplier.

Mandatory Rate Relief for Charities

Organisations that are recognised as charities, either by being a registered charity or acknowledged by HMRC as being a charity for tax purposes, can claim 80 per cent relief from business rates if:

- the charity (or trustees of the charity) is the ratepayer, and
- the charity uses the property wholly, or mainly, for charitable purposes.

Any organisation that qualifies for 80 per cent mandatory rate relief may also apply to their local council for discretionary relief for all or part of the remaining 20 per cent of its bill.

How are business rates calculated?

If you need to pay business rates, your property will have a 'rateable value' based on the rental value of your property. These values are set by an independent Government Agency, the Valuation Office Agency (VOA).

The last revaluation of non-domestic properties in England and Wales took place in 2016/2017, with the new rates applying from 1 April 2017. In 2018 the Government announced that the frequency of business rates valuations would be increased from every five years to every three years to prevent large changes in business rate bills caused by significant changes in property values. Although the next revaluation was scheduled for 2021, due to the COVID-19 outbreak this revaluation has been postponed until 2022.

You can obtain details of the rateable value of your property from your local Valuation Office or the business rates department of your local authority. The VOA website allows you to access entries in local rating lists: www.gov.uk/government/organisations/valuation-office-agency.

Transitional arrangements

There are transitional arrangements in operation which phase in the increase in business rates associated with the 1 April 2017 revaluation. This relief sets a limit to the percentage by which your business rate bill can increase each year until 2022.

The transitional relief is automatically included in the bill you receive from your local authority.

Lodging an appeal

You can make an appeal against the 2017 valuation of your property at any time during the life of the valuation (i.e. until April

1, 2022). You are advised to appeal as soon as possible as you will have to pay your rates in full until a decision has been reached and, for most appeals, there are limits on how far any resulting change in value will be backdated.

Appeals are made in the form of a 'proposal' to the local Valuation Officer or online through the VOA website. If an agreement is not reached within three months of receipt of your proposal, it will be automatically referred to the local Valuation Tribunal, which will hear the case and give a decision.

Seeking the advice of commercial valuers

If you feel that the valuation of your business is too high, and you are not satisfied with the advice you have received from the local Valuation Officer, you may wish to consult a private firm of valuers or rating consultants before deciding to lodge an appeal.

Before agreeing to employ any rating consultants, always confirm:
- the terms
- their expertise
- their professional indemnity insurance cover.

Fees for commercial valuers

The fees paid should depend on the amount of work needed and on whether the appeal can be resolved by agreement. If a firm is handling a number of appeals from a specific area, it may negotiate a settlement that includes all of them, which will reduce the cost of each individual case.

There have been a number of reports of 'unqualified' firms seeking to obtain rating instructions by offering to represent ratepayers on payment of a fixed fee (payable before any work is done) and 'guaranteeing' a successful outcome to the appeal. Often cold calls are made by telephone or in person to the property and you are best advised not to employ such organisations. No one, no matter how eminent, skilled or experienced, can guarantee that an appeal will be successful.

It is also important to note that, although rare, it is possible for appeals to lead to an increase in the rateable value of your property (e.g. when the records of the Valuation Officer are not up to date on the physical extent of the property or the fact that it is being used for short-stay accommodation). Only reputable firms should be used to help you appeal against your rating assessment. Members of the Royal Institution of Chartered Surveyors (RICS) and the Institute of Revenues Rating and Valuation (IRRV) are regulated to protect the public from misconduct, and are required to hold adequate indemnity insurance.

Further guidance

Valuation Office Agency

For information on the valuation of your property or appeals, contact your local Valuation Office (listed in the telephone directory), or visit their website: **www.gov.uk/government/ organisations/valuation-office-agency**

Your local authority

For any enquiries about your business rates bill, contact the business rates department of your local authority: **www.gov.uk/ find-local-council.**

Self-Catering Letting Options

KEY FACTS

- You need to consider self-catering letting options if you let a property for holiday purposes.
- Occupiers do not gain any rights to stay on in your property as long as it is actually let for a holiday.
- For out-of-season lettings, you may wish to consider an assured tenancy or an assured shorthold tenancy.

Holiday letting

If you let a property for holiday purposes, the law allows you to do this without the occupiers gaining any rights to remain in the property. There is no limit to the length of the holiday let, but it must actually be for a holiday. 'Holiday letting' is defined in the **Housing Act 1988** as 'a tenancy the purpose of which is to confer on the tenant the right to occupy the dwelling house for a holiday'.

You are recommended to have a basic agreement with the occupiers (this can be by letter), which includes a statement that you are letting the premises as a holiday let, with the start and end days of the let clearly stated.

> **Note:** while there is no limit to the length of a holiday let, to comply with the Furnished Holiday Letting Rules (see the *Tax Status of Accommodation Businesses* section) the letting must not be for longer than 31 continuous days.

If the occupier doesn't leave at the end of the let, legally you don't have to go to court to recover possession of the property. However, you would still be strongly advised to apply to the Courts for eviction.

Out-of-season letting

If you are thinking of supplementing your income by letting your property for a number of months out of season, you can opt for:

- an assured tenancy
- an assured shorthold tenancy.

> **Note:** the **Immigration Act 2016** requires you to check the immigration status of guests applying to occupy a property under a residential tenancy agreement. It is an offence to let your property under a residential tenancy agreement to anyone that you suspect is disqualified from occupying a property due to their immigration status.

Assured tenancy

Assured tenancies are designed to give tenants the right to remain in your property until you have reason, or grounds, to seek possession. The relevant grounds, in this case, would be that the property has been let temporarily 'out of season' (such lets are often called 'winter lets', although they occur during any time of the year).

There are two forms of assured tenancy:
- a periodic tenancy - this rolls over on a week-to-week or month-to-month basis
- a fixed-term tenancy - this is a set period such as 12 or 18 months.

When a fixed-term tenancy expires, it continues as a periodic tenancy unless you sign up for a new fixed term.

Setting up an assured tenancy

You must give the tenant written notice before the start of the tenancy (or include a simple declaration in the tenancy agreement) that says the tenancy is not an assured shorthold tenancy and that possession might be recovered on the basis of Ground 3 of the Grounds for Possession in the **Housing Act 1988**.

To ensure that you have a mandatory right to repossess a property if a tenant refuses to leave, the let must be for a period not exceeding eight months and the property must have been used as a holiday let at some point in the preceding 12 months.

Ending an assured tenancy

You have the right to seek possession of the property at the end of the roll-over period or the fixed period of the tenancy.

If you seek possession, you have to give written notice of at least:
- 28 days, if the guest pays rent weekly
- one month, if the guest pays rent monthly.

If the tenant does not leave at the end of the notice period, you would have to start court proceedings to recover possession of the property.

Assured shorthold tenancy

Another form of assured tenancy that many landlords prefer to use is an assured shorthold tenancy. This allows you to seek possession even when there are no specific grounds for you to do so. However, this would mean that the tenant has the right to stay in the property on this basis for a minimum of six months (even if you have agreed a fixed term for less) or the length of the fixed term, whichever is the longer.

There are no special procedures for setting up a shorthold tenancy, but you must give two months' written notice to seek repossession. If the notice period expires and the tenant doesn't leave, you must still recover possession through the Courts. However, for recovering possession on a 'no-ground' assured shorthold basis, you can use the Accelerated Possession Procedure, which can be quicker and cheaper than a full court hearing.

Alternatively, you can set up a fixed-term out-of-season assured shorthold tenancy, by prior notice to the tenant, as for a full assured tenancy.

Note: to maintain the tax status of the property as being a Furnished Holiday Let, the total period that a property is let under either an assured tenancy or an assured shorthold tenancy must be less than 155 days in any given year.

Note: remember that planning restrictions may have been imposed on you as a condition of permission being granted for the property's use as a holiday let that prevent the property being used as a residential property.

Further information on tenancies

Professional legal advice

You should always take legal advice before you enter into any tenancy agreement.

Tenancy agreements: a guide for landlords

Further information in tenancies can be found at **www.gov.uk/tenancy-agreements-a-guide-for-landlords/tenancy-types.**

LICENCES & CONSENTS

MARKETING

CUSTOMERS

FOOD & DRINK

HEALTH & SAFETY

STAFF

BUSINESS MANAGEMENT & TAX

FURTHER INFORMATION

Houses in Multiple Occupation

KEY FACTS

- In some cases, your local authority may class your accommodation as a House in Multiple Occupation (HMO).
- If you feel that your property is being classed wrongly as an HMO by the local authority, you may appeal to a residential property tribunal.
- HMOs usually need to be licensed by the council.
- Environmental Health Officers are responsible for enforcing HMO legislation locally.

In a few local authority areas, guesthouses, bed and breakfasts and holiday flats have been classed as HMOs. When this happens, the implications for a proprietor can be far-reaching.

The **Housing Act 2004** introduced mandatory licensing and a new definition for HMOs. This legislation has been extended through the **Licensing of Houses in Multiple Occupation (Prescribed Description) (England) Order 2018**, so that a property to five or more people - from two or more separate households – is deemed to be a "large HMO" and the landlord must be licensed by their local housing authority.

What is an HMO?

A house in multiple occupation is defined in the Housing Act 2004 as:

- an entire house or flat that is let to three or more tenants who form two or more households and who share a kitchen, bathroom, or toilet facilities
- a house that has been converted entirely into bedsits or other non-self-contained accommodation and which is let to three or more tenants who form two or more households and who share kitchen, bathroom, or toilet facilities
- a converted house that contains one or more flats that are not wholly self-contained (i.e. the flat does not contain a kitchen, bathroom and toilet) and that is occupied by three or more tenants

LICENCES & CONSENTS

MARKETING

CUSTOMERS

FOOD & DRINK

HEALTH & SAFETY

STAFF

BUSINESS MANAGEMENT & TAX

FURTHER INFORMATION

who form two or more households
- a building that is converted entirely into self-contained flats if the conversion did not meet the standards of the Building Regulations 1991 and more than one-third of the flats are let on short-term tenancies.

Tenants

In order to be an HMO, the property must be used as the tenants' only or main residence and it should be used solely or mainly to house tenants. Properties let to students and migrant workers will be treated as their only or main residence and the same will apply to properties which are used as domestic refuges.

Therefore, holiday cottages let to families or other groups of people living together as one household for a holiday, who have a main home elsewhere, are **not** HMOs.

Where winter letting to groups of people who are not related is taking place, the premises may well be considered to be an HMO and you should seek advice.

What being an HMO means

Owners who intend anything other than holiday letting should seek advice and talk to their local authority. If the premises are deemed to be an HMO, they will have to meet some strict standards concerning amenities and fire precautions in the building. Usually, they will need to be licensed.

The great majority of holiday homes are not HMOs. Bed and breakfast accommodation may be if it is let to people who don't have another residence.

Licensing

Under the national mandatory licensing scheme, an HMO needs to be licensed if it is a building consisting of three or more storeys and is occupied by five or more tenants in two or more households.

The council will grant a licence to an HMO if it is satisfied that:
- the HMO is reasonably suitable for occupation by the number of people allowed under the licence
- the proposed licence holder is a 'fit and proper person'
- the proposed licence holder is the most appropriate person to hold the licence
- the proposed manager, if there is one, is a 'fit and proper person'
- the proposed management arrangements are satisfactory
- the person involved in the management of the HMO is competent

- the financial structures for the management are suitable.

Enforcement
Environmental health officers, who are responsible for enforcing HMO legislation locally, have the right to enter a property at any reasonable time after giving 24 hours' notice in writing. Also, they may serve legal notices requiring the provision or improvement of amenities.

Standards
Properties of the relevant type must be licensed throughout the UK, while local authorities have discretion to adopt additional licensing schemes in regard to lower-risk properties. Before granting a licence, they will need to be satisfied that a set of standards are met. If they are not met, they will judge the property not to be reasonably suitable and refuse to grant the licence.

The standards come from a Government circular. Most local authorities adopt similar sets of standards, but there are variations. The standards include requirements for fire precautions. See the *Fire Safety (General)* section for more information on fire safety

The recent **Licensing of Houses in Multiple Occupation (Prescribed Description) (England) Order 2018** also introduces rules that set minimum size requirements for bedrooms in HMOs to prevent overcrowding and require landlords to adhere to council refuse schemes in order to reduce problems with rubbish.

Appeals
If you feel that your property is being classed wrongly as an HMO by the local authority, you may appeal to a residential property tribunal.

Further guidance
Your local authority
Detailed advice on HMOs is available from your local environmental health officer: **www.gov.uk/find-local-council**

Guidance on private renting and HMOs
Your rights and responsibilities as a landlord can be found on the Gov.uk website: **www.gov.uk/private-renting/houses-in-multiple-occupation**

Guidance on minimum bedroom sizes
Guidance on extending mandatory licensing to smaller HMOs and introducing minimum bedroom sizes is available at: **www.gov.uk/government/publications/houses-in-multiple-occupation-and-**

residential-property-licensing-reform-guidance-for-local-housing-authorities.

Utilities and Waste Collection

KEY FACTS

● If the water supplies for your business come from a private supply, the **Private Water Supplies Regulations 2016** apply to you.

● Local authorities must take and analyse samples of private water supplies from groundwater sources.

● If you make a specific charge to your customers for gas or electricity, the most you can charge is limited by the 'maximum resale price' rule.

● The maximum resale price is the same price that you have paid to your own supplier.

● If you pay business rates, you need to pay for a commercial waste collection service unless you are exempt under the **Controlled Waste Regulations 2012**.

Private water supplies

Private water supplies include water:
● from groundwater sources
● drawn from privately owned boreholes or wells
● taken from surface water, such as springs and streams.

The **Private Water Supplies Regulations (England) 2016** consolidated and repealed the Private Water Supplies Regulations (England) 2009. Together with the **Water Industry Act 1991**, they apply to all private water supplies intended for human consumption, whether this is for drinking, washing or food production. The aim of the regulations is to ensure that all private water sources are safe and free from contaminants.

Do these regulations affect me?

Yes: if any part of the water supply for your business comes from a private supply.

Private water supply tests

The 2016 regulations are very similar to the previous regulations, in that they require local authorities to record the number of private supplies in its area, and for each supply must record:

- the name of the supply, together with a unique identifier
- the type of source
- the geographical location, using a grid reference
- an estimate of the number of people supplied
- an estimate of the average daily volume of water supplied in cubic metres
- the type of premises supplied
- detail of any treatment process, together with its location
- the name of the Health Protection Agency in whose area the supply is located.

After the initial assessment, the regulations require local authorities to monitor the supply on an ongoing basis. The regularity of the sampling will vary depending upon the volume of water used, from once a year for supplies of less than 10 cubic metres per day to 34 times a year for supplies of up to 10,000 cubic metres per day.

In addition, the local authority must also undertake a thorough risk assessment of each supply at least once every five years.

In addition to the previous requirements, the **Private Water Supplies Regulations (England) 2016** require local authorities to test private water supplies for radioactive substances (this usually means the level of naturally occurring Radon in the water) and undertake a risk assessment of new supplies, and supplies that have been out of use for more than 12 months, as soon as is reasonably practicable. The risk assessments of these suppliers will then be subject to review every five years as per the 2009 regulations.

Cost of samples

The local authority will contact the person responsible for the supply (this may be the landowner, a person using the water, or a person representing a group of water users) about sampling. The regulations set out the maximum amounts that a local authority can charge for undertaking risk assessments, taking and analysing samples and providing authorisations to use a private water supply.

The bill will be sent to the person responsible. If an authority decides to carry out tests over and above those required by the regulations, it has to bear the costs of these tests itself.

If test results show that the water is unwholesome, because it fails to meet the standards or other requirements, the local authority can insist the water supply is improved. If any private supply of water intended for human consumption constitutes a potential danger to human health, a local authority acting under these regulations will serve a notice to the responsible person. It is an offence to breach this notice. However, the regulations establish an appeal process if you wish to challenge a notice.

The resale of gas and electricity

Maximum resale prices

If you are reselling gas and/or electricity that has already been bought from an authorised supplier, the amount you can charge your customers is limited by the 'maximum resale price rule'. This means that the most you can charge a customer for the supply of gas or electricity is the amount that you yourself have been charged by your gas or electricity supply company. Put another way, you can only sell gas or electricity to your guests on a non-profit basis.

As the provisions relating to the maximum resale prices for electricity and gas are reviewed from time to time, you should also occasionally check the Ofgem website (see *Further guidance*) to see whether there have been any changes.

Do maximum resale prices apply to me?

Yes: if you make a specific charge to your customers for gas or electricity, whether or not you use individual meters to record their consumption. The rule typically applies to self-catering accommodation and caravan sites, although it affects all businesses where separate charging occurs. If you overcharge for electricity or gas, your customer can ask for a refund of the excess and can pursue the matter in the small claims courts if necessary.

No: if you do not make a specific charge for electricity and/or gas (e.g. if customers are charged a single rental figure for fully inclusive accommodation). The rule also does not apply to any gas or electricity that is used in communal facilities, e.g. for the use of a dryer in a laundry room or a shower in a washroom block at a caravan park. In other words, there is no maximum limit on what you can charge a guest for using a communal washing machine, provided that this use is billed separately to the charge for general gas and electricity use.

Price of energy units

If you are charged a **single unit rate** for gas or electricity by your own supplier, you must charge your customers the same rate. If the unit rate varies, e.g. if you pay on an economy 7 type tariff, or prices vary on a seasonal basis, you will need to calculate an average price for each unit used.

A copy of the explanatory publication, *The resale of gas and electricity – guidance for resellers* is available to download from the Ofgem website (www.ofgem.gov.uk). This gives further information and includes example resale price calculations.

Standing charges
In addition to the charge for units used, many authorised suppliers levy a standing charge to cover the cost of maintaining your connection and billing you for the fuel. You can recover this from your customers – the individual sums need to be calculated according to the number of units of electricity used by each consumer. Once again, the Ofgem publication gives further guidance.

Waste collection
If you pay business rates then, unless you qualify for an exemption under the **Controlled Waste Regulations 2012**, you will need to pay for a commercial waste collection service either through your council or with a private contractor. The Controlled Waste Regulations provide an exemption from waste disposal charges for small businesses that:
● were operating prior to 6 April 2012 and were eligible for free waste disposal at this date; and
● are eligible for Small Business Rate Relief (i.e. the property has a rateable value of less than £15,000).

Note: waste collection charges comprise of two components – a charge to collect the waste and a separate charge to dispose of the waste. Therefore, even if you qualify for the exemption from waste disposal charges, you will still need to pay for your waste to be collected.

Further guidance
Your local authority
Advice and information on private water supplies and waste collection, including exemptions, is available from your local authority: **www.gov.uk/find-local-council**

Private water supplies
Information on private water supplies can be found in *Keeping your private water supply safe*. It is free to download from the Drinking Water Inspectorate website: **www.dwi.gov.uk**

Reselling gas and electricity
The *Resale of Gas and Electricity – Guidance for Resellers* gives further information and includes example resale price calculations. It is free to download from the Ofgem website: **www.ofgem.gov.uk.**

WHERE TO FIND
FURTHER INFORMATION

Business support helpline

The Government's Business Support Helpline provides a quick response service if you have simple questions about starting or running a business. It also provides a more in-depth service if you have more complex enquiries:

- Business Support Helpline (England)
- enquiries@businesssupporthelpline.org
- Telephone: 0800 998 1098
- Monday to Friday, 9am to 6pm

Growth Hubs

The Local Enterprise Partnership (LEP) network has established 38 Growth Hubs throughout England which are the central repository of information, advice and support for business within a defined local area.

The aim of the Growth Hub network is to provide a single point of contact for local business that will provide all the information, advice or support they require including compliance with legislation.

You can find contact details for your local Growth Hub in VisitEngland's Business Advice Hub:

www.visitbritain.org/business-advice/find-local-support.

Legal advisors

The Law Society is able to provide you with a list of solicitors within your area: **solicitors.lawsociety.org.uk**. Your local Destination Organisation may also be able to give you names of suitable local firms.

Independent financial advisors

The IFA consumer website is able to forward you a list of independent financial advisors, accountants or solicitor in your area:

- **www.unbiased.co.uk**

Utilities/Facilities

These include the following:

Gas Safe Register

- Tel: 0800 408 5500
- register@gassaferegister.co.uk
- **www.gassaferegister.co.uk**

OFGEM (The Office of Gas and Electricity Markets)

- Tel: 0330 440 1624
- **www.ofgem.gov.uk**

WHERE TO FIND FURTHER INFORMATION

OFCOM (Office of Communications)
- Tel: 0300 123 3333
- **www.ofcom.org.uk**

OFWAT
The economic regulator of the water sector in England and Wales.
- Tel: 0300 034 2222
- **www.ofwat.gov.uk**

Waste and Resources Action Programme (WRAP)
- Tel: 0808 100 2040
- **www.wrap.org.uk**
- For any matters to do with collection of rubbish or recycling, contact your Local Authority.

Trade associations
These include the following:
Association of Leading Visitor Attractions - ALVA
- email@alva.org.uk
- **www.avla.org.uk**

Bed and Breakfast Association
- Tel: 0174 981 4908
- **bandbassociation.org**

BACTA - trade association for the amusement and gaming machine industry
- Tel: 0207 730 6444
- info@bacta.org.uk
- **www.bacta.org.uk**

British Association of Leisure Parks Piers and Attractions - BALPPA
- Tel: 0207 403 4455
- **www.balppa.org**

British Activity Providers Association (BAPA)
The BAPA monitors safety standards and quality within the activity sector throughout the British Isles. BAPA also provides a detailed consumer guide which is available on request.
- Tel: 0174 676 9982
- **www.thebapa.org.uk**

British Holiday and Home Parks Association (BHHPA)
The BHHPA is the representative body of the parks industry including caravans, chalets, tents and all types of self-catering park accommodation.
- Tel: 0145 252 6911
- **www.bhhpa.org.uk**

British Destinations

British Destinations represents the interests of resorts and destinations throughout the UK.
- Tel: 0151 934 2285 / 2286
- **www.britishdestinations.co.uk**

Farm Stay UK Ltd

Farm Stay UK Ltd is a co-operative of 1200 farmers throughout the UK who provide serviced and self-catering accommodation on working farms.
- Tel: 0247 669 6909
- **www.farmstayuk.co.uk**

Holiday Home Association (HHA)

The HHA is a trade association for self-catering operators, from individual owners through to the agencies and associations.
- Tel: 0207 078 7329
- **www.holidayhomeassociation.org.uk**

Tourism for All

Tourism for All, a national charity, is the UK's central source of travel and holiday information for disabled people, older people and carers.
- Tel: 0845 124 9971
- **www.tourismforall.org.uk**

People 1st

People 1st is an employer-led skills and quality assurance expert for the hospitality and tourism sector. It is the lead agency on all issues relating to education, training and qualification within the sector.
- Tel: 0203 074 1222
- **www.people1st.co.uk**

National Caravan Council (NCC)

The NCC is the representative trade body for the UK caravan industry involved in setting standards and promoting quality. NCC operates the Product Approval Scheme for new caravans to ensure compliance with minimum health and safety standards.
- Tel: 0125 231 8251
- **www.thencc.org.uk**

UKHospitality

UKHospitality represents accommodation providers, restaurants, catering establishments and leisure companies.
- Tel: 0207 404 7744
- **www.ukhospitality.org.uk**

Publications Contact List

The publications mentioned within individual legislation sections are available from the following organisations:

Advisory, Conciliation and Arbitration Services (ACAS)
- **National helpline: 0845 747 4747**

WHERE TO FIND FURTHER INFORMATION

- Orderline: 08702 42 90 90
- **www.acas.org.uk**

Advertising Standards Authority (ASA)
- Orderline: 0207 492 2222
- **www.asa.org.uk**

Equality and Human Rights Commission (EHRC)
- Tel: 0808 800 0082
- **www.equalityhumanrights.com**

Food Standards Agency (FSA)
- Tel: 0207 276 8829
- **www.food.gov.uk**

Health and Safety Executive (HSE)
- Incident Contact Centre on 0845 300 9923 (Note: this can only be used to report serious or fatal accidents)
- **www.hse.gov.uk**

HM Revenue and Customs (HMRC)
- VAT Helpline: 0845 010 9000
- Employer Helpline: 0845 714 3143
- **www.gov.uk/government/organisations/hm-revenue-customs**

Home Office
- Tel: 0207 035 4848
- **www.gov.uk/government/organisations/home-office**

Information Commissioner's Office (ICO)
- Helpline: 0303 123 1113
- **www.ico.org.uk**

Pay and Work Rights Helpline
- Tel: 0800 917 2368
- **www.gov.uk/pay-and-work-rights**

TSO (formerly The Stationery Office)
- Orderline: 0333 200 2425
- **www.tsoshop.co.uk**

Trading Standards Institute
- Consumer Direct helpline: 0845 404 0506
- **www.tradingstandards.uk**

Valuation Office Agency
The VOA is an agency of HMRC.
- Tel: 0300 050 1501
- **www.gov.uk/government/organisations/valuation-office-agency**

Index

Legislation is in *italics*
Major page references in **bold**

A

ACAS (Advisory, Conciliation and Arbitration Services) 191, 208, 220
accessibility 35, 82, 85–9, 91, 92
accidents
duty of care 129, 130
reporting 139
slips and trips **151–2**
accommodation
accepting customers **81–3**
booking contracts 37, 39, 43, 48–9, 53–4, **57–9**, 75, 77–9, 83
cancelled bookings **57–9**, **75–9**
disabled customers **85–92**
houses in multiple occupation **245–8**
letting options **241–3**
pricing and charging **51–5**
tax status **231–3**, 243
television licences 13–15
unfair trading practices 34
utility supplies **249–52**
accommodation offset (National Minimum Wage) 194
adoption leave 205–6
Adventure Activities Licensing Regulations 2004 166–7
advertisements
online endorsements 36
paid promotions 36
signage **29–32**
unfair trading practices **33–8**
see also direct marketing
advertising codes 38
age discrimination 201
agency workers 138–9
alcohol **1–8**, 11, 166, 217, 219
Alcohol Wholesaler Registration Scheme 8
allergies 90, 114, **118–20**

alterations to buildings 21, 22, **24–5**, 172, 176
Alternative Dispute Resolution (ADR) Regulations 2015 103–5
apprentices 194, 195, 196
asbestos 21, **26–7**
assistance dogs 85, 88, 89–90, 201
assured tenancies 241, **242–3**

B

baby-sitting/baby-listening 100–101
bed and breakfast accommodation
business rates 235–6
'change of use' consent 22–4
fire safety 169, 173, 179
food 107, 109, 110
health and safety 148
houses in multiple occupation 245, 246
licences 16, 17
marketing 37, 47
smoking 186
tax status 231, 232
bedsits 245
belongings, customers' **93–7**
bills, non-payment 96
bonds 54–5
booking contracts 37, 39, 43, 48–9, 53–4, **57–9**, 75, 77–9, 83
booking fees 60, 82
breastfeeding 199
Brexit 67
British Standards Institute (BSI) 179–80
building regulations 21, 23, **24–5**, 246
Building Regulations 1991 246
Building Regulations 2000 23–4
business management
assured tenancies 241, **242–3**
business rates **235–9**, 249, 252
charities 228–9, 230, 235, 237
income tax **225–6**, 228,

230
legal form of the business 229
self-catering letting options **241–3**
tax status **231–3**, 243
utility supplies **249–52**
Value Added Tax (VAT) **226–9**, 230
Business Protection from Misleading Marketing Regulations 2008 33, 35
business rates **235–9**, 249, 252

C

cancelled bookings 57–9, **75–9**
caravans 3, 14, 17, 133, 158, 181, 186, 251
carbon monoxide 136, 157, 159
carers, discrimination 82, 85, 87, 199, 201
cash basis accounting 226
caving 166
CCTV 4, 62–3, 70–1, 73
change of use **22–5**
charging
bonds/damage deposits 54–5
debit and credit card charges 55
displaying prices 52–4
energy units 252
misleading information 51–2, 53–4, 59
charities
business rates 235, 237
data protection 63, 67
establishing 228, 230
Gift Aid 228–9, 230
Charity Commission 228, 230
children
and alcohol 7–8, 219
childcare **99–101**, 207
employment of 136–7, 190, **217–20**
health and safety 130, 136, 144, 166
hotel bookings 83–4
minimum pay 218
Children Act 1989 99–101

Children (Protection at Work)
Regulations 2000 217
cleaning materials 111, 138,
144–5, 152, 171
climbing 166
cold callers 41, 153, 238
Committee of Advertising
Practice (CAP) 38
Community and Ancillary Sales
Notices (CANs) 2
comparison marketing 35
Competition and Markets
Authority (CMA) 36, 58
Conservation Areas 24, 31
Consumer Contracts
(Information, Cancellation
and Additional Charges)
Regulations 2013 39, 43, 60
Consumer Protection
(Amendment) Regulations
2014 53
Consumer Protection (Distance
Selling) Regulations 2000 39,
43
Consumer Protection from
Unfair Trading Regulations
2008 33, 36, 51–3, 59
Control of Asbestos
Regulations 2012 26
Control of Substances
Hazardous to Health
Regulations (COSHH) 2002
144–5
Controlled Waste Regulations
2012 249, 252
'cookies' on websites 42
Copyright, Designs and Patents
Act 1988 15–16, 20
copyright licences, music 3, 8,
13, 15–18
cotton buds, plastic 121
COVID-19 1, 147, 196, 209,
237
credit and debit card charges
55
credit cards and cancellations/
no-shows 76–7
  data security 67–9, 73
curtailed bookings 57, 75,
76, 77
customers
  accepting 81–3

Alternative Dispute
Resolution (ADR)
Regulations 2015 103–5
booking contracts 57–9
cancellations and no-shows
57–9, 75–9
childcare 99–101
consumer rights 43, 61
damages claimed by 37, 54,
79, 86
data protection 61–73
disabled 62, 81–2, 85–92
discrimination 81–2, 85,
86–7, 89–90
dispute resolution 103–5
hearing-impaired 89, 174
luggage and belongings
93–7
pricing and charging 51–5,
59–60
privacy 62, 70–2
refusing accommodation
81, 87, 90
registration 69–70
selling tickets 59–60, 77
surveillance equipment 61,
70–3
'walk-in' 83

D
damages
  bonds/damage deposits
  54–5
  cancellations and no-shows
  77–8, 79
  curtailed bookings 77
  customers' claims 37, 54,
  79, 86
dancing 3
data protection 61–73
Data Protection Act 2018 61–4,
66, 67, 70–2
  see also General Data
  Protection Regulation 2018
data security, credit cards
67–9, 73
Department for Business,
Energy and Industrial Strategy
(BEIS) 45, 49, 182, 183, 196,
197, 198
Department for Education
(DfE) 101

deposits 54–5, 57, 58–9, 75–8
Destination Organisations
(DOs) 32, 229
direct marketing 39–44
Direct Marketing Association
(DMA) 40, 44
disabled customers
  assistance dogs 85, 88,
  89–90, 201
  definition 85–6
  discrimination 81–2, 85,
  86–7, 89–90
  Equality Act 2010 81,
  85–9, 92
  fire safety 87, 171, 172,
  174, 177
disabled employees 200
disclosure, tips and service
charges 196–7
discrimination
  accepting customers 81–2
  age 201
  disabled customers 81–2,
  85, 86–7, 89–90
  employees 199–201
  Equality Act 2010 85–9
  indirect 82, 86
display screen equipment 141,
142, 171
dispute resolution 103–5
distance selling 43
dogs see assistance dogs
domestic premises, food
preparation 110
Drinking Water Inspectorate
(DWI) 252
drink stirrers, plastic 121
duty of care 126, 129, 130
DVDs, licences to show 13,
14,18, 19–20

E
Early Years Foundation Stage
(EYFS) 101
EC Online Dispute Resolution
(ODR) platform 103, 104
Electrical Equipment (Safety)
Regulations 1994 160
electrical systems/equipment,
safety and maintenance 149,
152–5, 157, 160–1, 171
Electricity at Work Regulations

1989 152, 160
electricity supplies 251–2
email addresses 62, 103, 105
email, direct marketing 39–40
emergency procedures
  disabled employees 137
  employee training 138
  employees with poor
  English 137
  fire safety 169, 172–3, 174
  health and safety 130, 137,
  138, 150, 166, 167
  outdoor activities 167
employees
  under 18s 190, **217–20**
  adoption leave 205–6
  agency workers 138–9
  competent person
  appointment 138, 150
  disabled 200
  discrimination 199–201
  duties of 139
  employees with poor
  English 137
  flexible working 203,
  206–7
  harassment 126, 200
  health and safety 123–7,
  130, **132–4**, **135–9**,
  141–2, 147–50, 152, 157,
  159, 170–4, 185–7
  health surveillance 137–8,
  139
  holiday entitlement 190–1
  maternity/paternity rights
  199, **203–7**
  mental health 125–6
  migrant workers see
  migrant workers
  National Minimum Wage
  193–8
  new and expectant mothers
  137
  night-time workers 190
  parental leave **203–8**
  pensions **221–4**
  rest periods 189, 191, 195,
  218
  risk assessments 136–7
  tax 229
  temporary employees 139
  voluntary 193

wages *see* wages
working hours **189–91**,
218
young people 136–7, 190,
217–20
zero-hours contracts 191
see also self-employed
persons
*Employers' Liability
(Compulsory Insurance) Act
1969* 129, 132–3
*Employment (Allocation of
Tips) Bill 2019–20* 196
Energy Performance
Certificates (EPCs) 26
energy units, price 252
entertainment licences 3–4,
8–11
entitlement to work in the UK,
proof of 209, **210 –13**, 215
environmental health authority
  employers' liability
  insurance 133
  food safety 109, 110, 115
  health and safety 126, 127,
  133, 136, 152, 168, 186
  houses in multiple
  occupation 245, 247
  licences and consents 2,
  4–5, 31
  smoking 186–7
  swimming pool safety 168
*Environmental Protection
(Plastic Straws, Cotton Buds &
Stirrers) (England) Regulations
2020* 121–2
Equality Act 2010 81, **85–9**,
92, **199–201**
Equality and Human Rights
Commission (EHRC) 83, 90,
92, 201
equipment
  hazards from 141–2, 160–1
  maintenance and safety
  130, 142–4, 152–5, 157–63
EU/EEA countries, transferring
personal data 67
EU Settlement Scheme 211–12
EU-UK Trade and Cooperation
Agreement 67
eye tests 142

F
*Fairgrounds and amusement
parks: Guidance on safe
practice* 155
falls from height 142–4
Family Entertainment Centres
(FECs) 9, 10–11
family-friendly working **203–8**
faxes, direct marketing 39, 40
filing systems, Data Protection
Act 63
Filmbank Media 18–19, 20
films, showing 13, 18–20
financial advisors 225, 226, 229
Financial Conduct Authority
134
Fire Action Notice 169, 172
*Fire and Rescue Services
(Northern Ireland) Order 2006*
169
fire safety **169–77**
  alarm systems 172, 174–5,
  176
  building regulations 25
  disabled customers 87, 171,
  172, 174, 177
  emergency lighting 174
  emergency procedures
  169, 172–3, 174
  fire-fighting equipment 174
  fire-inhibiting sprays 182
  furniture and furnishings
  171, **179–83**
  houses in multiple
  occupation 170, 246, 247
  means of escape 174, 176
  notices 169, 172, 176
  precautions 173–5
  regulations 169–70, 176
  responsible person 169,
  170, 172
  risk assessments 136, 168,
  169, **170–7**
  self-catering
  accommodation 169, 172,
  173, 179, 180, 181
  smoking 171, 174, **185–7**
Fire Safety Officers 4, 176, 180
*Fire safety risk assessment:
large places of assembly* 173
*Fire safety risk assessment:
small and medium places of*

assembly 173
Fire Safety (Scotland) Regulations 2006 169
Fire (Scotland) Act 2005 169
first aid 135, **139**
flags 31
flexible working 203, **206–7**
food and drink
    allergies 90, 114, **118–20**
    genetically modified 117–18
    inspections 113–14, 115, 122
    labelling 107, 114, **117–20**
    late night licensing 3
    local authorities 107, 109, 110, 113, 115, 120, 122
    pre-packaged 114, **119–20**
    premises requirements 110
    ready-to-eat foods 112–13
    record keeping 108, **109–10**, 113
    safety and hygiene **107–16**
    'Scores on the Doors' 115
    single-use plastics **121–2**
    temperature control 111–13
    unpackaged 120
Food Hygiene (England) Regulations 2006 107, 111
Food Safety Act 1990 107, 108, 114, 118
Food Safety and Hygiene (England) Regulations 2013 107
Food Standards Agency 107, 108, 110, 115, 118
foreign workers **209–13**
'free' alcohol 1
Furnished Holiday Letting (FHL) Rules 231, 232
furniture and furnishings 136, 162, 171, **179–83**
Furniture and Furnishings (Fire) (Safety) Regulations 1988 179, **180–3**

G
Gambling Act 2005 8–9, 11
gaming machines 1, 8–11
gas safety **157–60**, 162–3
Gas Safety (Installation and Use) Regulations 1998 157–8

gas supplies 158, 159
General Data Protection Regulation 2018 61, 66–7, 73
General Food Law Regulation (EC) No 178/2002 107, 108, 114, 118–19
General Food Regulations 2004 107, 108
General Product Safety Regulations 2005 161
genetically modified (GM) food 117–18
Gift Aid 228–9, 230
glass, safety 150–1
guests see customers
guide dogs *see* assistance dogs
gym safety 165–6

H
HACCP principles 107, 109
harassment of employees 126, 200
hazardous substances 138, 141, **144–5**
hazards
    from work activities **141–5**
    in the workplace **149–55**
Health Act 2006 185
health and safety
    children 130, 136, 144, 166
    cold callers 153
    competent person appointment 138, 150
    duty of care 126, 129, 130
    emergency procedures 130, 137, 138, 150, 166, 167
    employees 123–7, 130, 132–4, 135–9, 141–2, 147–50, 152, 157, 159, 170–4, 185–7
    employer responsibilities 123–5
    employing children 136–7
    environmental health authority 126, 127, 133, 136, 152, 168, 186
    first aid 135, **139**
    gas safety **157–60**, 162–3
Health and Safety at Work Act 1974 **123–7**, 135, 152, 157, 165, 166

Legionnaires' disease 134, **147–8**
legislation **123–5**
liabilities **129–34**, 159–60
Management of Health and Safety at Work Regulations 1999 **135–9**, 142, 150, 157, 165, 166
mental health 125–6
notices 125
outdoor activities 166–7
policy statements 125, 138
product safety **157–63**
risk assessments 125, 135–7, 139, 143, 145, 147–8, 150, 165–6
safety management **135–40**, 167
self-employed persons 123–4, 135, 139, 141, 155
transportation of customers 131–2
    see also fire safety; hazards
Health and Safety at Work Act 1974 **123–7**, 135, 152, 157, 165, 166
Health and Safety (Consultation with Employees) Regulations 1996 124
Health and Safety (Display Screen Equipment) Regulations 1992 141, 142
Health and Safety Executive (HSE)
    accident reporting 139
    Adventure Activities Licensing Regulations 2004 166–7
    asbestos 21, **26–7**
    COSHH 144–5
    employers' liability 133
    gas and electrical safety 155, 160–1, 163
    health and safety notices 125
    health and safety policy statements 125, 138
    Incident Contact Centre 139
    Legionnaires' disease 148
    new and expectant mothers

137
publications 140, 152
swimming pool safety 166
health surveillance 137–8, 139
hearing-impaired customers 88, 89, 174
height, working at 141, 142–4
Highways England 31–2
HM Revenue and Customs (HMRC)
  Alcohol Wholesaler Registration Scheme 8
  cash basis accounting 226
  helplines 229
  income tax 196, 197, **225–6**, 228, 230
  National Quality Assessment Scheme 91, 133, 159, 170
  tax status of accommodation businesses **231–3**, 243
  Value Added Tax (VAT) 7, 18, 19, 38, 51, 52, 53, 76, 226–9, 230
holiday accommodation
  houses in multiple occupation 245, 246
  out-of-season letting **241–3**
  self-catering letting options **241–3**
  tax status **231–3**, 243
holiday entitlement, employees 190–1
holiday packages **45–9**
Home Office 7, 71–2, 173, 175, 209–11, 213
Hotel and Mobile Units Television Licence (hotel licence) 13, 14–15
Hotel Proprietors Act 1956 83, 93, 94–5
hotels
  accepting customers **81–3**
  booking contracts 37, 39, 43, 48–9, 53–4, **57–9**, 75, 77–9, 83
  data protection **61–73**
  discrimination **81–9**
  long-term residents 14, 15
  luggage and belongings

93–7
  registration of customers 69–70
  surveillance equipment 61, **70–3**
  television licenses 13–15
houses in multiple occupation (HMOs) 171, **245–8**
Housing Act 1988 241, 242
Housing Act 2004 170, 245–6

I
illuminated signs 30
Immigration Act 2016 242
Immigration (Hotel Records) Order 1972 69
income tax 196, 197, **225–6**, 228, 230
independent financial advisors 229
indirect discrimination 82, 86
indoor sporting events 3
Information Commissioner's Office (ICO) 40, 41, 42, 61, 63, 66, 67, 73
inheritance tax 232
inspections, food hygiene 113–14, 115, 122
insurance
  cancellation 76
  employers' liability 129, 132–4
  indemnity 238–9
  insolvency 49
  public liability 129, 133–4, 170
  transportation of customers 131–2, 134
insurance brokers 133–4

L
labelling, food 107, 114, 117–20
ladders 142–4, 145
late night refreshment 3
Legionnaires' Disease 134, **147–8**
letting agents 161, 182–3
liabilities 58, 93–5, **129–34**, 159–60
licences
  adventure activities 165,

166–7
alcohol **1–8**, 11
entertainment 3–4, 8–11
gaming machines 8–11
Family Entertainment Centre (FEC) operating licence 10–11
houses in multiple occupation 245, 246–7
music copyright 3, 8, 13, **15–18**
personal licence 3, 4
premises licence **4–7**, 11
showing films and DVDs 18–20
sponsoring overseas workers 214
television 13–15
Temporary Event Notices 3–4
transportation 131–2, 134
Licensing Act 2003 2–4, 6, 7
Licensing of Houses in Multiple Occupation (Prescribed Description) (England) Order 2018 245, 247
Linked Travel Arrangement 38, 45–6, 47–9
Listed Buildings 26, 30, 82, 89
Live Music Act 2012 8
local authorities
  business rates **235–9**
  childcare 101
  food and drink 107, 109, 110, 113, 115, 120, 122
  health and safety 127, 135, 142, 162–3, 168, 183, 186–7
  planning permission **21–4**, 25
  premises licence **4–7**, 11
  serving alcohol 219
  signage **29–32**
Local Environmental Health Officers (EHOs) 126, 136, 152, 247
London Local Authorities Act 2004 94, 95
luggage and belongings **93–7**

M
mailing lists, buying 65

Making Tax Digital 230
Management of Health and Safety at Work Regulations 1999 **135–9**, 142, 150, 157, 165, 166
Mandatory Code for the sale of alcohol 7
Manual Handling Operations Regulations 1992 141, 142
marketing
  direct marketing **39–44**
  distance selling 43
  holiday packages **45–9**
  unfair trading practices **33–8**
  unfair comparisons 35, 38
  see also advertisements; signage
maternity rights 199, **203–7**
  maternity leave 203–4
  Statutory Maternity Pay 203–4, 205, 206
mental health 125–6
migrant workers
  documentation 209, 210–11, 212–13
  employers' responsibilities 209–13
  EU Settlement Scheme 211–12
  houses in multiple occupation 246
  points-based migration system 209, 213–14
  proof of entitlement to work in the UK 209, **210 –13**, 215
  sponsoring overseas workers 214
Minor Variation Application (premises licence) 6–7
misleading signs 29, 31
misrepresentation **37–8**
Motion Picture Licensing Company (MPLC) 18, 20
motor vehicles *see* vehicles
music
  copyright licences 3, 8, 13, **15–18**
  Live Music Act 2012 8
  recorded 3, 8, **15–18**

N
National Accessible Scheme (NAS) 91, 92
National Employment Savings Trust (NEST) 222
National Food Hygiene Rating Scheme 115
National Living Wage 193, 194, 195, 197
National Minimum Wage **193–8**
Next Generation Text Service (NGT) 88
night-time workers 190
no-shows 57–9, **75–9**
non-optional charges 52, 60
Notice of Underpayment 193
notices
  customers' property 94–5
  employers' liability 130
  fire safety 169, 172, 176
  health and safety 125
  smoking 186

O
Occupier's Liability Acts 1957/1984 129
Ofcom (Office of Communications) 41
Ofgem (Office of Gas and Electricity Markets) 251, 252
Ofsted 99–101
Online Dispute Resolution (ODR) platform (EC) 103, 104
online reviews 36
out-of-season letting 241–3
outdoor activities, safety 166–7
overseas workers, sponsoring 214

P
Package Travel and Linked Travel Arrangements Regulations 2018 38, **45–9**
paid promotions 36
painting 143
parental leave **203–8**
Passenger Service Vehicle (PSV) licence 131
passenger vessels, music

copyright licences 17
paternity rights 204, 206
Payment Card Industry Security Standards Council 68
PayPal 54, 68
Pensions Act 2008 221
pensions, workplace **221–4**
Permitted Development Rights 25
personal information 61–2, 64–5, 67
personal licence (alcohol) 3, 4
Phone-paid Services Authority 41–2, 44
planning permission **21–4**, 25
plays 3
points-based migration system 209, 213–14
police
  customer registration 70
  customers' property 96
  detaining customers 96
  licences 2, 4–5, 7
PPL PRS Ltd 13, **15–18**
premises licence **4–7**, 11
pre-packaged food 114, **119–20**
Prepacked for Direct Sale (PPDS) food 114, **119–20**
Prevention of Illegal Working 211
pricing and charging **51–5**
Privacy and Electronic Communications (EC Directive) Regulations 2003 39
Privacy and Electronic Communications (Amendment) Regulations 2018 41
Private Water Supplies Regulations (England) 2016 249–50
product safety **157–63**
proof of entitlement to work in the UK 209, **210 –13**, 215
Protection of Freedoms Act 70–1
Provision and Use of Work Equipment Regulations 1998 151, 153–5, 166
PRS for Music licence 13, **15–18**
public liability insurance 129,

133, 170
Public Register of Authentic Identification and Travel Documents Online (PRADO) 212

R

rateable values 235, 236, 237, 238, 252
ready-to-eat foods 112–13
'reasonably practicable' 123, 124, 136, 137, 142, 149, 152
record keeping
 accidents 139
 customer registration 69–70
 data protection 61, 63–4, 66, 69–70
 electrical testing and maintenance 153
 employee wages 197
 fire risk assessments 170, 172, 175
 food 108, **109–10**, 113
 gas appliance maintenance 159
 migrant workers 212
 risk assessments 125, 135, 136, 138
 working hours 189, 191
registration of customers 69–70
Regulatory Reform (Fire Safety) Order 2005 24, 169–70, 174, 176, 177
resale of gas and electricity 251–2
rest breaks 189, 191, 195, 218
return to player (RTP) 10
RIDDOR website 139
risk assessments
 adventure activities 167
 fire 136, 168, 169, **170–7**
 hazardous substances 138
 health and safety 125, 135–7, 139, 143, 145, 147–8, 150, 165–6
 Legionnaires' disease 147–8
 private water supplies 250
 record keeping 125, 135, 136, 138
 swimming pools 165–6
 work at height 141, 142–4

rolled-up holiday pay 191

S

Safer Food, Better Business 110, 111
safety
 food **107–16**
 hazardous substances 138, 141, 144–5
 management **135–40**, 167
 manual handling 141, 143
 risk assessments *see* risk assessments
 work at height 141, 142–4
 work equipment 141–2
safety data sheets 144
safety glass 150–1
safety management **135–40**, 167
Safety Representatives and Safety Committees Regulations 1977 124
same-sex couples, parental rights 204
'Scores on the Doors' 115
second-hand equipment 160
security of data **67–9**, 73
self-catering accommodation
 assured tenancies 241, **242–3**
 business rates 235–6
 customers' property 96
 electrical equipment 152, 160–2
 fire safety 169, 172, 173, 179, 180, 181
 gas safety **157–60**
 immigration status of customers 242
 insurance 133
 letting options **241–3**
 music copyright licences 16
 Occupier's Liability Acts 1957/ 1984 129
 out-of-season letting **241–3**
 tax status **231–3**, 243
self-employed persons
 accident reporting 139
 cash basis accounting 226
 health and safety 123–4, 135, 139, 141, 155

income tax 225
National Minimum Wage 193
work equipment 141
working hours 189
selling tickets **59–60**, 77
service charges 48, 53, 78, 194, **196–7**, 201
serviced accommodation, definition 21
shared parental leave 205
shift work 194
signage 24, **29–32**, 154, 166, 174, 186–7
single-use plastics **121–2**
skill with prizes machines (SWPs) 1, 9
slips and trips 151–2
small businesses
 business rate relief 235, 236, 252
 cash basis accounting 226
 food safety 109
 health and safety 144
small claims procedure 78, 96, 251
smoking 171, 174, 185–7
social media 33, 38, 40, 214
sponsoring overseas workers 214
sporting events 3
staff *see* employees
Statutory Adoption Pay 206
Statutory Maternity Pay (SMP) 203–4, 205, 206
Statutory Paternity Pay (SPP) 204, 205
straws, plastic 121–2
streaming services 13, 18
surveillance equipment 61, **70–3**
swimming pool safety 130, **165–6**, 168

T

tax
 business rates 236, 237
 cash basis accounting 226
 and employees 229
 income tax 196, 197, **225–6**, 228, 230
 Making Tax Digital 230

status of accommodation businesses **231–3**, 243
see also Value Added Tax (VAT)
taxis 79, 90, 132
Telephone Preference Service (TPS) 39, 40, 41, 44
telephones
accident reporting 139
bookings contracts 57, 59
direct marketing 39–40
hearing-impaired customers 88
premium rate numbers 41–2
selling tickets 60
television licences 13–15
temperature control, food 111–13
Temporary Event Notices (TENs) 3–4
temporary employees 139
tenancy agreements 26, 242–3
tenants, houses in multiple occupation 246
text messaging, direct marketing 39–40, 41, 42
tickets, selling **59–60**, 77
tips 194, **196–7**
Tourism Quality Services Ltd (TQS) 167
tourism signs (white on brown) 31–2
Town and Country Planning Act 1990 24
Town and Country Planning (Control of Advertisements) Regulations 2007 29–30
Town and Country Planning (Use Classes) Order 1987 22
trade associations 104
trademarks/trade names 35
Trading Standards
cancellations 79
dispute resolution 105
gas and electrical safety **157–60**
misrepresentation 38
package travel regulations 46, 49
premises licence 5
pricing of goods and

services 52, 53, 55
unfair trading regulations 36, 38
transferring personal data to and from EU/EEA countries 67
transportation of customers 131–2, 134
trekking 161, 166
TV licences *see* television licences

U
UK Borders Act 2007 209
under 18s see children
unfair trading practices **33–8**
pricing and charging 51, 52
signage 29, 31
unfair comparisons 35, 38
unpackaged food 120
unwinding contracts 53
utility supplies **249–53**

V
Valuation Office Agency (VOA) 237, 238, 239
Value Added Tax (VAT) 7, 18, 19, 38, 51, 52, 53, 76, **226–9**, 230
vaping 187
VDU work *see* display screen equipment
vehicles
damage to 94–5
transportation of customers 131–2, 134
VisitEngland
accessibility guides 91
National Accessible Scheme (NAS) 91
National Quality Assessment Scheme 91, 133, 159, 170
visitors' books 69–70
visually-impaired customers 88, 201
voluntary workers 193

W
wages
employing children 218
maternity pay 204–7
National Minimum Wage

193–8
pensions 224
'walk-in' guests 83
waste collection 249, 252
water
Legionnaires' disease 134, **147–8**
private supplies 249–51, 252
Water Industry Act 1991 249
water sports 167
windows
safety glass 150–1
window cleaning 143
work at height 141, 142–4
Work at Height Regulations 2005 141, 143
work equipment, safety 141–2
working hours **189–91**, 218
Working Time Regulations 1998 189–91
Workplace (Health, Safety and Welfare) Regulations 1992 149–50
Workplace Pension Scheme **221–3**

Z
zero-hours contracts 191

Getty Images

Looking to grow your tourism business?

Visit the Business Advice Hub for free resources, practical tips, case studies and local support

Start-up | Funding | Compliance | Health & Safety | Accessibility | Sustainability
Staff | Training | Accreditation | Awards | Marketing | Local Support

Go to visitengland.org/businessadvice
for more information

VisitEngland

VisitEngland ⊛

Legislation
for tourist accommodation and attractions
Do you really know what your legal obligations
are as a tourism business?

The Pink Book: Legislation for tourist accommodation and attractions includes clear guidance and practical information on the legislation that affects your business, including:

- new legislation on single-use plastics
- your rights and responsibilities if a booking is cancelled
- whether you can refuse a booking
- maintaining a customer database that complies with the General Data Protection Regulation
- the licences required to provide TV, play music or provide films to customers
- minimising your risk under health and safety legislation
- ensuring you have the right consents from your council
- what you need to do to employ someone living outside the UK, including the European Union.

www.visitengland.org/pinkbookonline

NOT FOR RESALE £9.99

ISBN 978-0-7095-8413-1

9 780709 584131 >